EUROPEAN IMMIGRANTS and the CATHOLIC CHURCH in CONNECTICUT, 1870-1920

EUROPEAN IMMIGRANTS
and the CATHOLIC CHURCH
in CONNECTICUT, 1870-1920

Dolores Ann Liptak

1987

Center for Migration Studies
New York

EUROPEAN IMMIGRANTS
and the CATHOLIC CHURCH
in CONNECTICUT, 1870-1920

First Edition
Copyright 1987 by
The Center for Migration Studies
All rights reserved. No part of this book may be reproduced
without permission from the publisher.

CENTER FOR MIGRATION STUDIES
209 Flagg Place, Staten Island, New York 10304-1148

Library of Congress Cataloging in Publication Data

Liptak, Dolores Ann
European Immigrants and the Catholic Church
in Connecticut, 1870-1920

Bibliography: p. 199.
Includes index.

1. Catholic Church — Connecticut — History.
2. Catholics — Connecticut — History.
3. Catholic Church — Archdiocese of Hartford (Conn.) — History.
4. Connecticut — Emigration and Immigration.
5. Connecticut — Foreign Population. 6. Connecticut — Church History.
I. Center for Migration Studies (U.S.)   II. Title.
BX1415.C8L56 1987   282'.746'0880693   86-6859
ISBN 0-913256-79-X (Cloth)   ISBN 0-913256-80-3 (Paper)
Printed in the United States of America

*To my brother David who has been
the spiritual and intellectual
inspiration of my life.*

Table of Contents

List of Tables   viii

Acknowledgements   ix

Introduction   1

1. Ethnic Catholicism   7

2. The Formation and Consolidation of the
   Multi-Ethnic Diocese of Hartford   24

3. The Making of Connecticut's Catholic Clergy   60

4. Accommodation and Accord: The Prevailing
   Pattern of Interaction Between the Diocese of
   Hartford and European Immigrants   84

5. Trials of a Multi-Ethnic Church: Episodes of
   Discord in Polish and French Canadian
   Catholic Parishes   104

6. Episodes of Discord Within Other European
   National Parishes in the Diocese of Hartford,
   1890-1920   132

Epilogue   153

Appendix A   158

Appendix B   160

Appendix C   162

Bibliography   164

Index   187

List of Tables

1. Ethnic Background of Seminarians, by Time
   Periods   67

2. Occupations of Fathers of Seminarians, by Time
   Periods   72

3. Occupations of Fathers of "New Immigrant"
   Seminarians, Period IV (1915-1921), by
   Categories   73

4. Geographic Background of Seminarians, Old
   and New Immigrant, by Time Periods   76

5. Old Immigrant and New Immigrant Seminarians,
   by Time Periods and Place of Origin   79

Acknowledgements

Many have made this book a reality. As my doctoral dissertation from the University of Connecticut (1978), the work was first guided by Bruce M. Stave of the Department of History. I wish to express sincere gratitude to Dr. Stave for his steady, sound direction at that time. Special thanks are also due to my religious congregation, the Sisters of Mercy, Hartford, Connecticut who encouraged, and still encourage, my historical vocation. Especially am I grateful to Mary Healy, RSM, DSW, whose continuous support and assistance as she worked in her own field of social work actually enabled me to keep my work in progress. Finally, I wish to thank Archbishop John F. Whealon, and all those at the chancery office of the Archdiocese of Hartford, who saw the importance of developing the archives and history of the Church in Connecticut. Without the opportunity freely to work with the important archival holdings, this book would have been impossible.

In the process of revising this study, I have continued to be in the debt of some who have helped me from the start. Important among these is the Reverend William Wolkovich-Valkavicius, now pastor of St. George, Norwood, Massachusetts. At both phases I was a privileged recipient of much of his scholarly research and writing on Lithuanian Americans; during the revisions, his generous contributions to my ethnic store of knowledge made an important difference. I must also thank the Reverend Silvano Tomasi, C.S., whose own fine work in Italian-American historical studies made the enthusiasm and support he rendered my work all the more important. The Scalabrinian Fathers are to be thanked as well for fostering my writings. I would like to express gratitude to one other religious congregation, the Marian Fathers and Brothers of Stockbridge,

Massachusetts. It was their interest in affirming research in Catholic topics and in publishing scholarly works that made it possible for me to find time and resources to work at the revising of the text. To my family, especially to my brother David, and to my friends I am, most assuredly, especially in debt. Regardless of my own feelings of inadequacy, they were always there to verbalize encouragement, somehow surer than I that the work begun a dozen years before would somehow find successful completion.

May, 1987
Washington, D.C.

Introduction

Those who have surveyed the story of the Roman Catholic Church in the United States generally have summarized the major developments that contributed to the rise of each Catholic diocese in the country. They also have studied the Church as a struggling institution that developed from a relatively insignificant numerical position at the beginning of the nineteenth century to represent 14 percent of the total population by 1890 and to account for approximately 20 percent of the nation's population during the twentieth century. Approaches that concentrate upon the Church's struggles, while more interesting in themselves, have produced an array of similar historical monographs. Thus, readers of American Church history, until very recently have been furnished with studies relative to "the impact of nativism", the struggle between public and private school education, internal conflicts such as those arising from "trusteeism" and the "German-Irish" struggle among Church leaders, and, finally the emergence of "liberal Catholicism" and the so-called heresy of "Americanism". Such repetition of topics seems to suggest that little new analysis about the nature of the Catholic Church and its experience in American history has been attempted; on the whole, the record reflects only routine reevaluations of the available historical data (*See,* Shea, 1886-1892; Maynard, 1941; Noonan, 1938; Barry, 1953).

Regardless of theme, most discussions of the American Catholic Church have tolerated a certain amount of mythology — the unwitting work of both defenders and critics of the Church. Yet two recurring assumptions that have served to unify Catholic Church history have become targets of a more recent development in historical revisionism. One entails the notion of the Catholic Church as a strong, monolithic structure safely enclosed within still another uncomplicated, tightly knit international organization whose headquarters are in Rome. The other views Catholicism in the United States almost as if it were a theological ethnic byproduct of an "immigrant religion" (Schaff, 1855).

America, published over a hundred years ago, exemplified the first assumption. Philip Schaff, wrote in opinionated, unfriendly terms concerning the organizational strength of the Catholic Church. He described the Church as using its concentrated power to "mix in politics and control the elections" and went on to warn:

> But this very effort for power and political influence may prove extremely dangerous to her, if not fatal. Quite lately, at the insistence of the National Council of Baltimore, she [the Church] has made systematic attacks, in the States of New York, Pennsylvania, Maryland, Ohio and Michigan, on the public elementary schools, conducted by the state, and mainly subject to Protestant influence. She has attempted, though thus far without the least success, to destroy them....(p.185)

From this, Schaff concluded that Protestants must expect to lose members to the Roman Catholic Church because of its "truly imposing organization" as well as its other impressive features. Since Schaff's time, many authors working from the same assumption have discussed the Church, namely, that it could somehow be seen within that narrow framework of unified power without reference to any of its significant differences as expressed from diocese to diocese.

Recent historians and sociologists have pointed out that this assumption of strong organization and unity has become increasingly difficult for serious students of Catholic Church history to support. For example, when the Reverend Thomas T. McAvoy, C.S.C. (1953), wrote of the Church, he consistently pointed out that the American Catholic Church experienced little real social or cultural unity well into the twentieth century. Other historians have reaffirmed the same in their writings. Contemporary sociologists have also acknowledged how erroneous it is to attach the "monolithic" label to the Church. (*See,* Gleason, 1970 and Abramson, 1977)

The "immigrant religion" description of the Catholic faith in the United States setting has also come under attack. Father McAvoy (1966) has challenged the notion that Catholicism is essentially immigrant faith by making a careful distinction between, on the one hand, the Catholic Church in its Anglo American origins during colonial times and in the early national period and, on the other hand, the Church during the nineteenth century immigrant influx, when its constituency was completely altered. As McAvoy pointed out, despite the fact that the Catholic Church, even in colonial times, was suspect for its being "different", and despite the fact that the Catholic Church today can be called an immigrant institution, it is important to recognize that the original reasons for "difference" and the ensuing developments that altered this situation should not be confused. To argue that the Catholic Church was essentially different from other indigenous religious organizations because it was a "foreign religion" adhered to by a "foreign element" is to emphasize some historical facts while ignoring others.

Although it is erroneous to consider the Catholic Church as a monolithic structure preaching an immigrant religion, it is also incorrect to argue that phrases like "immigrant institution" and "minority religion" should be totally discarded as descriptive of the American Catholic Church of either the nineteenth or twentieth century. Indeed, most historians of the Church in the United States have quite correctly depicted it as an organization drastically altered as it evolved throughout the last two centuries; consequently, they see it as a Church that, as the years passed, grew to have less and less in common with Protestant America, at least with respect to its history or membership. Often these historians, notably Sydney E. Ahlstrom in *The Religious History of the American People* (1972), have gone beyond a narration of the Catholic Church's difference from mainstream America and have even found grounds to commend the Church for being a chief instrument in the integration of minority groups within the Church structure, within American society, and especially within urban society. Unfortunately, some of these authors have tended to underestimate the difficulties that accompanied such plans or have not studied closely the complex struggles necessarily involved in the integration of many diverse groups (*See,* Dorn in Mohl and Richardson, 1973; McAvoy, Barry and Cuddy in Gleason, 1970; Cross, 1962).

Other historians, such as Colman J. Barry and, Jay P. Dolan (1977; 1975), have recognized that the internal conflict that existed among strong ethnic groups within the Church had much to do with reinforcing the perception that the Roman Catholic Church was a minority institution. These authors consequently have seen the disputes among certain ethnic groups within the Church as major episodes in themselves and, in some cases, have made the disputes the basis of their own specialized studies. Their investigations have, however, been based upon "old immigrant" constituencies. Unless subsequent studies concentrating upon later struggles among "new immigrant" groups complement such research, certain misleading impressions may be allowed to persist. For this reason, it seems imperative that students of American Catholic Church history perceive ethnic conflict along much broader lines than that of the historic nineteenth century confrontation between German and Irish Church leaders so that the full implications of ethnicity and its overall impact upon the entire American Catholic Church may be understood in its proper perspective. In light of the continuing integration of minority groups within the Church in modern times, it seems essential that the more complex episodes of accord and discord among minorities that preoccupied the Church in the decades spanning the turn of the twentieth century be given their due attention.

Only since the 1960s have scholars begun to investigate the Church as a multi-ethnic community with the mix of problems that such a multifaceted set of relationships suggests. Moreover, only recently has such an approach been seen as fruitful for a comprehension of the role of the Catholic Church in American society (*See,* Vecoli, 1969; Cada, 1964; Buczek, 1974; Wolkovich in Dyrud, Novak and Vecoli, 1978; Greeley, 1971; Smith, 1969).

It is now evident that it is necessary to go beyond the terms "minority" and "monolithic" so as to comprehend better the nature of the American Catholic Church and its place in American society. In the words of historian Moses Rischin (1976), "the almost unique cosmopolitan sweep" of American Catholicism can no longer be ignored as a serious topic for historical research. Attention must be drawn to the absorption by the American Catholic Church of peoples from many nations from the late nineteenth century onward that literally changed the face of American Catholicism, producing a "mosaic of ethnicity" and a special kind of American. The characteristics of this new American Catholic have not yet been properly recognized, appreciated, or investigated by historians of the Church.

In this study, investigation of the Catholic Church is restricted to the story of its development in one state, Connecticut, during the period when the most varied influx of foreign groups occurred. Through such a study, one may view the Catholic Church as it emerged as a multi-ethnic community of faith.[1]

Connecticut provides an excellent model for such a study. Unlike states such as Maryland and Pennsylvania, which boasted small, vital

---

[1] The history of the Catholic Church in Connecticut can be gleaned, for the most part, from two published works: H. O'Donnell, *History of the Diocese of Hartford*, Boston: The D.H. Hurd Company, 1900, and T.S. Duggan, *The Catholic Church in Connecticut*, New York: The States History Company, 1930, and articles written by J. Rooney, first editor of the *Connecticut Catholic* (the diocesan newspaper that began publication in 1876) as well as T. Shahan, bishop, and rector of Catholic University of America from 1909 to 1927, who was a priest of the Hartford diocese and its first historian. His research formed the basis of the O'Donnell work.

Roman Catholic communities since colonial times, the Catholic Church in Connecticut may be considered exclusively as a creation of nineteenth century immigration. Erected as a diocese only after the first influx of sizable numbers of Irish immigrants in the 1830s, it began its official existence in 1843 when, joined to its neighboring state Rhode Island, Connecticut was placed under the spiritual leadership of its first bishop, William J. Tyler. From the start, it was a "foreign intrusion" in the eyes of the host society, despite the fact that the bishop was a Yankee and that among its first missionary priests were several remarkably talented converts from American Protestant Churches or denominations. Composed primarily of Irish immigrants and a scattering of French Canadians and Germans, the Church in Connecticut was a classic example of a multi-ethnic faith community. Nor did this situation cease once the pioneer Catholics had yielded to second and third generations. By then the massive influx of other immigrant groups, especially during the period following 1870 and reaching to the 1920s, constantly reinforced its alien appearance.

From the first trickle of immigration in the nineteenth century, and through the great influx that spanned the turn of the century, Connecticut proved to be a remarkably receptive environment for immigrants of Irish, Slavic, and Italian backgrounds. Even those who came in smaller numbers, such as the Lithuanians and Hungarians, found Connecticut a suitable place to establish themselves. Thus, by the turn of the twentieth century, ethnic neighborhoods, clustering around their own churches, influenced by Roman Catholic pastors who shared or identified with the same ethnic or national backgrounds as the newcomers, became part of the Connecticut landscape. What is more remarkable, Boston and the highly industrialized cities surrounding it did not sustain a similar pattern. Hence reasons other than purely economic must be offered to explain why the particular patchwork quilt of ethnicity came to typify Connecticut, and the role of the Catholic leadership within the state as a possible contributing factor for the favorable evnironment must be investigated.

How such a burgeoning, ethnically diverse religious organization met the challenge of development during each phase of its nineteenth and twentieth century growth, therefore, links immigration to the development of the institutional Catholic Church in Connecticut. Such a study advances our understanding of the Catholic Church not only in Connecticut but in the nation as well. For, if the purpose of this diocesan investigation is to bring into full relief the struggle of one segment of the American Church in accommodating itself to the vast challenges posed to immigration in the midst of rapid industrialization and modernization—a story worthy of being recorded in itself—it also invites other historical and contemporary comparisons. Whatever brought together peoples of all nations into one religious body in Connecticut probably occasioned similar developments in other dioceses of the United States. With the increased interest in exploring the consequences of religious identity within ethnic groups, it is appropriate to scrutinize and to isolate those elements that made possible the development of the Catholic Church in twentieth century United States. Finally, such a study, within the limited context of a diocese confronted with the issue, should help answer the question as to whether the American Catholic Church positively or negatively affected the assimilation or acculturation of the immigrants.

1 Ethnic Catholicism

The identity of the American Catholic Church has been linked traditionally to immigration and ethnicity. Despite its fragile Anglo American roots in the colony of Maryland, and despite its ability to attract some native born Americans since colonial times, the U.S. Catholic Church has been perceived as an "immigrant institution", especially after the decades following the German and Irish immigration of the 1840s. Not to understand this is not to grasp the special mark of American Catholicism.[1] Furthermore, to tell the story of American Catholicism without consistent reference to the ongoing tradition of ethnicity within the United States Church would be to practice an ethnocentrism totally oblivious to the multicultured and socially distinct character of the American Catholic Church.

This study of the development of the Diocese of Hartford, Connecticut, in light of its rapid growth through immigration between the years 1870 and 1920, will necessarily emphasize the ethnicity of the American Catholic Church. Before the investigation of the Diocese of Hartford can begin, however, it is necessary to reflect upon the unique phenomenon of American ethnic Catholicism and to review its historic development in the United States.

Ethnic Catholicism can be described as that special intrinsic quality of Catholicism which acknowledges, accepts and, at times, celebrates the differing sociocultural boundaries of language, nationality, and faith

---

[1] Since the 1970s, scholarly efforts at ethnic research have produced solid results. Included among these more recent first studies are H. Abramson, *Ethnic Diversity in Catholic America*, New York: John Wiley & Sons, 1973; M. Novak, *The Rise of the Unmeltable Ethnics*, New York: The MacMillan Company, 1972; and R. Miller and T. Marzik, eds., *Immigrants and Religion in Urban America*, Philadelphia: Temple University Press, 1977.

practice which distinguish one Catholic congregation from another. Historically, it has most often revealed itself in two ways: through the proliferation of parallel church structures or institutions within close geographic proximity, and by a liturgical and spiritual diversity which has influenced the way Catholics relate to one another, to their Church, and to the larger environment. Of the very essence of the American religious experience, ethnic Catholicism is a phenomenon little understood within the American Catholic Church and, consequently, overlooked and undervalued.

The institution which most symbolizes the differences predicated by ethnic Catholicism is the national parish. Distinguished from the territorial parish which designates a congregation of Catholics strictly with reference to geographic boundaries, the national parish is a church unit of organization expressly initiated by proper Church authorities to join into one congregation those Catholics who are already united to one another for specific religious and sociocultural reasons. A variant of the primary organizational unit (the territorial parish), the national parish has been an integral part of Church jurisdiction for centuries (*See,* Ciesluk, 1944).

The historic precedents which gave validity to the national parish in the United States were certain parochial accommodations developed by the medieval Church in Europe. Since the Middle Ages, for example, "personal" or "non-territorial" parishes have been established by bishops wherever the specific quality of the group of people to be served determined its necessity. Such was the case when peasants who were bound by service to the manor were considered members of the Lord's private chapel. First recognized in the Fourth Lateran Council and in the thirteenth century decretals of Gregory IX, and later acknowledged by the Council of Trent in the sixteenth century, the "non-territorial" principle of formation meant that parishes were organized not on the basis of numbers and locations but according to the particular character of the people or families requiring service. When the common ties that bound a particular group of people became the primary reason for the formation of a separate parish, bishops had the power to establish non-territorial, or personal, parishes.

In the United States, the national parish became a particular American version of the nonterritorial parish. In the missionary environment of the nineteenth century American Catholic Church, more than a few bishops quickly saw the need and value of an alternative to the unusual pattern of parish building.

The national parish made its first appearance during the episcopacy of the first ordinary of the United States, John Carroll, the first Bishop of Baltimore. As early as 1791, specific legislation to provide for non-

English speaking Catholics was incorporated within the original code of laws issued by the American Catholic clergy. Mentioned again at the Third Plenary Council of 1884, the national parish became the accepted response to the spiritual needs of immigrants during the decades of massive immigration at the century's end.

By the 1920s, the national parishes had become the hallmark of Catholic diversity and difference. But their special demarcation of ethnicity also led to numerous complications. Because Irish Americans predominated among the nation's expanding Catholic population, for example, it often happened that even territorial parishes began to be perceived as national "Irish" parishes. This confusion alone served to strengthen the popular notion that American Catholics constituted a "foreign breed". For Catholics, however, the belief tended to have more divisive effects, suggesting to new immigrants that one ethnic group within the U.S. Catholic Church had managed to gain ascendancy over all the rest.

Still, it was within the structure of the designated national parish that the celebration of ethnicity occurred and where the various aspects of ethnic Catholicism were developed. In this setting, ethnic Catholics found courage to proclaim both their belief in the authority of the Church and their dynamic use of it. Within their own parishes they developed liturgies pleasing to them because they incorporated musical and ceremonial treasures and provided spiritually uplifting devotional traditions. Here, too, new social and cultural societies were initiated and unique religious perspectives expressed freely. Here the pastor, as an agent of progress and a symbol of continuity, represented the link between the congregation, other Catholics and the larger society. To the degree that a spirit of openness to new ideas, attitudes, and behavior predominated, therefore, the national parish has been the means used by both ethnic and diocesan leaders either to bridge or to avoid differences between Catholics. Through a dialectic exchange, it has proclaimed both the bonds of unity and the validation of the social boundaries which distinguish Catholics.

In a certain sense, then, the establishment of national parishes has produced the contemporary American Catholic Church. It not only insured a pluralistic approach to religious practice, it also has explicitly proclaimed ethnic Catholicism as a valid mode of faith expression. The decision to create national parishes and to construct a policy related to the service of immigrants was not, however, brought about without struggle and controversy. It is time that the phenomenon set in motion by the American Catholic bishops be examined; their acknowledgment of ethnic diversity more fully understood and evaluated. This chapter reviews the historical development of ethnic Catholicism and attempts to analyze the reason why the building of ethnic Catholicism has been such a difficult task for the American Catholic Church.

So very much a part of the history of American Catholicism after the mid-19th century, the concept of ethnic Catholicism was far from the mind of the Church's first leadership. The Church evolved at a time when revolution brought religious freedom for all, allowing room for growth regardless of historical, ethnic, or political advantage. Joining the ranks of religious denominations newly protected by the guarantees of the Bill of Rights, the Catholic Church organized under the auspices of an Anglo American, John Carroll of Baltimore (1735-1815). Under him, it took its first — albeit cautionary — official steps. With his episcopal blessing, it attempted to identify as closely as possible with the American character.

For its first forty years, the American Catholic Church continued to follow Anglo American leaders. In faith, doctrine, and sense of universality, it seemed Roman Catholic, but in identification with culture and society, it worked to portray itself as representing another American faith. During the last years of the 19th century, however, the rather independent American stance which the Church had assumed came abruptly to an end. With the appointment of the first permanent apostolic delegate from Rome to the United States in 1893, an official, explicit link between the American Church and the Vatican was forged. Ironically, one of the key motivations prompting this change of relationship was the increasing criticism expressed by American ethnic minorities that the predominant Irish American leadership of the U.S. Church prevented them from experiencing a true sense of equality among their fellow Catholics (Hennesey, 1981: 69-101, 184-234).

In point of fact, it was considerably before the naming of the apostolic delegate and the forging of explicit Roman ties that the American character of the U.S. Church had been seriously questioned by both Catholics and non-Catholics alike. Throughout the nineteenth century a demographic revolution had taken place, the consequences of which had a particularly awesome effect upon the Church, constantly eroding its American identification. As the swelling tide of immigration added greater numbers and greater diversity to the Catholic population, the strain of coping with difference began to take its toll. Much of the internal turmoil that troubled the Church during this period was traceable to the sense of inferiority and alienation.

Even John Carroll was not spared confrontations with ethnic Catholics. As early as 1794, for example, a German pastor residing in Baltimore alleged that Bishop Carroll lacked jurisdiction not only over his German parishioners but with regard to any German American Catholics. On that basis, he made the claim that German American Catholics should enjoy ethnic immunity from episcopal control (McAvoy, 1969:93-94). Attitudes of a similar nature gained adherents among other ethnic minorities as the new century matured, exacerbating a spirit of competition among Catholics.

Ethnic divisiveness may even have been at the basis of one of the most frequently discussed controversies of the early U.S. Catholic Church. In detailing their complaints against Archbishop Leonard Neale, for example, the trustees of a Norfolk, Virginia, congregation in 1817 made it clear that they were not arguing against the rights of bishops as much as they were demonstrating their personal animus toward the French born priest who had been appointed to be their pastor. In Articles Six and Eight of their petition, Irish pride was implicit:

> .....that the great body of Roman Catholics in that State as all the other States of this country are Irish or their descendants; that they alone (with small assistance of a few members, Spanish, Portuguese, and French) have built all the Churches, save one in Philadelphia.

> .....that they feel it inconvenient, nay unreasonable, not to say intolerable, to be refused a clergy of their own nation *ad nominatum*, acquainted with their characters and dispositions....(Ellis Papers, May 31, 1817).

They should share authority with the clergy, they seemed to argue, because they were not only Catholic laymen but also because they were Irish Catholics. Moreover, as Irish Catholics, they should have more say than other ethnic groups in the choice of clergy to serve them.

The question of "which nationality should rule" began to disturb the nineteenth century Catholic leadership more and more as the century progressed. The earlier German and Irish complaints headed a long list of critiques based on alleged power blocs within the Church. John Tracy Ellis, dean of American Catholic historians, has viewed this tendency toward ethnic difference and divisiveness as taking firmer hold by mid-nineteenth century. According to Ellis (1955):

> ...willy nilly the American church had become Catholic in the broadest sense and the problems of how best to mold the congeries of nationalities that composed its faithful into a stable element of the American population became its most pressing preoccupation. p.50

For the remainder of the century, and well into the next century, as membership mounted to twenty million by 1920 and as the recruitment

of Irish foreign born clergy patterned the same increase, the multi-
ethnic "immigrant" complexion of American Catholics and the distinct
Irish character of its leadership became even more evident. By the century's end, the U.S. Catholic Church had to come to grips with the
baffling task of consolidating its assortment of nationalities into a compatible and united religious family.

The northeastern and midwestern dioceses of the United States were
the first to experience the consequences of ethnic Catholicism. After
the 1880s, rapidly increasing numbers of southern and eastern European immigrants added still new shapes to the American Catholic ka-
leidoscope. As the twentieth century dawned, these immigrants, now
making up 18 percent of the U.S. total population, claimed to be Catholic (Shaughnessy, 1925, 1969:155-172).[2] Some Americans, especially
those with British roots, reacted against the Catholic presence by re-
newing an endemic anti-Catholic posture, joining nativist organizations, or simply resorting to threats and political blacklisting. Furthermore, despite the fact that the main efforts of most Catholic leaders
were Americanist in perspective — following Carroll's American model
for the Church — ethnic variety was a reality that had to be faced both
inside and outside the Church.

It is not surprising that this multi-ethnic membership would generate
a new set of problems as the number and degree of the differences
multiplied. Although, for all too many Americans, the Catholic Church
in the United States had never ceased being a "foreign institution", the
new burst of ethnicity further complicated matters. The alien character
of the Catholic Church now reverberated in the halting conversations
of the newcomers and displayed itself in strangely ornate architectural
features in neighborhood ghettos and in the employment offices of both
factories and foundries. Here recent immigrants vied with one another
for the most menial of occupations while established Catholics voiced
their dissatisfaction with the strangers in their midst. In particular, the
old-timers were taken back by the affrontery of foreigners who argued
for equality. They also feared that any sign of willingness to incorporate
the newcomers fully would result in a loss of the social and political
status among their American peers for which they had worked so hard.

Reminiscent of the strident tones of an earlier time was the turn-of-
the-century rash of acrimonious debates and demands. Two of the more

---

[2] According to Shaughnessy, approximately one-third of those immigrating between 1870-1900
were Catholic. By the end of the century the ratio would become approximately one-half. According to Maynard (1941), between 1884 and 1921, the Catholic population increased from seven
million to nearly twenty million, while the number of priests rose from seven to twenty thousand,
and the number of bishops from 55 to over one hundred, p.523.

famous episodes were midwestern affairs. One was precipitated in 1886 by a Milwaukee diocesan priest, Peter Abbelen, who personally stated his case to Roman officials concerning the prejudiced status of German Americans. Another was presented two years later by Peter Paul Cahensly, a representative of an international missionary society. The basic position of both challenges was that American Church leaders had failed to provide appropriate services for recent immigrants. Not only did these protests point to a dearth of institutions for recent immigrants, they also stressed how little was being done in the U.S. Church to locate priests to serve immigrants or to promote ethnic priests to the ranks of the episcopate as a testimony to their equal status. What raised such arguments to a level beyond complaint was the charge that the faith and morale of immigrants had been compromised by the negative attitude of the American hierarchy and that, consequently, the total American Catholic membership was on the brink of experiencing an almost scandalous decline. In both the Abbelen and Cahensly incidents, arguments for separate national parishes and demands for a quota system so minorities could be adequately represented among the episcopate were put forward as essential conditions to resolve the pending crisis (Barry, 1953).

Despite the German American bias of these two famous cases, the ethnic locus of complaints and charges against the Church had begun to shift by the 1890s. By that time, divisions emanated from other groups and were usually couched in arguments that were even more graphic in style and symbolic in language. Thus, the French Canadians argued for *survivance* and Polish congregations insisted upon being allowed their "Polish kind of faith". From diocese to diocese differing aspects of the same drama unfolded. If German Catholics still complained of ill treatment in dioceses beyond the "German triangle", newly established Polish and Slovak congregations grew restive in Cleveland, Buffalo, or Scranton, while Franco Americans bristled against interfering New England prelates, and Italians and Lithuanians smarted under signs of discrimination in Boston, Brooklyn, or Baltimore. (*See,* Blejwas, 1982; Guignard, 1982).

In general, most immigrant groups argued on the basis of an obvious reality: the Irish clergy dominated Church leadership positions. This predominance forced other ethnic groups into what they often perceived to be second-class status. As a result, they argued, they were effectively denied certain rights within their Church. Sometimes through direct confrontations or protest, sometimes by means of petitions ultimately sent to Church officials in Rome (or Washington, D.C.), their spokesmen sought a redress of real or imagined grievances (McAvoy, 1969).[3] Inevitably a number of factors weakened the general effectiveness of their demands, not the least of which was the decentralized nature of the American Catholic Church which literally kept the struggle of one ethnic group within diocesan bounds. Thus, during this period of their greatest need for both assistance and incorporation, immigrant communities remained wholly at the mercy of their dioceses.

In an atmosphere where ethnic Catholicism was so poorly understood and where the very organizational structure of the Church provided no direct means of producing effective change, little seems to have been accomplished by immigrant protests. National parishes were established and immigrant priests were sought out, to be sure. But beyond this, there seemed to have been little episcopal initiative. Apart from actively searching for trained clergy, or sometimes even sending seminarians abroad to be educated in the language and customs of immigrant Catholics, bishops did not appear to consider immigrant needs or to develop policies based upon them. Even where there was a degree of enlightened leadership, and where national parishes had already been established, the relationship between new ethnic groups and their bishops seemed, at best, ill-defined. Thus it appears that, despite the best intentions of all concerned, the establishment of national parishes worked against the best intentions of both diocesan officials and immigrants as well. There are those who have, in fact, argued that no diocese where national parishes had been organized escaped disharmony. Consequently, the primary means used by both the Church and immigrants to create an acceptable Catholic community became a source of conflict and a sign of contradiction. Little wonder, these critics add, that in all too many cases, efforts to assist immigrants in a more organized way seldom went beyond the bare minimum.

Just how widespread was discord between immigrants and their Church in the early decades of the present century? What, in fact, was achieved by recourse to the national parish as a means of assuaging discord? These are the very questions upon which diocesan histories have tended to be conspicuously silent. So, too, have general studies of American Catholicism. Only some of the more recent investigations of the U.S. Catholic Church have attempted to evaluate their impact.

One diocesan history which has attempted to address this issue is a 1982 monograph on the Chicago Catholic experience by Charles Shanabruch. In his study, Shanabruch draws a fascinating picture of Chi-

---

[3] According to McAvoy, one-third of the clergy in 1852 were Irish or of Irish descent. They particularly dominated New England and areas of New York.

cago's prelates consciously adhering to a philosophy with regard to immigrants, which aimed at, and ultimately succeeded in, achieving both acceptance and integration. In particular, he points to the episcopacies of Bishops Thomas Foley (1822-1879), Patrick Augustine Feehan (1829-1902), and James Edward Quigley (1855-1915) as administrations when appropriate attention was given to the establishment of national parishes as well as to general immigrant needs. Archbishop Feehan, for one, made it clear that he prized diversity of language and nationality within the Church not only as a help to Catholic growth but as a determinant of the character of the archdiocese. His successor, Archbishop Quigley, also emphasized the welfare of immigrants and publicly acknowledged their diversity as treasure. So sensitive was Quigley to the particular needs of Polish Americans, that he became a strong advocate of nominating a Polish American candidate for the episcopacy. Most recent historians credit him as the prime mover behind the appointment of a Polish American candidate, Paul Rhode, as his auxiliary bishop in 1908. Despite occasional lapses or lack of enthusiastic response, Shanabruch believes that this episcopal pattern of accommodation and acceptance of ethnic differences has, in fact, persisted within the Chicago archdiocese to the present. Such a conclusion does not necessarily contradict the generalization concerning Catholic leaders' indifference to ethnic needs. Yet it does suggest that at least some dioceses did seriously address the problems of growing ethnic diversity but that, for some reason, their efforts have been largely overlooked.

Research concerning the diocese of Newark, New Jersey, has uncovered a similar pattern. There the creation of national parishes became both a logical and efficient tactic used by several bishops who viewed the concept as ministerially sound and who, therefore, cared for immigrant needs with both consistency and sensitivity. Even at the turn of the twentieth century, for example, largely because of the wisdom of Bishop Winand Michael Wigger (1841-1901), 35 language parishes had been founded in the diocese. During the next 25 years, coinciding with the administration of Bishop John Joseph O'Connor (1855-1927), an average of two national parishes per year were added to the diocese (New Jersey Catholic Historical Records Commission, 1978). Well before 1930, the Newark diocese could boast not only about the impressive number of national parishes per Catholic population but also that 20 percent of its clergy were of new immigrant background — perhaps the highest percentage of any diocese in the United States (*The Official Catholic Directory*, 1930).

In the nearby metropolitan area of New York, the efforts of the sometimes controversial Archbishop Michael A. Corrigan to provide for Italian immigrants distinguished that urban area. Because of the missionary endeavors of such outstanding leaders as Bishop Giovanni Scalabrini and Mother Francesca Cabrini, much is known about the development of Italian American Catholicism there. But the record of these early apostles should not divert observers from recognizing that their work would surely have been impossible had it not been for both the encouragement and sponsorship given by Corrigan and other archdiocesan leaders. Two recent historical studies of the Italian American experience in New York substantiate the archdiocese's pro-immigrant view and its benefits for New York Italians (Tomasi, 1978; DiGiovanni, 1983). Among positive, albeit fundamental, signposts of these early accommodations of immigrants, were the more than forty Italian national parishes which had already been established in New York by the mid-1920s.

Other investigations into diocesan immigrant policies have unearthed some of the less favorable consequences of episcopal attitude and action giving more substance to the perception that Church leaders could behave poorly with regard to immigrants. According to those who have documented this tendency, the assimilationist rhetoric of some prominent American bishops, coupled with their occasional insensitive enforcement of certain Church policies, easily persuaded many ethnic Catholics that, despite their acceptance as members of national or territorial parishes, they could not expect full acceptance from American Catholic bishops. In a recent article, Philip Silvia (1979:414-435) reviewed one blatant example of this as it occurred in the Flint area of Fall River, Massachusetts, then under the jurisdiction of Thomas Hendricken, Bishop of Providence (1827-1886). In this case, Hendricken and the French Canadians of Notre Dame parish reached such an impasse over disputes involving the naming of a suitable French speaking pastor that the bishop employed drastic measures against the immigrant community. Frustrated by his continued failures, he finally placed the entire parish under interdict. If it were not for the necessary intervention of Cardinal Giovanni Simeoni, Prefect of the Sacred Congregation of the Propagation of the Faith, the scandalous Flint Affair might have outlasted the Hendricken administration. As it was, memories of episcopal ill treatment have continued to negatively influence the Fall River Franco Americans.

In his study of Canadian migrants to Biddeford, Maine, Michael Guignard (1982) documents a strikingly similar example of recalcitrance and authoritarian behavior on the part of another New England bishop, Louis Walsh, Bishop of Portland. As Guignard points out, even before being named bishop, Walsh had already made a poor impression among ethnic Catholics because of his strong assimilationist views of Catholic education. Thus, when Franco Americans heard of his nomination to the see of Portland in 1906, they anticipated trouble and publicly protested his nomination. In his first years as bishop, Walsh lived up to their worst expectations; his parochial policies, in particular, managed to embitter them still more. By reorganizing one parish to their distinct disadvantage, by enforcing a ban which prohibited ethnic societies from performing at liturgical and other societies, as well as by challenging some of the national parish methods concerning finances, Walsh reinforced their view that he believed in rewarding administrative efficiency over pastoral concern. But it was his decision to acquire Church property as sole owner, known as the Corporation Sole controversy, which particularly earned him their enduring animosity. For generations after property disputes based on their differences of opinion with him were settled, the fights and shoving matches which first erupted in Biddeford's Irish and French ethnic neighborhoods lingered on as bitter memories. To this day, French Canadian and Irish parishioners refrain from visiting each other's Church — seldom, certainly, do they participate in ceremonies other than their own.

In the process of their investigations concerning interaction between bishops and national parishes, moreover, historians have been required to study the national parish as a phenomenon itself. In questioning assumptions regarding the causes of unrest within ethnic parishes, they have tried to discover the basic characteristics underlying unrest as another way of evaluating episcopal moves to incorporate the nation's Catholic immigrants. If the establishment of a national parish headed by a priest "of their own" was so crucial for immigrants, why was it, researchers have asked, that episodes of conflict emerged in apparently firmly established national parishes? Why, furthermore, did discontent continue even among those national parishes where there was no apparent interference or lack of sensitivity on the part of bishops after establishment? In fact, evidence derived from virtually every study of ethnic Catholics suggests clearly that the establishment of national parishes was not, in and of itself, a sufficient deterrent to a generalized mistrust of authority by immigrant Catholics. Research also underscores the complexity of the issues involved and the difficulty of assessing the reasons behind the alleged recalcitrance of bishops. In almost every case, there seemed to be a number of factors which set immigrant congregations against their bishops or one another regardless of solid beginnings or good intentions. Instead of placing sole responsibility for the failures of national parishes upon diocesan leadership, as has been typical, it now appears necessary to withhold judgment until every aspect of the ethnic conflict itself is thoroughly analyzed.

Studies reviewing the Slavic, Lithuanian, French Canadian, Italian or Hungarian immigrant experience have all highlighted the sustained climate of factionalism within national parishes and the potential for further escalation. Whether the complicating factors involved a *campanilismo* spirit which set Italian parishioners apart from one another, or an urban versus rural regionalism which separated Poles, or was based on status competition or a search for identity and self worth, the results ranged from debates to violent outbursts and proved that discord was apt to last beyond legal or episcopal approval. At the source of each instance there seems to have been a struggle that was at once psychological, political and cultural. (*See,* Miller and Marzik, 1977; *also,* De Marco, 1981; Sorrell, 1975; Cygan, 1983).

In many cases, one of the most significant sources of the conflict which often divided ethnic parishes seems to have been within the community itself. Sometimes difficulties developed between the pastor of one parish and the pastor of the other. At other times discord was the result of disagreements between curate and pastor. In both instances, the members of the congregation inevitably took sides until the parish became divided into competing factions. A newly appointed pastor might find himself an object of disapproval simply because the removal of his predecessor as well as his assignment to the parish forced a factional realignment within the parish. Or, he might be confronted with a full-scale rebellion, instigated by an ambitious curate, but carried forward by parishioners equally anxious to gain power in the parish. At still other times, a priestly co-worker might advance the cause of revolt for his own purposes, hoping to focus the parish on his superior leadership capabilities. Until agendas and issues such as these were resolved, the smooth functioning of the parish involved remained illusive, a tense atmosphere prevailed, and the aims of the bishop were thwarted. In this mood of disappointment and dissatisfaction, smoldering discontent could easily surface at the least provocation on the part of the bishop.

Leslie Woodcock-Tentler (1983) provides an example of the kind of divisiveness which consistently plagued Polish national parishes in their first years of development. Involving St. Albertus, the oldest Polish parish in Detroit, Michigan, this particular dispute ostensibly originated over the removal of the pastor at the request of one group of parishioners. Yet the reasons for the split may have had more of a basis in the growing social and economic divergence within the parish itself. As the verbal and physical abuse intensified, observers were amazed to discover the degree of animosity exhibited and the effects of their ill will: one parishioner had been killed; a secessionist parish had been established blocks away; and there were numerous examples of harassment, personal injury, and property damage.

Woodcock-Tentler suggests a variety of reasons for such protracted and violence-prone discord. It might have arisen because of feelings of frustration exaggerated by a sense of inferiority and experienced by the more recent arrivals. But it was undoubtedly also sustained by a fear of losing status on the part of the well-established. In the Detroit case, those who wanted to oust the pastor were established Prussian Polish immigrants while those who wished to retain the pastor were more recently arrived Australian Poles, themselves barely struggling to survive in the new surroundings. That both Bishops Caspar H. Borgess (1826-1890) and his successor, Bishop John S. Foley (1833-1918), remained insensitive to these subtler motivating factors of tension and seemed to be looking merely for signs of obedience and repentance from the secessionists only intensified the division. For whatever reason, however, immigrant Catholics had turned against one another and their Church as well. In the end, it was the deep love and loyalty which the Polish secessionists had for their Church, and the diplomatic skills of the apostolic delegate, which saved the situation. Still, for almost a decade, ill will had wreaked havoc within the Polish community. Neither episcopal intervention nor the Polish desire for resolution had been able to bring peace until the psychological and sociological needs of destruction had been somehow assuaged.

Even the movement toward schism and the creation of independent Churches was often an outgrowth of tensions which had their origins in national parishes. It was in the national parish, for example, that an ambitious ethnic priest might first refine his arguments and develop his strategies to achieve his personal goals. In fact, the history of most major schismatic or separatist movements among American Catholics supports this contention. Thus, the co-founder of the Polish National Catholic Church, Franciszek Hodur, used the national parishes where he had served as both curate and pastor as the staging ground for his independence movement. Another dissident, Anton Kozlowski, developed his protest against the Church during his curacy years in Chicago. Furthermore, Hodur, Kozlowski, and a third rebel priest, Stephen Kaminski eventually combined their forces to form a national schismatic Church in 1907, not so much that they had found themselves prohibited from functioning in approved national parishes but because they had already tasted success there.

From his investigations of Slovak Americans, M. Mark Stolarik (1978) concluded that a similar phenomenon was at work among Slovaks. His research has unearthed several vivid examples of rivalry within established national parishes based on competition between pastors and abetted by the bias of the ethnic press. Often it was this very combination of factors that became the potent force in the creation of an atmosphere conducive to schism. Further complicated by the efforts of some Slovaks to remain independent of Hungarian influence, such internecine rivalry sometimes permanently divided Slovaks. One such incident occurred, for example, in the small Pennsylvania town of Maltby. There Slovak Catholics found their loyalties divided between two Slovak priests, to a great extent basing their viewpoints on information gleaned from the pages of the local Slovak newspaper. In the end, neither pastor met with Slovak approval. A similar situation developed in Cleveland, Ohio, where priest-journalist Jan Stas managed to influence Slovaks against a leading Slovak missionary priest, Stefan Furdek, successfully undermining the early years of a remarkable career and delaying the development of an entire Slovak congregation as well.

In his extensive writings on the Lithuanian experience, William Wolkovich-Valkavicius (1983) has joined Stolarik and other ethnic historians who have analyzed the effects of factionalism within immigrant parishes. He argues that Lithuanian Americans were often prepared to transform a national parish setting into a testing ground for confirming their own leadership roles rather than as a means of drawing their fellow Lithuanians closer to the American Catholic Church. He had, in fact, isolated one technique demonstrated by a number of Lithuanian clergymen: using the pulpit to criticize fellow countrymen, thereby advancing their own careers. According to Wolkovich-Valkavicius, there were several "bogus" immigrant priests who used temporary assignments in Lithuanian parishes to marshall support for themselves. Such was the case when a seminarian, Vincas Dilionis, managed to incite protests among Lithuanians in Pittston, Philadelphia, and Baltimore by merely exploiting local dissension. This kind of intramural squabbling seemed to be directed against Church authorities, blaming them for actions which Lithuanians, themselves, might have originally brought into being.

There was still another way in which national parishes tended to render disservices to the American Catholic community. Even if they succeeded in creating unified congregations, the very establishment of the national parish might inevitably result in preventing ethnic Catholics from gaining a sense of full membership in the Church. This is a thesis suggested in an article on Polish ethnic leadership by William Galush (1984). According to Galush, Polish immigrant clergy often shared the same paternalistic attitudes towards recent immigrants as did many of the American hierarchy; they also held strong convictions concerning the universality of the Church. For these reasons, a number of Polish priests aligned themselves squarely with the American bishops. In the eyes of certain Poles, this was a form of treason since it seemed as if their clergy had chosen loyalty to the American Church over a Polish faith perspective. When this choice occurred because of faith convictions, the record of history bears witness to its wisdom. Consistently, strong parochial institutions were created. But when such motivation was not clearly the case, a whole new set of complications tended to short-circuit their growth. In the short run, the decision to keep dissent from moving toward separatism worked. The bishop was temporarily satisfied; an atmosphere of calm prevailed. In the long run, purity of intent on the part of all participants was essential if the parish was to prosper and grow. Finally, even if good will remained the continual pastoral pattern, the very atmosphere created by the contentment could produce its own set of problems — not the least of which was a sense of isolation on the part of both congregation and clergy. Only if incorporation was the long range goal of everyone involved in the establishment of national parishes could the negative consequences of this narrowing of options for both ethnic leaders and members be avoided.

For a number of reasons, therefore, the establishment of national parishes seemed, at best, only a partial and imperfect answer to the crisis of accommodating immigrants within the structure of the American Catholic Church — only one step in the process of creating a Catholic community. It was not enough to insure the general health and vitality of the American Catholic Church. Even when the purest of motivations prevailed, the true purpose of providing a particular accommodation for the ethnic difference seldom seemed the uppermost concern. In light of such pessimistic conclusions, some basic questions remain. When so little seems to have been accomplished by their establishment, was permission to form ethnic parishes really a constructive episcopal contribution? Moreover, since the making of a strong U.S. Church clearly depended upon surmounting the divisiveness inherent in utilizing the national parish as a solution to its multi-ethnicity, what can be said for other kinds of decisions which bishops made concerning ethnic Catholics? Were any of these, in fact, implemented during this crucial period of growth through immigration as convincing proof that American Catholic leaders understood the direction they should take in their response to ethnic minority members?

The episcopal record of other pro-immigrant choices is even more bleak. The degree to which ethnic minority clergy were incorporated into chancery and other administrative offices, for example, can be used as a measure of episcopal determination to convey an attitude of respect for immigrants. Thus, confirmation of leadership upon ethnic clergy would carry with it profound psychological and social effects.

However, there seems to emerge no clearly positive picture concerning episcopal intentions to incorporate ethnic minority or immigrant clergy into diocesan leadership structures. Rather, prestigious assignments or promotions of ethnic clergy were few and far between.

This apparent bypassing of qualified clergy by the Irish American hierarchy suggests a myopic view which necessarily had negative implications for the non-Irish clergy of their dioceses. The same attitude also seemed apparent on the national level. It especially characterized appointments to the American Catholic hierarchy. The disregard of ethnic clergy at the time of the diocesan or hierarchical promotions was taken by certain ethnic groups as the ultimate convincing proof that the recent immigrants from central and southeastern Europe were, indeed, second-class members within the American Catholic Church.

One example of this disinterest with respect to Polish clerical advancement within the Church should suffice. Using 1924 *Catholic Directory* figures, the Reverend M.J. Madaj (1978) investigated the number of Polish clergy in leadership positions during a decade in which their membership had reached considerable proportions nationwide. Since Polish Catholics accounted for approximately one sixth of all United States Catholics in the 1920s, he based the expected ratio of leadership upon that figure. Instead of 20 Polish members in the American hierarchy, however, he found there was only one Polish American bishop among the nation's 119 hierarchical members (98 bishops, 17 archbishops, and 4 cardinals). On the administrative level, below the episcopate, he discovered that Polish clergy fared as poorly. There were no vicars general or chancellors of Polish background; among diocesan consultants, Poles numbered 15 of 595. According to Madaj, only with the German and French Canadian clergy were the statistics somewhat more favorable. In the face of such figures it is not difficult to understand why minority Catholics tended to agree with critics who questioned the sincerity of the American Catholic hierarchy or with the claim that bishops were trying to respond appropriately to immigrant demands.

There were other ways in which episcopal leaders could model the proper attitude which Catholics of their dioceses should follow with respect to the new membership. Chief among these would be: calling attention to the achievements of national parishes in the diocesan press; accepting invitations to participate in ethnic festivals and other celebrations; singling out prominent ethnic clergy or laypersons for honors, etc. To develop such tactics, however, there would have to be a conscious decision by the bishop involved. For a number of reasons, much of the constructive efforts of dioceses have been unrecorded. Whether these omissions were motivated by embarassment over the more typical pattern of discord involving ethnic minority Catholics or were sustained by a general indifference concerning the affairs of its newest members, the end result is the same. A clear picture of the place of ethnic Catholics within the American Catholic Church remains illusive. It is, therefore, very important to continue the recent efforts of historians to investigate diocesan action in this regard.

The following study of the development of the Catholic Church in the Diocese of Hartford from the time when it first faced large scale immigration into Connecticut until the rush of new Catholics subsided in the 1920s is a further attempt to sharpen this ethnic focus of the American Catholic experience.[4] It aims to examine one diocese in the light of the description of ethnic Catholicism that has been highlighted in this chapter, taking as given that the experience of immigrant Catholics has often been misread and mistold by Church leaders, ethnic members, and onlookers. It concentrates upon the record of Church leadership as preserved in diocesan archives and other historical sources, asking the same questions of the Diocese of Hartford as historians and sociologists have already begun to ask of other dioceses. In an effort to understand what was really accomplished by episcopal immigrant policy, it elucidates the underlying motivations behind the reported words and actions of the majority Irish constituency of the diocese. It evaluates the official approaches taken: the number and kind of national parishes established; the types of outreach employed to find and to promote ethnic clergy within the diocesan administrative structure; and means taken to convey explicit messages of belonging and acceptance of the ethnic Catholic members of the diocese; and the celebration of ethnicity itself. Finally, this study analyzes some of the conflicts and controversies which originated within national parishes of the diocese in an effort to uncover the reasons behind both ethnic and episcopal response or action.

In this way, the present investigation attempts to advance the understanding of the specific processes involved in the incorporation of Catholics generally and to clarify the variety of means Church leaders utilize to address the more pressing needs of their newest immigrant members. By thus presenting the historical record of strategies used to assist immigrants, it is hoped that Catholic planners, aided by a more concentrated focus on the complex dynamic that once shaped the American Catholic Church, will have a pattern to follow as they develop immigrant policies that reflect the highest aspirations of the American Catholic Church.

[4] The diocese of Hartford, comprising the states of Connecticut and Rhode Island, was first created in 1843; in 1872, the Diocese of Providence, Rhode Island was separated from it. From that time until 1953, when another subdivision occurred within Connecticut, the Diocese of Hartford was coterminous with Connecticut state boundaries.

2 The Formation and Consolidation of the Multi-Ethnic Diocese of Hartford

The history of the Diocese of Hartford reveals a close relationship between ethnicity and Church development. In this sense, it reflects in miniature a relationship between immigration and the Catholic Church that is characteristic of Catholicism's general development in the United States.

The history of Catholicism in Connecticut begins with the arrival of immigrant workers during the 1820s, more than a quarter-century after the American Constitution had first guaranteed religious freedom. A vital community composed of a handful of well-to-do lay leaders and a much larger almost exclusively Irish immigrant following intruded into the Yankee environment and made itself heard in a way that would eventually command respect far beyond the confines of the state (Fitton, 1872).

On July 11, 1829, Catholic leaders launched *The Catholic Press*, the first such newspaper established in New England and the second in the United States. Through this journal Connecticut Catholics announced their intention to present themselves in an almost militant stance not only to their Protestant Yankee neighborhoods of Hartford but also to the reading public everywhere. This ambition, implemented in the first issues of the newspaper, must have surprised the respected citadel of Puritanism that Connecticut proudly claimed to be, and caused comment among New England's Protestants. For the Catholics of Connecticut it represented even more than a bold statement of religious identity; it virtually constituted a formal affirmation of their existence.

There had been a scattering of Catholics residing in Connecticut long before 1829. While the only acknowledged Catholics to have spent any time there during the colony's first century were authorized priests on special assignments, in all probability a few Catholics did reside in Connecticut in colonial times (*See,* Thwartes, 1959; O'Donnell, 1900). Port cities such as New London and New Haven were the favored residences of such "foreigners". In cities such as these, maritime labor crafts encouraged the development of an ethnically diverse populace.

Circumstances discouraged most Catholics from openly acknowledging their religious allegiance, even when they did take up residence in the colony. In both the seventeenth and eighteenth centuries, legal prescriptions, easily enforcible whenever Connecticut's "Standing Order" felt threatened, prevented the outright profession of the Catholic faith. Despite some efforts toward toleration in the early part of the eighteenth century, Connecticut's lawmakers did not relax the colony's anti-Catholic policy. For example, to ensure that no Catholics might ever aspire to political office in the state, lawmakers specified, as a limitation of office, those who would not renounce the Pope or refuse to abjure Catholic doctrines and practices. In so intolerant an atmosphere, the most prudent posture for the few Roman Catholics in Connecticut was undoubtedly to remain as inconspicuous as possible.

As late as the 1750s, Connecticut's authorities continued to indicate that their attitudes toward Catholics had in no way softened. When one contingent of the Catholics exiled from England's newly acquired Acadia were dispatched to Connecticut in 1755, lawmakers met in emergency session in New Haven to enact legislation designed to protect the colony from any possible religious or economic threat. They scattered the several hundred Acadians in small groups among fifty diverse locations in the colony. Since these few Acadians and other Catholics were dispersed throughout the colony, there was no identifiable Catholic community in pre-Revolutionary Connecticut. Thus, on the eve of the American Revolution, Catholics remained a tiny minority still suspect, still deprived of freedom of worship, and still subject to arbitrary legislation.

The American Revolution altered the status of Catholics and other religious minorities. When the War of Independence was finally over, Connecticut's Catholics enjoyed some of the reforms that had affected so many other aspects of colonial society. For example, although they had to await Connecticut's later legislation for a complete release from legal restrictions Catholics almost immediately experienced a sense of relief due to changed attitudes within the colony. Contact between Yankees and French soldiers, especially when Rochambeau's army and the Duke of Lauzun's troops camped in and traveled through the colony in the 1780s, had been but one factor that helped improve the Catholic image. So, too, had the presence of Irish soldiers in Connecticut regiments and in the Continental army. Where a few years before a "Popish priest was thought to be the greatest monster in creation", now the sight of a Catholic priest in a New England town could even arouse interest and polite curiosity.

Even though it was still possible for a Catholic missionary "to be hooted and occasionally stoned, by urchins who had imbibed the prejudice of their parents" as late as the early nineteenth century, the first evidence of toleration in Connecticut were already apparent after the 1790s. Some priests even took up residence in Connecticut. During the 1790s, French emigré priests lived briefly in New London, New Haven, Wethersfield and Windsor. That same decade, John Thayer became the first American born and English speaking priest to serve Catholics in Connecticut. It was Thayer, in fact, who earned one prominent's Connecticut native's special mention. While visiting the West Hartford home of Noah Webster, his former Yale classmate and famous lexicographer, Thayer celebrated the Eucharist. Thus, Connecticut Catholics can authenticate the year 1791 as the first recorded Eucharistic liturgy by citing the following Webster diary entry: April 9d° Mr. Thayer (classmate, Catholic, written subsequently) arrives and lodged with me. 10. Sunday. I attend high Mass in his room. Go to church (Cesaro, 1965:43).

After 1800, however, most priests found it more convenient to bypass the state because of the small numbers of Catholics in residence there. Except for the possibility that the Reverend Francis Matignon had preached at the Congregational Church in Hartford on several occasions, and the fact that John Cheverus, bishop of Boston (under whose jurisdiction Connecticut belonged after 1808) had stopped to celebrate liturgies in Hartford, New Haven, and several smaller towns, records of priestly visitations in any area of the state during the first quarter of the nineteenth century are lacking (Fitton, 1872:188-189).

A number of reasons may be cited as to why Catholics did not elect to live in Connecticut until the late 1820s. Lack of economic incentive certainly curtailed in-migration; little industrial or commercial development occurred until the canal building "mania" affected Connecticut's business elite. Moreover, "that spirit of exclusion" that was "a distinguishing characteristic of all New England, but, perhaps, especially of Connecticut" easily dampened any desire of Catholics to settle in the state (Noonan, 1938:6). Another almost compelling reason deterring Irish, German, or French Canadians from living in the state was the body of statutory limitations imposed upon resident "foreigners". Although released in 1818 from the burden of taxation for the maintenance of the established Congregational Church, Catholic immigrants still were not allowed to acquire real estate without special permission of the legislature, nor could they be admitted to a local franchise without meeting certain requirements set by town magistrates. Thus, while political, social, and economic factors worked against Connecticut's overall expansion during the first quarter of the nineteenth century, it also curtailed the further development of the Catholic Church in the state.

Nevertheless, in 1823, a small but resourceful community of Catholics did gather in Hartford. In a letter to John Cheverus, the bishop of Boston, they expressed their frustrations over being without a resident priest. In his reply, the bishop acknowledged their situation but encouraged them to prepare for the future. His letter read, in part:

To the Roman Catholics residing at and near Hartford...

> Your letter of the 3d. inst. has been duly received, and has afforded me great gratification. I wish I could go immediately...In the meantime, you will do well to procure a room and meet every Sunday to perform together your devotions. Let one who reads well and has a clear voice, read the prayers of Mass, a sermon, or some instruction out of a Catholic book...

> I am happy to hear that you openly profess your religion. Never be ashamed of it or of its practices; and above all, do honor it by irreproachable conduct. Be sober, honest and industrious; serve faithfully those who employ you, and show that a good Catholic is a good member of society, that he feels grateful to those who are kind to strangers, and sincerely loves his brethren of all persuasions, though he strictly adheres to the doctrines of his own church....(O'Donnell, 1900:182)

Once Irish laborers had been recruited for work for canal companies and other transportation projects, the hopes of the Hartford community finally began to be realized. From official visits of both Bishop John Cheverus and his successor, Benedict J. Fenwick, which occurred after 1823, to the appointment of a resident pastor in 1829, the steady development of the Church in Connecticut proceeded. During those years, Irish laborers began to arrive in ever-increasing numbers, first to dig the canals, then to work for the steamboat companies that plied the waterways between New London, New Haven, and New York. Soon after Irish workers came to construct the new railroads. Because of Connecticut's continuing economic progress, they stayed on to become permanent residents. In these efforts they were joined by both German and French Canadian laborers who also became new members of the Connecticut Church.

Although still numbering only a few dozen in the Hartford area during the later 1820s, the Catholics were ready to organize their first Church. Through Deodat Taylor, whose brother had earlier formed the Catholic Tract Society, and the Reverend Robert D. Woodley, who had been assigned to them in 1829, they requested the assistance of Boston's purchasing, for $900, a small wooden church building that the Episcopalians of Hartford had outgrown. In 1830, this structure was formally dedicated as the Church of the Holy and Undivided Trinity. On June 17, Bishop Fenwick preached to an overflowing congregation made up not only of enthusiastic Catholics but also of interested, approving, and curious Protestants. To the Reverend James Fitton, the most prominent of Connecticut's early missionaries, who would shortly become the pastor of the new Church, the dedication appeared "truly sublime and strikingly significant". For leading Hartford families like the Taylors, for other benefactors, such as Nicholas Devereux, whose loan had made the first business transactions possible, and for the immigrant Catholics who made up the bulk of the Trinity Church's first congregation, the day was the climax of years of anticipation and labor. After so long a time in which Connecticut's Catholics had lived in a state "where our holy religion was scarcely known" and little appreciated, there was finally, "a chosen and sanctified place" (Fitton, 1872:192-193).

After this splendid beginning, the increase of Catholics throughout the state proceeded so rapidly that Churches and missions were soon established in New Haven, Bridgeport, and other smaller communities, leading Father Fitton to caution priests who had come to assist him about the dangers of admitting new members too quickly. Despite his fears, however, by the 1830s converts accounted for over 80 adults, many with their families. Some who requested membership in the Church had apparently been attracted because of its "changeless nature" in otherwise bustling times, while others seemed to have been influenced by the faith of pious Catholics. Together with the immigrant laborers, these converts brought the total number of Catholics living in Hartford and New Haven to over three hundred members each, while Bridgeport had about one hundred more. Even the smaller towns of Derby, Middletown, New London, Norwalk, Norwich, Stonington, and Waterbury each claimed enough Catholics in the 1830s to warrant the occasional visitation of the missionary. Accounting for approximately five thousand members by the 1840s, the Church in Connecticut had proved so capable of independent growth that, in 1843, Bishop Fenwick petitioned Rome for a division of his diocese.

On September 8, 1843, the areas emcompassed by the states of Rhode Island and Connecticut were combined to form one diocese, with Hartford as the episcopal city. For the next thirty years, under the direction of its first three bishops, William J. Tyler, Bernard O'Reilly, and Francis Patrick McFarland, the Diocese of Hartford continued to expand in both states. When in the early 1870s the demands of its population grew too great for one bishop, the Roman office was once again petitioned for a change. In 1872, the Diocese of Hartford was separated according to state boundaries and a new diocese, that of Providence, was formed to provide for the Catholics of Rhode Island. Thus the years 1843-1872, representing the time when the diocese included both states, may be considered the initial phase in history of the Diocese of Hartford.

From the start, the Diocese of Hartford created its own way of presenting itself within Protestant New England. Despite the first bishop's Protestant American background, as well as a spirit of religious revivalism that had caused a number of outstanding Protestants to consider Catholicism seriously for the first time, there is no evidence that Bishop Tyler or his successors made any concerted effort to attract a Protestant following or identification with Protestant New England. Nor did the presence of certain prestigious families, many of whose members had become outstanding converts, move the Church in the direction of assimilation or initiation of Protestant ways and values. Either to avoid arousing antagonism among the Protestant majority or to maintain internal harmony by attending to new Catholics, leaders concerned themselves from the very beginning with the Church's immigrant membership. Thus, as the years moved on, the Connecticut Catholic Church became even more sharply set apart from its Anglo Protestant neighbors.

One factor that contributed to the Irish appearance of the diocese was that most of the clergy immediately available to assist early bishops with the spiritual work of the diocese were Irish immigrants. Certainly, the diocese's first bishop, William J. Tyler (1806-1849) found this to be the case; in fact, five of the first six priests he assigned to work in the diocese were Irish born. Moreover, although he petitioned European mission societies (such as the Leopoldine Mission Society of Vienna and the Propagation of Faith in Paris), for financial aid, he learned early in his career that the best way of acquiring priests would be through contacts with the Reverend John Hand, rector of the newly opened All Hallows Seminary, Drumcondra, Dublin, Ireland. Yet even with this assistance — the seminary would send fourteen priests during Tyler's administration alone — the bishop complained that the diocese was still experiencing a serious shortage of priests.

The recruiting of priests for the diocese continued during the brief career of his Irish born successor, Bernard O'Reilly (1803-1856), who traveled to Ireland not only for that purpose, but to negotiate for religious communities as well. Only during the career of the Irish American Francis P. McFarland, who was bishop of the diocese from 1858-1874, was this overwhelming Irish immigrant character of the diocesan clergy somewhat altered as native clergy and missionaries from Europe and Canada joined the ranks. In the formative years of the diocese almost the entire leadership (bishops, priests, religious and lay leaders) had their roots in Ireland; the influence of these leaders reinforced the already solidly Irish character of the diocese.

Another factor that contributed to the "Irishness" of the Diocese of Hartford during its missionary period was the personality of Hartford's second bishop, Bernard O'Reilly. After tuberculosis and heart disease ended the brief career of Bishop Tyler in 1849, any "American" appearance that the first bishop might have conveyed about the ethnic character of the diocese was quickly dispelled. Under the leadership of the flamboyant, occasionally irascible, and often stubborn Bishop O'Reilly, the Diocese of Hartford began to be ever more clearly perceived as an immigrant church.

Born in Ireland, O'Reilly not only personified certain dynamic qualities of the Irish temperament, but also assumed leadership of the diocese at the very time when one particular trait — his penchant for dramatic confrontation — would draw wide public notice. During the six turbulent years of his administration, nativist incidents such as those that had earlier caused disturbances and violences in Philadelphia, Charlestown, St. Louis, and other Protestant strongholds occurred within the diocese. In each case, Bishop O'Reilly reacted with characteristic style; his tactics served to intensify the Protestant view that the Catholic Church was a "foreign" intrusion.

If occasionally there were times when Bishop O'Reilly seemed to skirt confrontations with his Yankee hosts (the visit of Gaetano Bedini, papal nuncio to Brazil, to several cities of the diocese was an unexpectedly amicable and incident-free experience), he more often used the tactics which gained him public notoreity.

As Know-Nothing political triumphs in Rhode Island and Connecticut in 1854 and 1855 resulted in discriminatory legislation against Catholics, Bishop O'Reilly continued to speak out concerning injustices against the Catholic immigrant minority. In a case involving some Norwich Catholics for example, he directed an open letter to the Connecticut General Assembly concerning the importance of the doctrine of separation of church and state. He met other Know-Nothing threats as directly, on one occasion taking a stand before a Protestant mob that had gathered in front of a Providence convent of Mercy to storm the building. Such confrontations — verbal or otherwise — reinforced the notion that the Diocese of Hartford was willing to accept its image of being different from the prevailing Yankee environment and affirmed its readiness to suffer whatever unpleasant consequences might result.

The personality of Hartford's second bishop was reflected in many of the Catholics in his diocese. One example is that of the Reverend Michael O'Neill, the first resident pastor in Waterbury, who in 1855 was found guilty of trespassing, for entering the home of a Protestant in order to administer the Sacrament of Penance or Reconciliation to his Catholic wife. What seemed to have jeopardized O'Neill's case, was his steadfast refusal to divulge information linked to the seal of confession, despite the Judge's admonition. The ongoing organization of parishes even in the face of repeated intimidations and harassments as well as persistence in rebuilding churches mysteriously destroyed were other indications that the people of the diocese found Bishop O'Reilly's example appropriate for imitation. The founding of over twenty-five parishes, several schools and orphanages, and the inauguration of temperance societies, military associations and social clubs all reflected the growing sense of solidarity that permitted Catholics to present themselves as distinctly Catholic additions to Yankee New England.

By the time Francis P. McFarland, the third bishop of Hartford, assumed office in 1858, the prevailing Irish ethnic character of the diocese was already an unquestioned assumption. In a report submitted to Rome in 1862, McFarland described his constituency thus:

...In the Diocese there are about 100,000 Catholics. These are all foreigners, or their sons. Thirty years ago there was neither a Church nor a priest within the present limits of the Diocese. Nine-tenths of the Catholics are Irish, and they are generally attached to their faith and attentive to their religious needs, although often rude and ignorant. The other tenth is composed of about an equal number of Germans, French, and Italians...

All our Catholics are poor and generally laborers. They suffer much from the prejudices of Protestants who are four-fifths of the population. Yet they generally show much zeal in behalf of their religion.

...there are six native priests of the United States and 45 of other countries; but the majority of these are in part educated in the United States.

Of the priests born outside, 43 are from Ireland and 2 from
English America.

...There is a society of religious women, the Sisters of Mercy
founded by Madame McAulley (*sic*) in Ireland....They
number about 60 members and are involved in instruction,
in the care of the sick and of orphans (Bernard Smith Papers).

An Irish American, Bishop McFarland had little difficulty accepting
the notion that the American Catholic Church was an immigrant institution. Receiving his early education in Pennsylvania's public schools
and most of his seminary training in Maryland, he apparently realized
that his Irish heritage could blend easily into the image of the "new
American". His admiration for the yeoman farmer and the common
laborer also helped to convince him that the destinies of both natives
and immigrants in American society would eventually be compatible.
First assigned after ordination in 1845 to teach at St. John's College
(Fordham, New York), he soon left to volunteer as a circuit-riding missionary in rural upstate New York. Later, when offered other academic
positions — he was even invited to become the president of a college to
be established in Rochester, New York — he chose instead nomination
as bishop of the still impoverished missionary Diocese of Hartford.
From 1858 to 1874, he assumed the challenge of leading the fledgling
diocese from poverty to its greatly enhanced status during the post-
Civil War period.

The transformation of the Diocese of Hartford during Bishop Mc-
Farland's administration was, to a great extent, the result of the Civil
War and its aftermath. An increase in the number of Catholic immigrants in the diocese was largely due to the urgent need for laborers in
war-related industries. Their continuing and enthusiastic welcome in
Connecticut and Rhode Island was ensured by their readiness to enlist
for military service throughout the war. Bishop McFarland's own attitude toward the war effort definitely aided the Catholic position in the
diocese in general. Aware of his responsibility as a "Northern" bishop
(yet not an acknowledged admirer of Lincoln), he did his best to rally
his people to patriotism without ever enunciating his personal views.
Undoubtedly subscribing to the verdict of one of his brothers, that "war
is passion and passion is the opposite of wisdom", and that the Civil
War should be seen "as a national disgrace for the sins of the nation",
he nevertheless actively sought out chaplains for the Irish regiments
from Connecticut and Rhode Island, called upon his people to pray for
the preservation of the Union, and formally invoked the divine bene-

diction upon the troops (Conley and Smith, 1976:91). These actions were apparently sufficient to convince Connecticut's Yankees that they could count upon the Catholic Church to support the Union cause.

This is not to say that Bishop McFarland's attitudes with regard to the problems raised by the Civil War are easily analyzed. In the voluminous records of his episcopal career, for example, one can find little mention made of the war itself, as if the problems which it generated were merely peripheral aspects of his administration. His major efforts during the war and post bellum period, instead, were concentrated to the internal affairs of his diocese. Specifically, the needs of his immigrant population seemed to require his constant attention. A petition he received in the early 1860s well illustrates the nature of his more typical business. Sent by a small committee of Irish Catholics from Thompsonville, the intensely expressed yet error-ridden request spoke of the problems of being a Catholic community trying to find acceptance in a thriving mill town. Concerning their children, the committee members wrote:

> The Catholic boys and girls are mixed at work with the Juveniles of the Other Religious Sects, our simple youths imbibe the sceptic notions of the latter and are led away beyond the controul (*sic*) of their parents untill (*sic*) they become reckless, those children generally despise their parents and pay no attention to advice...(Episcopal Papers)

For the adults of the parish, like concern was expressed:

> There are a great many of our Countrymen coming to Mass on Sundays from several localities surrounding this village, unfortunately and ignorantly they have got a way of testifying friendship towards each other by drinking from the fatal cup of rot gut and inhale from this mixture poison which often causes them to be frantic for a time, they give room to their enemies to say that they are a cursed race and the religion they belong to cannot be good. (Episcopal Papers)

Their request to the bishop was a simple one. If they had a resident pastor "all this disrespect for parish and religion thro' his advice would disappear" and "this evil of Gin selling on Sundays would also be stoped (*sic*)". As he would do in so many of the areas of Connecticut and Rhode Island, Bishop McFarland responded favorably, appointing a resident pastor, the Reverend Bernard Tully, in January of 1863.

For the French Canadians who had become migrant workers in factories and mills in eastern Connecticut during the war years, Bishop McFarland recruited French and French speaking priests. The first of these, the Reverend Florimond De Bruycker, a Louvain professor whom he had met in England, came to the United States at the bishop's personal bidding in 1863. Thereafter the bishop corresponded with the rector of the American College in Louvain, Belgium, and was able to acquire eight priests, the first of a series of graduates to begin their work in the diocese. He also acquired several German speaking priests who began to work in parishes among German Catholics in New Haven and Hartford. Before the 1860s came to an end, both French Canadian and German Catholics were being served by priests who spoke their languages and understood their national traditions.

By the close of the Civil War, not only property gains but improved morale, financial status, and increased membership indicated that the missionary phase of the Catholic Diocese of Hartford had virtually come to an end.[1] For the first time, the diocese was in a position to contribute to funds ranging from seminary building drives in the North to collections for impoverished parishes in the South. So generous were some of these responses that on one occasion the bishop of Newark asked, "What *modus operandi* do you use to accomplish such a feat?" The bishop could also work with expanding local parishes. In cities and towns where mills, iron and brass works had been in operation, new churches and schools could be built. In factory areas, as well as in rural areas, Catholic families could finally be called upon to support their local churches.[2]

A degree of affluence became especially apparent among Catholic city residents. The Reverend Luke Daly in New Britain, Thomas Hendricken in Waterbury, and Matthew Hart in New Haven became well known for their pastoral work, especially among urban Catholics, and in some cases in the development of missions in outlying areas as well. Moreover, there were so many Catholics in the larger cities that second and third parishes had to be organized. Both Hartford and New Haven had several churches and parochial schools; both also supported large

---

[1] Because the total population of Connecticut in 1870 was 537,454, this meant that the Catholic population of 140,000 was about one-fourth of the total. For statistics, *see,* U.S. Office of the Census, *Ninth Census, 1870,* I, 93-94, 475-484, 489, 512.

[2] Catholic population in the diocese in the year before the separation of the diocese was estimated at 200,000, with 95 churches, 74 church buildings or chapels, 10 academies, 45 parochial schools, and 4 orphan asylums. At McFarland's death, there were 145,000 Catholics in Connecticut (total population in 1870 was 537,454), 80 churches, 76 priests, 38 parochial schools, 10 religious and literary institutions, and 3 orphan asylums.

orphanages. Moreover, parochial schools were founded or enlarged in such diverse localities as New Britain, Meriden, Wallingford, Middletown, Stamford, Danbury, Bridgeport, Waterbury, and Winsted. Besides these parish schools, chiefly staffed by Sisters of Mercy or lay men and women, there were girls' academies. This responsibility fell to the Sister of Mercy in Hartford, the Sisters of Congregation of Notre Dame in Waterbury, the Sisters of the Third Order of St. Francis in Winsted. To accomplish the many apostolic duties of the diocese were more than seventy priests, one hundred religious women, and scores of lay men and women. To such a degree had the diocese expanded, moreover, that in 1868 the largest ordination in the entire United States was reported to have taken place in the Diocese of Hartford.

Because the diocese had expanded so greatly, and also because its increased size began to tax his failing health, Bishop McFarland suggested to Roman officials, while he was attending the First Vatican Council in Rome in 1869-1870, that he be permitted either to resign his post or to receive the help of an assistant bishop. Instead, he was asked to remain as bishop with the provision that the Hartford diocese would be split into two jurisdictions, one coterminous with the state of Connecticut, the other with Rhode Island. Bishop McFarland consented, accepting the more difficult alternative of remaining bishop of Hartford, thereby necessitating his moving from Providence to Hartford. Because of this personal sacrifice, the city of Hartford regained the distinction of being the cathedral city for the diocese. On May 19, 1872, the feast day of the patron saint of the newly reconstituted diocese, Bishop McFarland returned to the city of Hartford to take up residence. With his arrival, a new chapter in the official history of the Diocese of Hartford, now comprising only the state of Connecticut, began.

If the immigrant cast had been set by the Irish, Germans, and French Canadians in the pioneer stages of the diocese, its multi-ethnic character would be newly molded during the episcopacies of Bishop McFarland's successors, especially those of Bishops Lawrence Stephen McMahon, Michael Tierney, and John J. Nilan. Of Connecticut's over 600,000 residents in 1880, there were 130,000 (or approximately 20%) listed as foreign born. A threat to some on the grounds that they were "a cheaper grade of laborers" than previous immigrants, this foreign born population would increase by 100,000 over the next two decades. By 1920 the percentage of foreign born to native born workers would reach approximately 25 percent of the entire population. Because the vast majority of the newcomers were of Italian, Slavic, or eastern European origins, even greater changes befell Connecticut society. Settling primarily in the urban areas of the state where they found jobs in firearms factories, carriage and custom-built specialty shops, foundries, metal-goods, and other businesses these new laborers transformed the appearance of the work force of the state and prompted its civic and religious leaders to question the "future promise" of the laboring masses. For no one was this question of Connecticut's ethnic makeup more critical than for the religious institution with which the vast majority of the newcomers identified: the Roman Catholic Church (Johnston, 1903).

Neither Bishop McFarland, who died on October 12, 1874, nor his successor Thomas Galberry, who administered the diocese for only twenty months before his sudden death, had to face the fullness of this challenge. During the period of their administrations, the acceptance of Catholics began to be a distinct possibility as, for the first time, the political, social, and economic status of many of the state's Catholics began to improve remarkably. Reports of its growing prominence appeared repeatedly after 1876, when the diocese inaugurated the *Connecticut Catholic*, later named *The Catholic Transcript*, a newspaper that has been in continuous publication since that date. According to the paper, the diocese was second only to the Archdiocese of Boston among the dioceses of New England in numbers of overall progress and effectively ranked with such rapidly expanding dioceses as Newark, Detroit, and Milwaukee.

By the mid-1880s, "Irish" (70,638 of the Catholic population of Connecticut) and "foreigners" (59,354) made up the Catholic membership of the diocese, and Irish hegemony seemed, for the first time, challenged by other ethnic groups. First evident during the administration of Lawrence Stephen McMahon (1835-1873), this change within the ethnic base of the diocese forced its leaders to come to grips with the implication of ethnic diversity and the impact of that phenomenon upon Connecticut society as well. Under Bishops Michael Tierney and John J. Nilan the policy of the diocese with respect to the accommodation of immigrants would be further tested and solidified.

For a diocese whose clergy and other religious leaders had been almost exclusively Irish (in this respect it was preeminently a microcosm of the American Catholic Church), the rush of newcomers to the diocese after the 1880s was a matter of real concern. Proud of the accomplishments of their Irish ancestors (both in Ireland and in the United States), diocesan leaders always found ample opportunities, especially through the Catholic press, to dramatize their personal and joint contributions to Connecticut society. By the 1890s, in fact, many had taken Irish predominance in the Church for granted. The additions of Slavic, Italian, and other European groups led the Irish leadership and membership of the diocese to the realization that their continued acceptance in Connecticut society would be challenged anew. Like Catholic leaders faced with the same problems in other American dioceses of the Northeast, Connecticut's Catholic leaders had to construct a policy that remained apostolic and catholic — that is, open to all — but did not seriously threaten the assimilation of the Catholic Church into American society.

Lawrence Stephen McMahon was the first of Hartford's bishops to confront this dilemma directly. The son of Irish immigrants who had settled first in St. John's, New Brunswick, and then relocated in Massachusetts, the future bishop had remote preparation for this dual task. He could have received no better initial formal training for his role as an American bishop than that of attending the public grammar and high schools of Charlestown, Massachusetts, where he first proved that it was possible for a Catholic immigrant to compete scholastically and culturally with the best Yankee society could offer. Moreover, his seminary experience (in Canada and Europe) taught him that the roots of the American Catholic Church reached back to every nation; hence, a crucial goal of the Church is to express that universality. For this reason, he could comprehend the problems that would arise if Catholic Church leaders joined the ranks of those who argued for the rapid assimilation of the immigrant either into American society or into the American Catholic Church.

Bishop McMahon's early service as a priest of the Archdiocese of Boston highlighted his perception of the "American" dimension of his apostolate. Ordained in Rome in 1860, he had been in Boston only several months before the outbreak of the Civil War. When the 28th Massachusetts Regiment appealed for a chaplain, he volunteered immediately, subsequently accompanying troops engaged in battles fought at New Bern, Fredericksburg, Second Bull Run, Antietam, and Richmond. Despite his succumbing to exhaustion and illness that prevented his returning to his troop for almost a year, he was back with his regiment at war's end. One of the few Catholic chaplains to have been so much involved in active duty, his personal participation in war helped earn for the Catholic Church as a whole an enhanced reputation in post bellum times. It served him well in his dealings with both civic and religious leaders throughout the remainder of this public career.

Bishop McMahon's early experience as a diocesan priest also strengthened his realization that the vast majority of American Catholics still had to endure the prejudices of Protestant Americans — regardless of the degree to which they had demonstrated their patriotism through war involvement. In the postwar years he became equally aware that new commercial and industrial opportunities had swelled the membership of the Church with individuals whose ethnic backgrounds encompassed a far wider variety of customs and traditions than ever before. Assigned pastor in New Bedford, Massachusetts, (a position he would retain for fourteen years) and having discovered that over half of his congregation was Portuguese, he learned their language so he could celebrate the liturgy, confer the sacraments, and otherwise communicate with his fellow Catholics. Dissatisfied with his own halting linguistic abilities he personally worked toward acquiring priests from Portugal, writing to both a bishop in Portugal and to clerical friends of persons in his congregation. He did not relax his efforts until he located Portuguese priests and had established a Church for them. It was this kind of persistence with groups whose traditions were alien to him that would continually characterize McMahon's episcopal efforts in Hartford.

During the sixteen years of his tenure as bishop, McMahon organized forty-eight parishes, dedicated seventy churches, completed construction of the diocesan cathedral, and supervised the founding of sixteen parish schools and convents. Many of these involved German, French Canadian, Italian, Slovak, and Polish minorities. Considering their needs as basic as those of the more established Irish constituency of his diocese, he responded to the petitions of every immigrant group that sought his help, supplying them wherever possible with priests of their own, assisting them in the establishment of separate national parishes (parishes where the language and customs of an ethnic minority dictated special status), and even helping to provide schools.

To some of the more established members of the diocese who felt threatened by the organization of national parishes, Bishop McMahon seemed almost unsympathetic. Perhaps his seminary experience in Canada and abroad had helped him appreciate the language, customs, and traditions of the French Canadians, French, Germans, and Italians far better than those of other American Catholics; certainly his experience as a priest in Massachusetts had especially readied him for work with cultures viewed by Americans as foreign. Thus, according to an impressionable young priest who described the bishop as a man who could not "confound what was essential with that which was non-essential", the bishop's typical response to those who worried over the negative impact of new immigrant parishes was a curt "I don't care..." (Duggan, 1930). The historic record suggests that the bishop's sense of universality of the Church, as well as his formulative pastoral experiences, simply dominated his perceptions of the future direction of the diocese.

Following in the tradition of Bishop McFarland, Bishop McMahon turned for his first recruits to the graduates of the seminary at Louvain, Belgium. In particular he sought out French and German speaking priests to assist in the establishment of parishes, especially in the urban areas of the diocese. By the end of his administration, he had become involved in the establishment of five French parishes and three German parishes. Two of the oldest German congregations in the state — Sacred Heart, Hartford, and St. Joseph, Bridgeport — were named independent parishes with full parochial rights. When the new immigrants asked permission to organize independent parishes, the bishop was also open to their requests. Thus, during this tenure, the first Slovak Church in New England was incorporated, and the initial stages of Polish and Lithuanian Catholic parishes were completed.

A typical example of Bishop McMahon's method of dealing with immigrant requests can be detected in his negotiations with the French and German speaking congregation in Meriden. When this group petitioned him for a priest in 1880 (the first year of his administration), he authorized Reverend J.J. Van Oppen, a Louvain graduate already stationed in the diocese,

> ...to take spiritual charge of the French speaking Catholics of that city and see if you cannot organize them into a congregation by themselves. And as you speak and understand the German language you may take charge, also, of the Catholics of that nationality. Perhaps it would be better to have a separate service for each of the two elements but I leave matters of detail to your zeal and prudence in which I have the fullest confidence. (St. Thomas Seminary Library)

Thus commissioned, Father Van Oppen began his work in Meriden and plans for the Church of St. Laurent were set in motion. According to parish legend, the men of the parish dug the entire foundation for the church on one summer evening. Then, shouldering picks and shovels, they proceeded in parade, marching through the neighborhood to the music of the same band that had accompanied them during the excavation chores. At the cornerstone ceremonies in 1881, Bishop McMahon congratulated the congregation in their native tongue and encouraged their continuing endeavors.

Perhaps one of the most interesting anecdotes indicating Bishop McMahon's quick, even impulsive, response to immigrant needs is one concerning his granting permission for the religious community of the Missionaries of Our Lady of LaSalette to make their first American foundation in the Diocese of Hartford. This community of priests and brothers, whose origins were in Grenoble, France, had sent two priest-agents to the United States in 1892 to contact bishops both there and in Canada with a view toward seeking admission to establish themselves in American dioceses. Unable to persuade the bishops of New York and New Jersey, they were returning to Canada when they met some priests of the Hartford diocese who introduced them to Bishop McMahon. When the bishop heard their story, he immediately volunteered to accept their community into the Hartford diocese. By 1894, the first foundation of the LaSalette Fathers was made in the city of Hartford; the pioneer group took up residence in what had formerly been the bishop's residence. Soon afterward, the community was put in charge of several parishes in the diocese. To this day, the LaSalette Fathers have continued to function in pastoral and various missionary roles among Irish, French, and other ethnic minorities (St. Thomas Seminary Library).

In a similar, matter-of-fact and sometimes abrupt manner, Bishop McMahon responded to the requests of Italian, Slavic, and other European peoples whose growing numbers in the state also demanded his special concern. As in the case of French Canadians and Germans, his decisions were made in response to expressed needs. Largely because of the added language barrier, there were some instances of misunderstanding on the part of either Bishop McMahon or the parishioners involved in new parishes. For a number of reasons, a period of testing did occur and some problems did develop in the formation of the first parishes organized for these groups. Upon Bishop McMahon's shoulders fell the difficult task of easing the entry of all Catholic newcomers into the diocese.

One would have expected that Bishop McMahon's years spent in Italy would have helped him expedite the formation of Italian parishes in the diocese. In one respect it did provide somewhat of a headstart. Unfortunately, like other bishops of American dioceses, he also found himself in rather embarassing situations with respect to his Italian constituency. In one letter to the prefect of the Propagation Office in Rome he wrote of the difficulty that developed after he attempted to find a priest for an Italian congregation in New Haven:

> Having a considerable number of poor Italian immigrants who, because of their language, were almost wholly deprived of religious and spiritual help, I suggested to him that he try to bring them together in order to preach to them the word and administer the sacraments to them so that they would not lose their Catholic faith, hoping that later perhaps they might form a distinct parish. Since the Italians had neither Church nor rectory and were too poor to pay the salary of a priest, the good pastor of...received this Mr. R....into his house and gave him lodging and food, intending that he re-

ceive no salary from these poor people, and he told me that if Mr. R...asked a salary, certainly the pastor would ask him to pay his board. After a little time, it was evident that Mr. R....had more zeal for his own interests than for the salvation of souls. The principal object of his exhortations was the obligation on the part of the people to give money to the priest. He claimed injuries against his Italian compatriots, not only of the flesh, but also in the Protestant newspapers. He made no secret in public for his contempt of the poor and unhappy people. In consequence, a great many stayed away from holy Mass, and almost no one came to the sacraments. Finally, as he had shown himself altogether devoid of the apostolic zeal, tact, and prudence in caring for people, and as he was perfectly useless for the ministry, in spite of several repeated warnings I told him on March 23, 1887, that his time of testing was past and that I had no further need of him. He made no objection but merely repeated his desire to remain in the diocese for some weeks because the season, he said, was not favorable for his return to R...I have allowed him to remain among us until the month of July 1887, but without any duties. He has served the Italians in one way or another for seven or eight months and has received in his time 750 *lire* besides his board and lodging. He has received more than these works have merited according to justice and more than he would have received if he had been fully Rector (Episcopal Papers, February 10, 1888).

The pastoral failure of the priest mentioned above did not, however, keep Bishop McMahon from looking for beneficial solutions for the Italians of New Haven. The year after this letter was sent to the Roman Propagation Office (and after other Italian priests had succeeded the mysterious Reverend Mr. R....), Bishop McMahon secured the aid of an Italian religious community that had been founded only two years previously in Piacenza, Italy, by Bishop Giovanni Battista Scalabrini. This Congregation of St. Charles Borromeo, known popularly as the Scalabrinians, was to become a highly successful missionary society organized to help Italians and, subsequently, all immigrants in foreign lands. In New Haven, the Scalabrinians were able to take charge of the Italian parish in 1889 and to help in its organization as St. Michael's, the first Italian parish of the diocese (Schiavo, 1949).

Another example of the bishop's unhappy experiences in helping Italian immigrants occurred in the beginning days of the Hartford Italian community and involved an immigrant priest who presented himself to Bishop McMahon, with letters of recommendation from the Archbishop of Cincinnati, but who nevertheless left his assignment abruptly, being pastor in Hartford for less than one year. Only after several unsatisfactory attempts to place Italian priests over congregations, would later bishops of Hartford turn to non-Italian diocesan priests, trained in Italian seminaries, to take charge of Italian parishes.

Bishop McMahon also displayed concern for the needs of immigrants from central and eastern Europe. In these efforts as well, he was often unable to translate his concern into satisfactory results. Because the initial stages of the establishment of the first Slovak parish in the diocese exemplified a typical phase of episcopal-immigrant relationships, the notarized petition sent to Bishop McMahon by a lay committee and representing a midpoint of the dialogue is reproduced below:

Bridgeport, Connecticut Sept. 13, 1890
To the Right Reverend Mc'Mahon, Bishop of Hartford Conn.
Highly Honored Holy Sir:

> The undersigned Slovanian Roman Catholics of the city of Bridgeport, Conn., again appear before your holiness with the repeated request, that you may give ear to our woes and assist us in keeping up our beloved religion, which will otherwise be neglected by about 1200 good souls who are here now awaiting your highly esteemed orders and advice, and still more are flocking into our midst with the expectations that the time is not very distant when your holiness will assist us in building a church on the beautiful and well located lot of land purchased by us for that purpose nearly two years ago for money collected only among our own people who have given this money with delight in the expectation that as soon as our land will be paid for by us, that you will assist us in buiding a neat and according to our standing suitable church, and will furnish us with a priest who will be able to speak our native tongue so that we may not be straying around like lost sheep with our hearts bent on our beloved religion but no one to lead us in the right road so that our souls may remain pure and not be condemned by Jesus Christ our savior. It is true there is a priest in this city who is well versed in the language we speak but he is not doing anything for us and by all appearances he is restricted from assisting us in the work we earnestly dsire (*sic*) to reach.

We are now about 1200 souls of the Roman Catholic faith in this city and have good chances for more to come especially when they hear that we are working for the possession of a church to which purpose we have already purchased and paid for land situated as heretofore mentioned. Furthermore have we transferred the said land to your holiness as Right Reverend Bishop of the State of Connecticut, in trust: and that there are several hundred more souls of our faith living in the visinity (*sic*) who would gladly join our parish, if such would be established here for us, we are now well able to support a church with a priest who is able to lead and advise us in our well beloved faith. We therefore again appeal to your holiness for protection and for furnishing us with a priest who will be enabled to establish for us a standing in our beloved faith, so that our children may not be lost to the faith of which their parents and ancestors have been born and raised. We further state to your holiness that if we were able to understand the English language we would not attempt the above request and would with pleasure join any parish in which we may live, but under the circumstances it is utterly impossible for us to do so, and if we want to remain good Catholics and get the acknowledgement from our savior Jesus Christ we must be provided for, and your holiness is the empowered with the desired remedy.

Michael Simko, President
Joseph Rooko, Secretary
Andrew Hunyady, Fin. Sec.
83 Willard Street, Bridgeport, Conn. (Episcopal Papers, Sept. 13, 1890)

This petition for a parish—the first written directly to the Bishop of Hartford by any representatives among the new immigrant groups—reveals much about its authors. For one, it indicates the degree to which the petitioners were conscious of their ethnic character as somewhat distinct from the European groups to which they had traditionally been associated in this country. As "Slovanians"—not as Czechs, Bohemians, or Hungarians—they had presented their initial request. Although the bishop had refused to acknowledge an earlier request made through an Irish lawyer hired for that purpose, he had informed them that "if they act like other Catholics, I will help them all I can". Their response was the request shown above. Their persistence and willingness to achieve their goal in conformity with episcopal desires was rewarded. By granting them permission to organize St. John Nepomucene parish in Bridgeport in 1891, Bishop McMahon became the first bishop in New England — perhaps in the entire United States — to establish a parish for "Slovanians" who would years later begin to refer to themselves as "Slovak".

Perhaps influenced by Slovak example, other new immigrant groups organized Catholic fraternal societies in Connecticut and sought out the assistance of the bishop to set up parishes. Polish Catholics in Meriden who had already located their own priest were possibly encouraged by the Slovak success to begin their negotiations with Bishop McMahon. Moreover, the establishment of St. John Nepomucene's might have motivated the Lithuanians of Waterbury to petition the bishop in 1893. Even if there is no connection between the establishment of the Slovak parish in Bridgeport and the subsequent organization of other Slavic, Lithuanian, and Hungarian parishes in the 1890s, it is still clear that immigrant groups did find the Hartford diocese sensitive to their first tentative probes for recognition.

Perhaps there is no clear link between the formation of these first Slovak, Polish, Lithuanian, and Hungarian parishes and, the continuing flow of more and more central, southern, and eastern Europeans into Connecticut after 1890. After all, the foundaries and factories of the state were constantly in need of strong and able-bodied workers. Yet the facts that the city of Bridgeport began to be known as the "cosmopolitan city" even by the turn of the century and that similar immigration trends were also occurring in Waterbury, Meriden, and New Britain suggest that factors other than the purely economic were motivating the "immigrant" population to remain in the state. For, as sociologists have generally remarked, minority groups traditionally sought out institutions where they could find a certain sense of belonging. In the unfriendly Yankee American environment the Slavic, Hungarian, Lithuanian, and Italian immigrants who came to find work in Connecticut could turn to the Catholic leadership in the diocese for a certain degree of acceptance and understanding. These good experiences with diocesan authorities, were, in turn, communicated to friends and relatives. It is probable that the initial cooperation accorded by Bishop McMahon to these first petitions played a more significant part in attracting new immigrants to the state than has ever been sufficiently acknowledged.

If one of the major accomplishments of Bishop McMahon's episcopacy had been the creation of a climate conducive to the formation of a multi-ethnic Catholic Church in Connecticut, the chief challenge of subsequent episcopacies would involve the forms that the Diocese of Hartford would assume as more and more of the new immigrants followed the pattern of earlier immigrants. Aware of the strong possibility that the institutional Church would lose much of its newfound acceptance in American society if it continued to accommodate immigrants, subsequent bishops of Hartford nevertheless pursued the same policy as their predecessors. Moreover, especially during the administration of Bishop Michael Tierney (1894-1908), the diocese not only addressed the problem of accommodation more systematically and sympathetically than ever before, but it actually led other dioceses in the execution of policies consciously designed to ease the entrance of immigrants into the American Catholic Church. Under Tierney's successors, the diocesan response to the accommodation of immigrants remained basically the same.

In 1890, the Diocese of Hartford included about 150,000 Catholics, accounting for one-sixth of the state's total population, and it ranked fourteenth among states where there were significant Catholic populations. As immigration and natural increase almost doubled the numbers of American Catholics by 1920, it would be expected that the number of Catholics in Connecticut would increase proportionately. Not only did this prove to be the case but the increase in numbers per capita was among the highest in the nation. For example, during a peak period of immigration to the United States (1906-1916), while the national percentage increase of Catholic population was 10.6 percent, Connecticut's Catholic increase was 37 percent, or third highest in the nation (only New Jersey and Arizona surpassed Connecticut). Furthermore, while other New England and Middle Atlantic states, such as Rhode Island (13.5%), Massachusetts (11%), Maine (11.3%), and Pennsylvania (28%) did not show increases in Catholic population above the national norm, figures for New York (2%), New Hampshire (-4%), and Vermont (-18.5%) indicated that Connecticut's Catholic growth was exceptional for the Northeast and East (Shaughnessy, 1925:206). Moreover, the fact that from 1901 on, Catholics would represent one-third or more of the total population of the state also meant that the increase of Catholic population had occurred apart from factors that would have prompted similar increases among other Christians. The steady, substantial growth of the Catholic Church in the Diocese of Hartford must be explained by factors other than pure economic considerations; it would appear that among the reasons Catholic immigrants preferred Connecticut as their permanent residence was a sense of accommodation they perceived in their dealing with the Diocese of Hartford. Somehow, they felt comfortable as members of the Church in Connecticut.

Bishop Michael Tierney's early upbringing, previous pastoral experience, and gregarious personality had done much to prepare him to confront the varied situations that would become the almost daily concerns of his administration. Like Bishop McMahon, Tierney had also been an immigrant, emigrating as a youth from Tipperary with his family. He also had the experience of growing up in a small, bustling American community (Norwalk, Connecticut) and of competing with Americans and Canadians in seminaries in Kentucky, Montreal, and Troy, New York. Early in his priestly career, he, too, had been singled out for his special talents. When Bishop McFarland negotiated with the new Bishop of Providence at the time of the division of the diocese, for example, Michael Tierney was the only priest McFarland specifically requested.

If Bishop McMahon would be noted subsequently for a certain brusqueness that alienated him from many, Michael Tierney drew the opposite reactions from priests and the laity. Extremely popular, his appointment as bishop was greeted with great enthusiasm, especially on the part of the diocesan clergy who had nominated him as their choice.

His former parishioners in New London, Stamford, Hartford, and New Britain also agreed with the appointment. In Michael Tierney, Connecticut's Catholics had already seen a leader whose primary concern was the well-being of the people he served. If Irish Americans rejoiced, so, too, did Poles, Lithuanians, Germans, and other new immigrants rest confident that the bishop's pastoral experience — especially that gained during his New Britain pastorate — would provide him with the skills he needed for his episcopal office.

Though popular among his people, Michael Tierney's standing among the nation's more influential bishops was somewhat ambiguous. In this heyday of "liberal" Catholic bishops (the American triumvirate consisted of Cardinal James Gibbons, Archbishop John Ireland, and Bishop John J. Keane), it was becoming more necessary for like-minded churchmen to recommend as candidates for the office only those bishops who actively subscribed to the position that the American Catholic Church should be in the forefront of political, economic, and social reforms within the American system. Tierney's emphasis on simple pastoral concerns and the apparent lack of support for the so-called "Americanists" (especially with regard to any emphasis on rapid assimilation of immigrants) seemed so unprogressive that some liberal spokesmen informed Monsignor Dennis O'Connell, the most influential American in Rome, of the rumor that Tierney was an "anti-Satolli" man — thus, presumably, anti-Americanist. While criticism did not prevent Tierney's appointment as bishop, it also did not strengthen his position among American prelates then in favor. Fortunately for Tierney, his preferences had little negative consequences in the long run, as Americanists also soon found themselves in the opposite camp from Satolli — albeit for presumably different reasons.

Throughout Bishop Tierney's administration — and following in the tradition of both Bishops McFarland and McMahon — practical diocesan concerns were of far greater significance to the bishop than theoretical debates over national issues, and building his diocese was more important than the way he was perceived outside the Diocese of Hartford. In particular, pursuing the business of balanced institutional growth seemed to be his major goal. Thus, by the end of his episcopate, important structural development had occurred. Besides the incorporation of sixty-nine parishes, and the establishment of eighty-three new parishes, Tierney supervised the inauguration of several new diocesan institutions. Among these were a diocesan seminary for students in high school and their first two years of college; five hospitals in Hartford, New Haven, Bridgeport, Waterbury, and Willimantic; and protective homes for neglected youth, such as the House of Good Shepherd for girls and St. John's Industrial School for boys. But one of the most significant developments during Bishop Tierney's episcopate involved the gradual unfolding of what would become diocesan policy regarding the incorporation of new ethnic minorities into the diocesan structure.

To accommodate the new immigrants, Bishop Tierney pursued three basic tactics: 1) providing qualified clergy to work among ethnic minorities; 2) establishing national parishes wherever certain requirements could be fulfilled; and 3) encouraging a general attitude of respect and appreciation for the newcomers. With regard to each of these approaches, the bishop personally committed himself to the task of finding the most favorable solution to the "immigrant problem".

Like other American bishops who also understood the Church's responsibility toward immigrant Catholics, Tierney constantly sought out appropriate personnel to help in the organization of immigrant parishes. European seminaries were, therefore, his first source for the recruitment of pastors among the immigrant Catholics of the diocese. Correspondence from the rectors of the American College, Louvain, to the bishop bear out Tierney's interest in identifying seminarians with strong leadership and moral qualifications for special training for the Diocese of Hartford. Among Louvain seminarians who would later become prominent priests in Polish parishes of the diocese were the Reverend Witold Becker, first pastor of St. Michael's, Bridgeport, and the Reverend Stanislaus Musiel, who served as pastor in both Middletown and Hartford. Other seminarians sent from Louvain included Herbert Dahme, who would subsequently become a language teacher at St. Thomas Seminary as well as the pastor of St. Joseph (German) Church, Bridgeport, and Arthur DeBruycker, a nephew of the more renowned Florimond DeBruycker, who would work with French Canadians in Willimantic.

Major American seminaries also prepared candidates for ordination. Some early graduates of St. John's, Brighton, Massachusetts, were Lucyan Bojnowski, perhaps the most successful of the pioneer Polish pastors, whose work was concentrated in the New Britain area; Ulderic O. Bellerose, a pastor among the French Canadians in Putnam; John Joseph Ambot, who took charge of Holy Trinity (Lithuanian) parish, Hartford; and Reinhard Bardeck, pastor of St. Cecilia's (German) Church, Waterbury (Sexton and Riley, 1945).

In an attempt to avoid incidents in which congregations were misled by "bogus" priests, Bishop Tierney did not accept ordained immigrant priests unless their canonical transfer papers were in perfect order. The few occasions he altered this policy proved disastrous (Father Bojnowski's career was almost permanently jeopardized by troubles instigated by a priest on "temporary" leave from Europe) (Buczek, 1974). Because Bishop Tierney realized that immigrant priests could be substantial assets to the diocese, he traveled throughout Europe on several occasions in quest of both priests and seminarians. In the summer of 1903 he moved from diocese to diocese, in Poland in search of priests. Although turned down repeatedly (he was told there was an even greater shortage of priests there), he finally managed to persuade one religious community, the Vincentians (or Lazarists) to establish a branch of their order in New Haven. Moreover, desperately in need of a replacement for a young pastor who was dying, he also prevailed upon a community of Polish Franciscans who had recently established a foundation in Buffalo, New York, to take over St. Michael's parish, Bridgeport. In both cases, his decision to give parishes over to the care of religious orders indicated his determination to strengthen the chances that Polish parishes would receive firm, steady leadership from the start — albeit at the loss of some diocesan control.

Bishop Tierney also looked for other ways whereby his priests might be better equipped to serve in ethnic parishes and better able to find acceptance among immigrants. Thus, only two years after he became head of the diocese, he announced the establishment of a minor seminary to begin the preparation of his own candidates for the priesthood; it was designed to be a six-year seminary, beginning with the first year of high school and extending to the close of the sophomore college year. From the opening of St. Thomas Preparatory Seminary in Hartford in 1897, one of the major aims of the school was to provide specialized study in modern languages. Included among its first faculty were two exceptionally gifted linguists, the Reverend Paul E. Roy, French scholar who would later be named an auxiliary bishop in Quebec, and the Reverend Hubert Dahme, whose pastoral experience further qualified him to prepare future priests for work among the German minority.

As Bishop Tierney had hoped, his minor seminary gradually became a primary source for a continuing flow of candidates from Italian, Slavic, Lithuanian, and Hungarian backgrounds. During Tierney's episcopate alone, fifty-one of the two hundred ninety-six students at St. Thomas were of non-Irish immigrant background.[3]

By no means satisfied that this minor seminary would be sufficient to prepare future priests to appreciate other cultures, Bishop Tierney also embarked upon an equally enterprising plan designed to continue the language training of graduates and give them firsthand experience with other cultures. Instead of following the tradition of assigning most graduates of St. Thomas to complete their last two years of college and the four years of the theologate to American seminaries, he began to assign some members of each seminary class to complete their studies in Europe. As more and more priests were needed to serve southern and eastern European immigrants, moreover, he determined to seek out more appropriate provincial seminaries than those previously used by the diocese. For this reason, he personally visited more remote and unheralded seminaries in Italy, Switzerland and the Austro-Hungarian and Russian Empires in order to find new academic settings where seminarians could acquire "the language of the natives" and experience their "national customs" and traditions. Satisfied that he had found schools that would fulfill the dual purpose of preparation for the priesthood and training for missionary apostolates within his diocese, the bishop began to assign most candidates abroad to these seminaries. By 1903, when his policy was formally announced, in *The Catholic Transcript*, he had already sent forty students abroad to study, and the plan had been in operation long enough for evaluation. According to one article:

> This is a wise and practical recognition of a condition of things which has developed within the last decade. French and German speaking Catholics we have had for over a quarter of a century. But the last ten years of the old century and the opening years of the new witnessed so great an influx of Italian, Polish, and Lithuanian emigrants that flourishing communities of these people have their own parochial autonomy and some of them are not without imposing

[3] Besides the eighty Irish candidates who entered St. Thomas Seminary in the first three years of its operation (1897-1900), there were five French, one Polish, and two German students. Three of the French students (Bellerose, Matthieu, and Perreault) as well as the Polish (Paul Piechocki) and the German (Wollschlager and Baumeister) students went on to ordination. From 1901 to 1908, forty-three more of the students would be "non-Irish".

> church edifices. They are happily provided with priests of
> their own nationality. Lesser communities of non-English
> speaking Catholics are to be found all over the State. They
> are not numerous enough to maintain their own parish
> plants. The faith of such settlements will be immensely
> strengthened, and, in many cases saved, by the presence of
> and contact with clergy men who are able to speak to them,
> instruct them and exhort them in their native tongues and
> in the language in which they learned their prayers and their
> catechism (Catholic Transcript, Sept. 24, 1903).

Despite suggestions by some that the purpose of training abroad was
to ensure Irish predominance over immigrant minorities, Bishop Tierney persisted in his efforts to educate as many priests as possible in
Europe. Thus, over the years, a procession of seminarians with names
such as Kelly, Sullivan, Mooney, and Piechocki were sent to seminaries
in Tarnow, Cracow, Lemberg, Eichstadt, Budapest, and Guyla-Feher-
var in central or eastern Europe; to St. Brieuc in Brittany, France; to
Bedonia, Piacenza, and Nepi in Italy; and to Freiburg and Lugano in
Switzerland.

Few dioceses imitated this program in any noticeable degree or gave
any public support to it. In fact, the opposite of bringing European
candidates to the United States to complete their studies seemed to be
favored. Still, there were other American bishops who pursued similar
plans and a few openly acknowledged Bishop Tierney's leadership in
this regard.

If Tierney had need of formal ecclesiastical approval for his ethnic
strategy, he certainly received it from the highest of sources, Pope Pius
X. Asked personally by Pope Pius what he was doing for the welfare of
the immigrants in Connecticut, the bishop explained his program. According to *The Catholic Transcript:*

> ...When the Bishop informed His Holiness that eight differ-
> ent tongues are spoken by the Catholics under his jurisdic-
> tion, the Pontiff inquired: How can you minister to them?
> When told seminarians are studying in foreign countries,
> the Pontiff answered 'the proper way, and the only way' (Oc-
> tober 5, 1985).

That Bishop Tierney's ethnic policy was continued by his successors for
decades in the Diocese of Hartford can be readily understood by reference to this brief papal remark, as well as to the continuing success

of the program as verified by the subsequent pastoral work of seminarians who prepared for the priesthood according to the Tierney model.

Like Bishop McMahon, Bishop Tierney also understood that he must respond to the requests of new ethnics to form Catholic parishes where their languages and customs could be given priority. Thus, on March 28, 1894, only one month after he was consecrated the sixth bishop of Hartford, Bishop Tierney granted the Reverend Joseph Zebris and the Lithuanian Catholics of Waterbury permission to organize their first parish in the diocese. This premier venture by the new bishop represented a milestone for the Lithuanians; St. Joseph's can be considered the first Lithuanian parish founded according to all the proper ecclesiastical and civil procedures in the combined areas of New England, New York, and New Jersey.[4]

The bishop's readiness to assist other ethnic minorities was equally evident from the first years of his administration. Moreover, he never succumbed to the temptation of requiring ethnic groups to combine into one parish — even with respect to those grounds that had, at time, collaborated in fraternal organizations or other social ventures. Thus, when the Lithuanian and Polish groups separately sought permission to establish their own parishes in New Britain, they were permitted to proceed. Within the same year (1896), the two national churches, St. Andrew's (Lithuanian) and Sacred Heart (Polish), were both dedicated.

Still, the bishop's recognition of the differing needs of immigrant groups and his efforts to locate qualified priests who would also be acceptable to the immigrants were often misunderstood. The most significant of the conflicts that did arise during his episcopate will be developed in subsequent chapters. But a narration of minor incidents that confronted him illustrate the lengths to which the bishop and parishioners would go to achieve their aims. During the ceremony of the blessing of the cornerstone of the Lithuanian Church in New Britain, for example, a group of Polish dissidents interrupted the ceremony to introduce their demands, thus forcing the bishop's immediate response. Time after time, in his attempts to work with immigrant communities, Bishop Tierney would be subject to the same kinds of harassment or pressure. Aware that his presence was still necessary if he

---

[4] The author is greatful to the Reverend William Wolkovich-Valkavicius for much of the specific and painstaking data on the Lithuanian parishes in Connecticut and for a biography of Father Joseph Zebris (unpublished materials to date). Wolkovich's principal sources are city directories, vital statistics, parish records, correspondence in the Episcopal Papers, Lithuanian newspapers (including one founded by Zebris, *Rytas*), the *Connecticut Catholic,* the *Catholic Transcript*, and local newspapers of Connecticut; Wolkovich Materials.

were to convey his personal concern, he persisted in participating at ethnic celebrations — even to the extent of attending minor events. When Father Bojnowski invited him to a baptismal celebration honoring a prominent teen-aged convert, he graciously accepted the invitation. One might wonder what the bishop's thoughts were as he watched the young girl, supposedly a member of the Polish royal family, ceremoniously baptized.

The bishop's continued willingness to attend such events as well as to wait out protests and harangues improved his relationship with immigrant communities and their leaders, prevented crises from escalating, and, in the long run, defused organized dissent. With the support of pastors like Father Bojnowski and Zebris, whose trust in him was confirmed by their continued loyalty, Bishop Tierney helped prevent major schisms from developing in the diocese. In fact, with the exception of some Polish and Hungarian groups that did affiliate with national schismatic churches in subsequent years, separation from the Diocese of Hartford never received widespread acceptance among Connecticut's ethnic minorities.

Toward the Lithuanian, Polish, Slovak, Hungarian, Italian, and French Canadian peoples who had concentrated in other large urban areas of the state, Tierney showed the same interest and concern that he developed with regard to the New Britain multi-ethnic community. By the end of his administration — twenty-eight national parishes had been organized. Eleven of these were Polish; seven were Italian. Among others founded under his direction were four Lithuanian, two French Canadian, two Hungarian, and two Slovak parishes (*See,* Appendix). No New England diocese could boast the proportionately high distribution of immigrants from both southern and eastern Europe. Only the dioceses of Newark, Brooklyn, and New York could in any way approximate the pattern.

Further impressive developments occurred in the development of the multi-ethnic Diocese of Hartford. For example, in industrial cities with large foreign born populations, several national parishes, sometimes only blocks away from other Catholic churches, were organized in various neighborhoods. Even by 1900, four of Waterbury's nine Catholic Churches served ethnic minorities. Within the next few years, almost one-half of Hartford's and New Haven's parishes were classified as national parishes, with Hartford listing five national parishes and New Haven having two Italian parishes, and one each for German, French or French Canadians, and Polish Catholics.

The most cosmopolitan city of all was Bridgeport. Although its foreign born population was approximately equal to Hartford's (around 50,000), its special character was due to the fact that so many ethnic groups had chosen to reside there. By the end of Tierney's administration, eight of the city's fourteen Roman Catholic parishes had been established as national parishes (*See,* Appendix C).

Still smaller cities and towns witnessed the establishment of second, and even third, Catholic churches as national parishes made their first appearance. With the bishop's approval, for example, new ethnic minorities in Terryville, Torrington, Derby, South Norwalk, Norwich, Rockville, and Union City organized separate parishes. Since an exceedingly large number of the most recent immigrants continued to be from Ireland, new territorial parishes were formed to accommodate them. Moreover, a growing number of both urban and rural parishes became ethnically integrated, thereby foreshadowing the different form of pluralism that would characterize the Church in the mid-twentieth century. In sum, almost one-half of the parishes inaugurated under Bishop Tierney served immigrants from southern and eastern European countries. Of the remaining churches, some had predominantly Irish American congregrations with mixed ethnic minority groups, while others were incorporated as national parishes for French and German Catholics.

Whether organized separately or not, however, the multi-ethnic constituency of the diocese had become unmistakably clear by the end of Bishop Tierney's administration. For years this complex situation had been highlighted by the diocesan press. But after 1900, it emerged as a constantly recurring topic. Especially through *The Catholic Transcript* which had become the official publication of the diocese in 1898, the bishop transmitted his optimistic attitudes and practical policies with regard to the demographic changes that had occurred. Undoubtedly following his lead, the diocesan press began to develop a decidedly pro-immigrant stance after the turn of the century, and by 1903 it not only closely mirrored the bishop's policies but became the chief means by which Catholic opinion on behalf of immigrants could be molded. From general comments such as "...Their (the immigrants') generosity and readiness to make sacrifices for their religion and for their native land are becoming more and more appreciated every day" to such specific comparisons as "...They are as ready to build their churches as were the Irish immigrants of forty and fifty years ago", the journal projected the bishop's beliefs and seconded his policies (Catholic Transcript, Nov. 8, 1945).

So clearly had the perception of the Diocese of Hartford as a successful model for the accommodation of varied ethnic groups been conveyed that the achievements of the diocese in this regard became the chief topic of comment at the time of Tierney's death in 1908. Then, in local and national news, the bishop's progressive immigrant policy was singled out as the main reason for the vitality of the diocese. For example, *The Boston Herald* emphasized the bishop's skill in meeting "the needs and demands of a state whose populations in the cities and large towns has changed...during the past fifteen years," while *The Bridgeport Telegram* commented on "the tact and patience with which he dealt with the non-English speaking congregations who have become so numerous in recent years...." (Duggan, 1900:153). Not only did *The Hartford Times* and *The Hartford Courant* both refer to his sensitive work for immigrants but newspapers as far distant as Pennsylvania, Ohio, and New Jersey also spoke of his "great work for immigrants" and his skill in preventing "much friction" by handling problems "in a masterly manner, paving the way for the future". The bishop's administrative skills, his capable leadership of the National Temperance Union, his various crusades against injustice and corruption, his spirit of ecumenism drew praise from the Protestant clergy of the state. His zeal for building schools, hospitals, and other welfare institutions — all these also received due credit. But, after all else was said, it was his ability to be a provident pastor of all his people, native and immigrant alike, that was emphasized as the one characteristic and crowning achievement of his episcopacy, and the key to the healthy condition of the diocese.

Not surprisingly, this was one of the principal themes developed by Matthew Harkins, bishop of the neighboring Diocese of Providence, in the sermon he delivered on the day of Bishop Tierney's funeral. Speaking on behalf of other American Catholic bishops, he remarked: "We are astonished at the number of languages spoken in that state; and we can but praise the foresight and zeal of the bishop, who has thus solved one of the greatest problems ever presented to the Church" (Catholic Transcript, Oct. 15, 1908).

John J. Nilan, a pastor during the previous fourteen years in Amesbury, Massachusetts, became the seventh bishop of Hartford in April, 1910. For the next twenty-four years as bishop he pursued a fundamental course of action that reinforced the policies and systematized the work already begun by previous bishops and that also found acceptance in secular cities. During Nilan's administration, a number of diocesan institutions, as well as several administrative offices, underwent needed modernization; but, apart from the establishment of a facility for infants and maternity patients, the coordination of Catholic Charities and some religious congregations, as well as the establishment of the first two women's Catholic colleges in the state, no innovative educational or social service institutions were founded. With regard to the Catholic immigrant population of the diocese, moreover, the bishop seldom took a course different from that charted by his predecessors. Bishop Tierney's policies concerning the education of seminarians and the pursuit of means to maintain or insure good interrelationships among ethnic minorities were especially imitated.

Nilan's pursuance of Bishop Tierney's ideas with respect to immigrants was straightforward, if unimaginative. Over the years, he maintained existing personnel policies, assigning diocesan candidates to various European and Canadian seminaries (except during World War I) and appointing authorized priests, conversant in foreign languages, to both national and territorial parishes. Albeit hesitantly, he also cooperated with ethnic leaders in the establishment of new national parishes. By the end of his administration an additional twelve Polish, ten Italian, two Lithuanian, and two Slovak parishes had been incorporated, while a number of parishes, especially in eastern Connecticut, had become *de facto* French Canadian national parishes (*See,* Appendix). Moreover, despite increased demands and restiveness on the part of certain immigrant groups, the bishop also worked toward developing an atmosphere in which the words "the Italian, the Pole, the Canadian, the Syrian, and the Slav are multiplying and making ready to possess the land" (Catholic Transcript, Jan. 12, 1913) would indicate that the pattern of ethnic diversity continued to typify the diocese. Faced with a growing number of domestic problems, the bishop closely monitored tense situations, managing to avoid schisms and to satisfy the basic demands of minorities, all the while maintaining the overall improved status Catholics had so recently achieved within the state.

The formation of St. Stanislaus Church, Waterbury, in 1912, was the first example of Nilan's procedures regarding minority requests. Because dissension had begun to develop in St. Cecilia's (German) Church, where Poles had earlier been welcomed by the Reverend Farrel Martin, the Polish Catholics of Waterbury had begun to negotiate with the diocese for the establishment of a separate parish. For several years, however, they had apparently met with no success. According to parish legend, a chance interview between the bishop and two "weeping" Polish women finally persuaded him to grant their wishes. Within a month after his conversation with the women, Bishop Nilan appointed the newly ordained Reverend Paul Piechocki, himself a native Meriden who had been educated abroad, to organize the parish.

Either because of the successful beginnings of this parish or because of the fear of "outside agitation" on the part of adherents of the Polish, National Catholic Church (a schismatic church), Bishop Nilan also decided to cooperate more fully with other Polish communities seeking permission to form their own parishes. Within the same year (1915), he approved the establishment of three Polish parishes — in Thompsonville, New London, and Southington. With the aid of Polish speaking priests who, in a number of cases, had already been assigned to parishes in these and other communities, Bishop Nilan began to assume the risks that had prevented him from establishing second parishes in smaller cities and towns. Thus, he finally helped organize churches in Suffield, Bristol, Torrington, Wallingford, Ansonia, Fairfield, and New Britain (*See,* Appendix B). In some cases he did this only to avoid further dissension; in other words it was simply because the establishment could no longer be postponed.

In areas where the number of Poles did not warrant the formation of separate parishes, the bishop continued his practice of appointing priests conversant in the Polish language and familiar with the customs. For this reason, a number of non-Polish priests, such as Fathers Mooney, Murray, and Tiernan, as well as the first of many Polish American priests who were natives of Connecticut—Fathers Kowalski, Sieracki, Topor, Bartlewski, and Karwacki—began their service to the Polish people in both urban and rural areas of the diocese. Eventually parishes were formally established under the leadership of native born Polish clergy, schools were organized, convents for Polish religious communities were built, and magnificent church structures were completed.

Bishop Nilan also provided in an extraordinary manner for the spiritual welfare of thousands of Italians residing chiefly in such urban areas of the diocese as New Haven, Waterbury, Bridgeport, and Norwalk. Not that the same pattern of requests or demands that had marked the Polish situation was specifically duplicated. The Italians were not as persistent as the Polish in demands for new parishes in the Diocese of Hartford. Either because of their Old World expectations of special treatment by the Church, or because of disillusionment with the leadership of immigrant priests, the Italians seemed to manifest a general disinterest over the development of national parishes. In spite of this, the bishop expressed concern over their welfare and responded to any overtures on their part. Gradually, the wishes of certain leading laymen, such as Carmine Palomba of Bristol, of diocesan priests, such as the Piacenza trained Charles Kelly, as well as of several Italian diocesan priests finally resulted in the incorporation of Italian parishes in Ansonia, New Haven, Bristol, Stamford, Hamden, East Haven, Waterbury, Bridgeport, and Middletown.

Providing for the great numbers of Italians who had settled in the New Haven area was a special challenge to Nilan's administration. With the cooperation of the Scalabrinian priests, together with that of some diocesan priests who had also worked with the Italians of New Haven for more than a decade, a third church for the Italians (St. Donato's) was established in 1915, and two additional churches, St. Ann's, Hamden (1920) and Our Lady of Pompeii, East Haven (1921), were organized. These five churches, as well as other city parishes, served the more than fifty thousand Italians who lived within the radius of the city. Furthermore, to assist the more recent immigrants as well as to care for Italian orphans and aged people, new institutions were organized in New Haven under the direction of an Italian community known as the Missionary Zelatrices of the Sacred Heart.

During Bishop Nilan's tenure the Hungarian minority finally developed its reputation as an outstanding Catholic community. St. Stephen's Church in Bridgeport had been founded during Bishop Tierney's administration but it was not until the advent of the Reverend Stephen F. Chernitzky in 1908 that the Hungarian Catholic community of the diocese first began to flourish. Under his excellent leadership, St. Stephen's became a "model Hungarian Catholic community", claiming preeminence among the Hungarian Catholic Churches in the North Atlantic states. This bishop's assignment of diocesan priests, some educated in Budapest, to other small communities where Hungarians had settled also proved advantageous. The leadership of such priests as the Reverend David Hutchinson, John A. Doherty, Joseph A. Degnan, and Peter J. Dolin among the Hungarians of New Haven, Middletown, Torrington, and Wallingford respectively, proved so effective the Hungarian Catholics did not push for the organization of their own parishes in these communities.

The Lithuanians also gained new pastors and new parishes during Nilan's time in office. Hartford's Holy Trinity parish, which had begun under the direction of Father Zebris, was granted the full time pastoral services of the Reverend John Ambot in 1912. As pastor of Holy Trinity for the next fifty years, Father Ambot would become a legendary figure. St. Casimir's, New Haven, in 1912, and St. Anthony, Ansonia, three years later, became the last two Lithuanian parishes to be incorporated within the diocese.

Thus, with regard to the Slovaks, Hungarians, Lithuanians, and other large groups of immigrants who had developed ethnic enclaves in various parts of the diocese, Bishop Nilan had implemented a standard plan. He cooperated with clerical and lay leaders in establishing parishes. Sometimes he even supported immigrants in specific causes not directly related to Church affairs. Thus, when the Reverend Andrew Komara invited former President Taft to Bridgeport during World War I to speak on behalf of American Slovaks, Bishop Nilan encouraged this as well as other plans aimed at improving the "alien" image that haunted immigrants in wartime. The same kind of encouragement was given to the work of the Reverend Charles Coppens, who, as pastor of the mixed German, French, and Austrian congregation in New Britain, managed to ease war-caused tensions by developing a spirit of harmony that excluded both "discrimination or recrimination" (Catholic Transcript, Sept. 17, 1914).

Although Bishop Nilan relied upon the diocesan press as the chief means by which he could indirectly appeal to all Catholics of the diocese to develop a cooperative spirit, he occasionally availed himself of other means of improving relationships among Catholics. This was particularly true with respect to his manner of dealing with groups that were, in some ways, exceptions to the more typical immigrant pattern of participation with the diocesan structure. For example, his practice of assigning French speaking priests to serve in bilingual parishes indicated his attempt to find an alternative to the establishment of national parishes in communities where mixed congregations had already existed for years. By assigning these younger French speaking or French priests as pastors of Catholic parishes already established in Taftville, Voluntown, Occum, Putnam, Baltic, Plainfield, Wauregan, and Jewett City, Nilan changed the image of these parishes, creating *de facto* French Canadian parishes.

Nor did the bishop neglect the more scattered groups of Catholics who did not identify with any of the more powerful ethnic groups already established in the state. For example, he agreed to the formation of Holy Cross parish, Bridgeport, for Slavonic Catholics who belonged to the Greek rite; he cooperated with Syrians of the Melkite rite in the establishment of St. Ann's, New London, and St. Ann's, Danbury; and he approved other parishes of Oriental rites. After 1907, when American Catholics who belonged to the Greek (Byzantine and Ukrainian) rite were placed under the jurisdiction of Bishop Stephen Soter Ortynsky, Nilan helped that bishop in the establishment of Eastern Rite Catholic Churches in Ansonia, Terryville, Hartford, New Britain, and other cities and towns of the diocese.

When the newspapers of the state reported Bishop Nilan's death in April of 1934, little mention was made of his ability to manage the "immigrant problem". Most of the tributes centered around his spiritual leadership, his brilliant administrative skills, his ability to cooperate with other churches and with civic endeavors, and his willingness to respect and work towards the same policies as those of his predecessors. That number of Catholics had grown from 370,000 to over 605,000, that Catholic Churches had increased from 218 to 289, that there were 26 more schools, four more communities of religious, several new academies, and the first two Catholic women's colleges were considered indicators of the bishop's organizing talents. What the statistics did not indicate was the number of national parishes. Had the list of 60 parishes founded during Nilan's episcopacy been published, the record would have shown that almost one-third were organized specifically to serve ethnic communities. Yet the proportionate increase in national parishes had not interfered with the growth of the diocese. To the contrary, it had helped the Diocese of Hartford deserve its reputation as being one of the strongest in the East where the apostolic duty of caring for all Catholics had been truly honored. Without Bishop Nilan's continued support of ethnic minorities, their customs, and their traditions, the healthy reputation of the diocese could hardly have been maintained uninterruptedly through the difficult restrictionist decade of 1910 and the turbulent 1920s.

Under its first seven bishops, the Diocese of Hartford had managed well the problems arising from changing immigration and had consolidated its diverse elements. Especially during the administration of Bishop Tierney it had settled upon its pro-immigrant stance and established its policies of accommodating to the needs of both old and new immigration, recognizing that the development of the diocese as a whole depended upon an appropriate response to immigrant requests. How these attitudes and policies became actualized on the local level was another question. The remaining chapters of this study focus on an investigation of how the overall philosophy of the diocese was reflected in the personnel attracted to serve the diocese, how this philosophy was communicated to specific ethnic communities, how it was translated into concrete, workable arrangements.

3 The Making of Connecticut's Catholic Clergy

During the years surrounding the turn of the century, Connecticut's population increased so dramatically that for the first time since the Revolution its rate of growth exceeded the average rate throughout the nation. Comprising 1,380,631 inhabitants by 1920, 38.6 percent of its population was foreign or mixed parentage and 27.3 percent was foreign born; thus, approximately two-thirds of its people could be designated as foreign stock. Only Rhode Island and Massachusetts had larger populations of foreign born or foreign born parentage in the nation. Moreover, Connecticut was becoming increasingly urban as most of the new immigrants sought the unskilled jobs available in the factories and foundaries of the larger cities of the state (VanDusen, 1961).

Bridgeport, incorporated in 1836 with a population of merely 27,643, rivaled New Haven as the largest city in the state by 1910; its population having grown to 102,054 (Bridgeport Chamber of Commerce, 1929). The net increase for both cities between 1890 and 1910 represented a 109 percent increase. Slovak, Polish, Hungarians, and Australians, in particular, sought out work in Bridgeport's diversified industries, especially those factories that produced machinery, tools, metal castings, sheets, and tubing as well as ammunition and hardware. New Haven attracted large numbers of Italians to work in its rubber companies, ammunition, and sporting goods factories, and railroad industry. Poles, Lithuanians, and French Canadians also found work and settled down there. Not to be outdone, Hartford continued to beckon immigrant labor for work in factories that produced typewriters, adding machines, firearms, electrical fixtures, and special machinery and tools. French, French Canadians, and recent Irish immigrants particularly chose work in its environs. In the nearby hardware factories of New Britain, large numbers of Poles (by 1930 one-fourth of New Britain was Polish), as well as Swedes, Ukrainians, and Armenians were offered employment, while in Naugatuck Valley, Waterbury's brass works occasioned the development of the largest Connecticut settlement of Lithuanians and the formation of Italian and Polish communities. Smaller cities and towns, such as Ansonia and Torrington, also provided many southern and eastern Europeans with work in the Naugatuck region's brass, metal, and other industries.

The Diocese of Hartford was the major beneficiary of the vast changes in Connecticut's population. As noted in the following table, its published increases of Catholics in proportion to the total population were consistently impressive:

Year	Total Population	Catholic Population	Percentage of Total
1890	746,258	152,945	20.5
1900	908,420	265,000	29.1
1910	1,114,756	370,000	33.1
1920	1,380,631	523,795	37.8

So quickly had its Catholic population increased by 1915, moreover, that only Massachusetts, New York, Pennsylvania, and New Jersey (all with much larger total populations) had larger Catholic populations in the Northeast; nationwide, numerically small Connecticut actually ranked as the twelfth largest Catholic state (Catholic Transcript, July 15, 1915).

Obviously recognizing the value of increased numbers (regardless of its negative sociocultural ramifications), spokesmen for the diocese could as easily comment on the changes in its ethnic base of membership. Thus, in a January 25, 1912 article, *The Catholic Transcript* was prompted to remark that "from the annual statements of the pastors of the state it is quite clear that the non-English speaking Catholics and their descendants are fast becoming a predominating element in our growth". The editor went on to specify that the French Canadians were at a point of outnumbering other inhabitants in eastern Connecticut, that the Polish people were also settling in that area, and there were twice as many baptisms of Italians in St. John's, Middletown, than of all other nationalities together. Thus, he suggested, "...the church of

the Italian, the Pole, the Canadian, the Syrian, and the Slav are multiplying and making ready to possess the land".

In case the editor's remarks might have suggested to some readers
that this increase should be the source of concern to Catholics, he added
what he believed to be the only foreseeable problem, namely, that the
"preaching of some modern economists with its terrible results" might
influence newcomers to adopt the language and methods of socialism,
or the more extreme measures pursued by such radical movements as
the I.W.W. If pushed to radicalism because they did not feel accepted
by those who shared the same religious tradition, the editor implied,
the Church in Connecticut would have to accept the responsibility for
the losses that would inevitably result. Even worse, however, would be
the harm done if Catholics joined those "Gilt-Edged Americans" whose
"retrogressive policies" advocated one hundred percent Americanism,
and would further set Catholics in opposition to one another.

The expression of concern for its new membership was a theme constantly repeated, especially during the tenures of the diocese's twentieth
century bishops, Michael Tierney and John J. Nilan. During their tenure there developed the solidification of the policy that eventually contributed to the making of the multi-ethnic characteristics of the diocese.
National parishes were established, priests were recruited or educated
to serve the newcomers, and every effort was made to cooperate with
the pioneer endeavors of such immigrant priests as Fathers Lucyan
Bojnowski, Gaspar Panik, Joseph Zebris, and Stephen Chernitzky.

During the same period, Bishop Tierney established St. Thomas
Seminary, a "minor" seminary (or *petit seminaire*) aimed at beginning
the formal training of young aspirants to the priesthood. The program,
open to students who usually ranged in age from fourteen to twenty,
involved the four years of high school and the first two years of college.
Upon the recommendation of a parish priest, along with the student's
personal acknowledgment of his desire to study for the priesthood, the
Catholic youth could enroll at the seminary, then located on Collins
Street, Hartford, in a class appropriate to the level of his previous educational experience. Almost every student was expected to pay a nom-
inal tuition; however, from the beginning a system that would allow
candidates to delay payments until after ordination was inaugurated.
With respect to minorities, sometimes even the deferred plan was
waived. As part of the first phase of the preparation for the priesthood
(the student would go on to two more years of college and four years of
theology at "major" seminaries in the United States, Canada or Europe
before ordination), a rigorous curriculum was devised. Although flexible with regard to the kind of education and number of years already
successfully completed before entrance, the course of studies followed

classical norms, with special emphasis on modern language training. Thus, the study of German, Italian, and French language culture was integral to the education of the young seminarians. From 1897 onward, St. Thomas not only provided the first formal seminary training but, more important, helped to set the attitudes for Connecticut's Catholic leadership. For this reason, a more precise study of the candidates who entered the seminary in the early decades of the twentieth century is the focus of this chapter.

In the period 1897 to 1921, 804 seminarians began their studies at St. Thomas. The vast majority of these students — at least during the first years of the seminary's existence — were of Irish background. Attracted by Irish priests who headed most of the parishes of the diocese, they were probably more influenced by parents whose greatest desire in life was to see that at least one of their sons would be ordained. Yet, from the start, patterns emerged concerning the future clergy of the Diocese of Hartford. The number of students from Connecticut's Irish majority and from other immigrant groups who enrolled in St. Thomas during the critical years of population expansion through immigration demonstrates the degree to which the policy of accommodation of immigrants was initially realized and subsequently encouraged. A statistical analysis of the socioeconomic background of the same students can help determine whether urban situations contributed to priestly vocations.

For the purpose of obtaining knowledge about the ethnic, socioeconomic, and demographic backgrounds of the young men who attended St. Thomas during the years 1897 to 1921, a study was undertaken utilizing the class register, which was painstakingly kept from the first years of the seminary's establishment. The tables and summaries that follow provide specific information about those members of the diocese who chose to take up leadership roles in the Church, will furnish a more precise picture of the Catholic constituency of the Diocese of Hartford and verify the pattern of accommodation espoused by diocesan officials.

Each table has been divided into four chronological periods to indicate changes that occurred over time; the date of the first Immigration Restriction Act (1921) has been chosen to end the study. Thus, the time periods for this investigation are:

Period I	1897-1902
II	1903-1908
III	1909-1914
IV	1915-1921

The categories involving economic class have been based on models used by Stephen Thernstrom (1973) in *The Other Bostonians*. City directories were utilized to determine the occupations of fathers (in some cases, mothers and siblings as well) of the seminarians. Because not all smaller cities and rural areas had directories, and because some fathers were not listed in available directories, it was possible only to designate the class background of approximately three-fourths of those in each time period (or 77.9% of the total 804 seminarians).

To determine the ethnicity of seminarians, the general rules of philology and linguistics were first applied. When there was a doubt, the nationality of sponsoring priests (if included in the register) was used as a clue to the seminarian's ethnic background. Through this means, it was determined that Father Bojnowski's candidates were Polish; Father Zebris' were Lithuanian; Father Komara's were Slovak, *etc.* However, this procedure was not without its limitations, because some Irish pastors also encouraged vocations among the new ethnic minorities. According to Dr. Michael Simko, a Slovak American who entered St. Thomas seminary in the Class of 1910, Father William H. Lynch of St. Charles (Irish) Parish, Bridgeport, influenced him as well as other members of St. John's, the Slovak parish, to enter the seminary. Along with the four Irish boys he sent to the seminary, Father Lynch also recommended at least four Slovaks for St. Thomas. Two of the latter, the Reverends Stephen Grohol and John Miklus, went on to the priesthood. Other Irish priests performed the same role among non-Irish constituencies.

In contrast, priests assigned to national parishes did not recruit Irish candidates for the seminary (national parishes were formed for people whose language and customs were different from the American norm). Therefore, the correlation between the nationality of the "new immigrant" priest and that of the seminarians directed to St. Thomas from the national parish is complete. Ethnic minority pastors and priests were encouraged by both the bishop and their own parishioners to seek out and nurture incipient vocations with their own parishes.

In the interests of highlighting the statistics involving the new immigrants, special care was taken to include in that category only those students whose ethnic identity was verified on several grounds. For this reason, personal reminiscences were used to supply documentary sources. Priests of a particular nationality who had reason to be familiar with the personnel of the diocese over a long period of time were consulted. Furthermore, parish histories, newspaper accounts, and other primary or secondary sources were also examined. As a result, the list of students enumerated as belonging to new immigrant stock is actually more accurate than that of the old immigrant stock; even those whose names may have appeared anglicized were detected by a variety of means used to determine background and set new immigrants and their sons apart from the Irish majority.

Nor are the final totals for new immigrants or first generation ethnics exaggerated. In fact, there were probably even more "new ethnic" students than are accounted for in the tables. For example, students with German names were placed in the "old immigrant" category despite the possibility that some of these might have been descendants of new immigrants. Furthermore, no attempts were made to consider the nationality of the mother, especially since the incidences of mixed-ethnic marriage during the period studied were quite rare; thus mixed ethnics, whose mothers were the ones who belonged to minority backgrounds, were classified according to the nationality of the father. One word of caution must be introduced: because an insignificant number of converts or children of converts of English background became seminarians (and because a consideration of them was not essential to this study), these students are not listed separately but are incorporated among the old (Irish) ethnic majority. Thus, these tables do not identify the Irish ethnic majority as clearly as they do the various old and new immigrant minorities represented.

To indicate the differences in geographic origin of the seminarians — and the correlation of those factors with ethnicity — six of Connecticut's cities have been selected for investigation. The largest cities in Connecticut — Hartford, Bridgeport, and New Haven — are enumerated first. Three other cities — Waterbury, Meriden, and New Britain — have been given separate categories for several reasons. First, they were considered urban factory and foundry communities. Second, they were recognized as "polyglot" or "cosmopolitan". Finally, more vocations derived from these cities than from other comparable flourishing Catholic centers, such as Middletown, Norwalk, Norwich, and New London. By contrast, the "small cities" category is composed of all cities and towns in Connecticut in which life was oriented around smaller factories, businesses, and related services, while the "rural" category is reserved for those areas where, by 1920, agriculture was the main occupation of the residents.

Although only a few of the seminarians were themselves immigrants, European birth was classified under separate heading. This was done in order to emphasize the fact that Old World origins by no means prevented aspiring students from pursuing vocations to the priesthood at St. Thomas Seminary. A follow-up of some of these immigrant students indicates that, on the whole, they were seen as assets to the diocese and given special consideration; a high percentage were sent to Canada or abroad for their major seminary training and, after ordination, many went on to become pastors in the national parishes of the diocese. According to the Reverend Alexis Riccio, who was himself an example of this pattern, one of Bishop Nilan's oft-repeated remarks concerned the value for a diocese of having priests of European background. Having a priest who could speak two languages, the bishop often repeated, was like having two priests. Because bilingual priests provided administrative flexibility in personnel management, constant efforts were made to encourage vocations among candidates who could serve in dual capacities.

Finally, it should be noted that approximately 25 percent of any class entering St. Thomas Seminary were ordained (representing the normal rate of persistence for seminarians). Although the rate was much lower when the entire six-year period is used as a basis (then perhaps only two or three of a class of fifty would continue to ordination), those "older" students who entered the seminary after high school tended to move on to ordination with greater frequency. A check for the fourth time period (1915-1921), when records of ordination were more easily available, bears out this conclusion. Of two hundred seventy-five seminarians, seventy-four or 26.9 percent continued to ordination. Whether ordained or not, however, the graduates of St. Thomas tended to further themselves in the professions, business, or public service. Especially true of the Irish majority whose parents provided role models of upward mobility, it was also true among the children of the newer immigrants. For example, among the seven Italian seminarians whose careers were traced (of a total of eleven who were in the seminary between the years 1897-1921), three became priests, two entered the professions (law and medicine), and two became business managers (one a director of a funeral home). Among Slovak and Polish candidates, the same pattern also prevailed, nor was the story less true with reference to other ethnic minority former seminarians.

The ethnic background of the seminarians who entered St. Thomas from 1897 through 1921 was predominantly Irish or Irish American. The number of Irish Americans was highest in the first five years (87.7%) and lowest in the last period (76.4%), corresponding with the drop in the percentage of Irish among the Catholic population in the state; by 1930 Irish or Irish Americans accounted for only 14.6 percent of the population of Connecticut, but still had the numerical leadership of the diocese. Because Irish Americans were in the position to maintain their leadership function in the diocese, the number of Irish candidates in the first years of the seminary is consistent with the number of Irish in the diocese. The same pattern would be maintained throughout the period studied. Although the number of seminarians from new

TABLE 1

ETHNIC BACKGROUND OF SEMINARIANS, BY TIME PERIODS

	Period I 1897-1902		Period II 1903-1908		Period III 1909-1914		Period IV 1915-1921		Total	
	Number	Percentage	Number	Percentage	Number	Percentage	Number	Percentage	Number	Percentage
Irish	107	87.7	138	80.7	191	80.9	210	76.4	646	80.3
French	6	4.9	11	6.4	13	5.5	12	4.4	42	5.2
German	3	2.5	6	3.5	5	2.1	9	3.3	23	2.9
Old Immigrant Total	116	95.0	155	90.6	209	88.5	231	83.6	711	88.4
Polish	4	3.3	8	4.1	16	6.8	14	5.1	42	5.2
Lithuanian	2	1.6	—	—	3	1.3	11	4.0	16	2.0
Slovak	—	—	7	3.5	3	1.3	11	4.0	21	2.6
Italian	—	—	1	.6	5	2.1	5	2.2	11	1.4
Hungarian	—	—	—	—	—	—	3	1.1	3	.4
New Immigrant Total	6	4.9	16	9.4	27	11.4	44	16.4	93	11.6
Total	122		171		236		275		804	

Source: All data have been derived from city directories, 1897-1921, Connecticut State Library.

immigrant stock appears small by comparison with the Irish majority, certain significant changes emerge. For example, from the first period onward, there were Poles and Lithuanian students enrolled in the seminary. Their persistence to ordination indicates that the original entrants from the "new immigrants" were seriously committed candidates for orders. By Period II there were also Slovak and Italian seminarians. The only group underrepresented for its numbers throughout all four periods was the Italian minority. Factors accounting for this defy strict statistical analysis. Two possible reasons can be advanced. According to most priests, the influence of dynamic, exemplary priests has always played an important part in the personal call to priesthood. Because few of the Italian priests who served in the diocese were able to establish lasting bonds in their parishes, it is probable that the youth of Italian parishes did not have the incentive of direct contact. Moreover, it is also generally accepted that vocations are nurtured in the home, where respect for priests and the sanctity of the priestly call is clearly communicated to the next generation. In the case of the Italian immigrant, the tradition of anticlericalism, which had become firmly grounded as a result of nineteenth-century Italian politics, militated against the promotion of vocations among Italian American youth.

The fact that there were few Hungarian candidates can be explained on the basis of total numbers — the Hungarian minority in Connecticut remained much smaller than that of the other new immigrant groups. Moreover, there were only two Hungarian Catholic parishes in the diocese during the period studied. However, the appearance of the Reverend Stephen Chernitzky — the first Hungarian priest to exert strong leadership among Connecticut's Hungarian Catholics as a whole — directly correlates to the appearance of Hungarian seminarians. A check of the class register reveals that the sole recommending priest for Hungarians is Father Chernitzky.

The relatively high number of Polish candidates sent to St. Thomas by their pastors is also interesting in light of the existence of several Polish seminaries in the United States (SS. Cyril and Methodius in Michigan as well as seminaries that were conducted by religious orders, such as the Polish Franciscans and the Polish Vincentians). Apart from the fact that the choice of St. Thomas might have been agreed upon simply because it enabled young candidates to remain closer to home, sending Polish youth to St. Thomas also indicated that the recommending priest saw the value of the seminary for Polish youths and its implications for diocesan service, and was not concerned that the seminary might discourage budding vocations. A similar case may also be made with respect to other non-Irish seminarians.

That the non-Irish ethnic minorities within the diocese were respon-sible for keeping the rate of ordinations at 25 percent of the total is another intriguing observation. Note the percentages of ordained priests among ethnic groups ten years after the last class used in the study had entered the seminary (and thus had spent the required eight to ten years in minor and major seminaries).

Ethnic Group	Number of Candidates	Number Ordained	Percentage Ordained
Irish	647	152	23.4
French	42	9	21.4
German	23	11	47.8
Polish	42	14	33.3
Lithuanian	16	6	37.5
Slovak	21	9	42.8
Italian	11	3	27.2
Hungarian	3	2	66.6

A study of data fails to reveal scientific reasons for the greater per-sistence of the sons of newer immigrants. One possible reason may be that the desire of members of minority groups to improve their social standing motivated them to pursue their vocation with even greater tenacity than those for whom other career options appeared possible. Another might be that the greater need for non-Irish priests motivated Catholic leaders to encourage persistence among ethnic minority can-didates. There are also faith considerations that must be taken into account. Perhaps the only certain conclusion that can be drawn from the above is that these immigrants or first generation Americans proved that it was possible for newcomers not only to aspire to clerical leader-ship within the Catholic Church in the Diocese of Hartford, but also to achieve their desires.

Using statistics contained in a report on the care of emigrants spe-cially prepared in answer to a communique from the Sacred Congre-gation of the consistory in Rome in 1914, some tentative conclusions may be drawn concerning the percentage of vocations from ethnic minorities as compared with the number of parishioners in national parishes. According to the report, there were 10,600 Poles, 1,350 Lithuanians, 800 Slovaks, 10,400 Italians, and 500 Hungarians who were considered "stable members" of the national parishes in ten Connecticut cities. Because 14 Poles, 11 Lithuanians, 11 Slovaks, 6 Italians, and 3 Hungarians were among the 275 students who had entered the seminary during the five years following the report, the percentage of "new immigrant" candidates for the priesthood is, in fact, proportionately higher than what could be anticipated from the ethnic minority Catholic population within the state as reported in the year 1915. Because new immigrant parishioners accounted for 5.3 percent of the total number of Catholics, the fact that 16.4 percent of the candidates to the seminary were of new immigrant background indicates that the number of seminarians from that background was even greater than might be presumed.

Finally, using the 1930 Catholic census data for the United States, one can compare the percentage of priests of new immigrant background among the total number of priests serving in the diocese with that of other dioceses with similar ethnic constituencies (especially southern and eastern European new immigrants), thereby indicating the degree to which the Hartford diocese attracted vocations of new immigrant background during the critical years of the study. In surveying the surrounding dioceses of New England (Boston, Springfield, Fall River, and Providence) as well as two nearby key ports of entry for immigrants (Brooklyn, New York, and Newark, New Jersey) and comparing the percentage of priests of southern or eastern European background serving in those dioceses in 1930 with that of the Diocese of Hartford, it becomes clear that Connecticut's Catholic leaders did meet the challenge of acquiring ethnic minority priests with impressive results. In fact, Hartford's average was well above those of every New England diocese; only the Diocese of Newark surpassed Hartford in its allocation of priests.

Archdiocese and Dioceses, 1930	Total Number of Priests Serving	Priests of Southern or Eastern European Background	Percentage of Total
Boston	1,149	69	6.0
Providence	329	34	10.3
Springfield	541	58	10.7
Fall River	206	12	5.8
Brooklyn, New York	746	89	11.9
Newark, New Jersey	715	135	18.8
Hartford	529	91	17.2

Another variable considered was the father's occupation (*See*, Table 2). Thernstrom's (1973) model, dividing occupation between white-collar and blue-collar categories, and his socioeconomic ranking of occupations became the basis for the various classifications used herein. The occupations of 178 (22.1 %) of the fathers could not be determined; moreover, 38 (4.7%) of the fathers were deceased. Therefore, the criteria for conclusions with regard to the socioeconomic background of the students were based on 73.2 percent of the seminarians. Although 48.7 percent of the fathers of seminarians for the entire twenty-five year period could be classified as blue-collar workers, this proportion fluctuates within the four time periods. During the first period (1897-1902), these fathers make up 57.4 percent of the total, while during the fourth period (1915-1921), they accounted for 49.8 percent. However, the two middle periods had proportionately few blue-collar workers (44% and 44.4% respectively). Thus, the statistics suggest that, although there was upward mobility evident until 1915, its rate was temporarily retarded during the period 1915-1921. One explanation for this might be the addition of candidates from new immigrant stock. For example, during the fourth period, the largest number of new immigrants entered the seminary. Although the fathers of the new immigrants belonged to all socioeconomic backgrounds (with the exception of the high white-collar category), there were more unskilled workers among the total new immigrant group while blue-collar workers clearly predominated. Where the occupation of fathers was listed in the directories, the results for the fourth period are shown in Table 3.

Another factor that may account for the discrepancy between the third and fourth periods is that there is a sharp increase in the number of skilled workers between the two periods, while there is little change between the numbers of white-collar workers. This would also account for the appearance of a slackening in the incidences of upward mobility. Thus, in Period I, 16.4 percent of all the fathers listed were represented among white-collar workers; in Period II, the percentage had increased to 23.4; in Period III to 25.0; while in Period IV there is a one point decline to 24.0.

During the period 1897-1921, the fathers of the seminarians derived, in almost equal proportions, from both white- and blue-collar backgrounds. On average, few fathers held high white-collar jobs (1.5%), but low white-collar occupations (21.5%) and unskilled jobs (22.8%) kept more fathers employed than any other kind of work.

The fact that a relatively high proportion of the fathers of Irish seminarians were in railroad-related jobs (4.6% within the four chronological periods), seems to hold little significance for the purposes of this study. Yet, it might suggest the community aspects of vocation. As has

TABLE 2
OCCUPATIONS OF FATHERS OF SEMINARIANS, BY TIME PERIODS

Occupation Group	Period I 1897-1902 Number	Percentage	Period II 1903-1908 Number	Percentage	Period III 1909-1914 Number	Percentage	Period IV 1915-1921 Number	Percentage	Total Number	Percentage
High White Collar	—	—	3	1.8	7	3.0	2	.7	12	1.5
Low White Collar	20	16.4	37	21.6	52	22.0	64	23.3	173	21.5
Skilled	20	16.4	13	7.6	27	11.4	45	16.4	105	13.1
Semi-skilled	15	12.3	17	9.9	35	14.8	32	11.6	99	12.3
Unskilled	35	28.7	46	26.9	42	17.8	60	21.8	183	22.8
Deceased	6	4.9	8	4.7	14	6.0	10	3.6	38	4.7
Unemployed	1	.8	1	.6	4	1.7	5	1.8	11	1.4
Farmer	—	—	1	.6	2	.9	2	.7	5	.6
Unknown	25	20.5	45	26.3	53	22.4	55	20.0	178	22.1
Total	122		171		236		275		804	

TABLE 3

OCCUPATIONS OF FATHERS OF "NEW IMMIGRANT" SEMINARIANS,
PERIOD IV (1915-1921), BY CATEGORIES

| Ethnic Group | Blue Collar | | | | Low White Collar |
	Skilled	Semi-skilled	Unskilled	Total	
Polish	3	1	1	5	3
Lithuanian	1	1	3	5	3
Slovak	1	1	7	9	1
Italian	2	—	1	2	1
Hungarian	—	—	1	1	2
Total	7	3	13	23	10

been pointed out, the call to the priesthood does not operate in a vacuum. The home setting and the personal contact of a respected priest have much to do with the cultivation of a vocation. However, the larger community's positive response is also needed. Because a network of Irish railroad workers had been formed, a kind of socioeconomic community among the Irish had, in effect, resulted. This group was in as strong a position to promote vocations to the priesthood as was the family and the parish. As suggested by the high incidence of vocations among its children, the railroad community performed this function well. Even when upward mobility altered the status of railroad workers, vocations from its ranks persisted.

In all four time periods, there were a few fathers who held positions in local government or in civil service. In Period I, for example, there were fathers occupied in the capacity of "voter registrar" and "superintendent of the poor"; in Period II, one father was a "city-sealer of weights and measures" and another worked in the office of the mayor; in each of the last two periods, six fathers are listed either as policemen or firemen. There were also a number of fathers who owned or managed small businesses, such as barber shops, butcher shops, food and meat markets, saloons, restaurants, hotels, or the more difficult to label "dealer" shops. Only in Periods III and IV, however, could any of the fathers be considered as moving into white-collar management positions. Other than business leadership, the most prestigious occupations that can be attributed to the fathers of the seminarians were those of medicine and law. In Period II, three fathers were physicians; five were either physicians or dentists in Period III. While no father is listed as a doctor in Period IV, one was a lawyer who held political office. Thus, the socioeconomic background of the seminarians corresponds roughly with that expected of immigrants and their descendants. The upward climb to more illustrious political positions, business occupations, or the professions was, characteristically, slow.

Although the role of the mother is highly significant in the cultivation of a vocation, little information in this regard could be ascertained from the sources used in this analysis. Seldom were the mothers of seminarians listed in city directories. Only if the father was deceased or the mother was the head of the family, did the mothers' names appear. Thus, in Period I, two mothers are reported as running small stores; in Period II, there were three teachers and one clerk listed; in Period III, one mother is listed as a storekeeper, one as a registered nurse, and two as working in unskilled capacities. In other cases, mothers are listed as widows, while the occupations of the other members of her immediate family are mentioned. This sparse information only seems to underscore what is already assumed about career options for women at the end of the nineteenth century and in the early twentieth century. Because of the lower socioeconomic standing of Catholic families over this entire period, mothers in need of work simply moved into the only legitimate occupations available to them. Thus, although some mothers are listed as teachers in Period II, it is not until Periods III and IV that the first mothers professionally trained in other fields, such as nursing, are listed. One does wonder how non-working mothers managed to send sons to the seminary. The policy of deferred payments — at least by the time that the candidate reached a major seminary — probably made the option possible. Indeed, many young men whose fathers could not keep up with payments must have also received their seminary training by taking advantage of the same system.

In sum, the economic background of the St. Thomas seminarians corresponds roughly with that of all immigrants and their descendants. At first, the vast majority of the seminarians derived from lower- or lower middle-class background. Over time there was some evidence that their fathers were able to move upward along the occupational ladder. But the change in economic status did not apparently affect the option of pursuing a priestly career because substantial increases in total numbers of seminarians occurred within each time period. There is also no evidence that the entrance into the seminary was a consciously chosen means of gaining status at any given time period.

Apart from the accepted notion that most Catholic mothers (Irish mothers in particular) dreamed of at least one son becoming a priest, there was nothing to support the idea that a Catholic youth was forced into that option or prevented from choosing alternative careers that could also bring considerable honor to his parents. Judging from the options chosen by brothers of seminarians or even by seminarians who left St. Thomas, a variety of other choices was always available. As for children of new immigrant stock, the situation was similar to that of Irish Americans, although persistence in the seminary was higher among the minority groups. Those new immigrants who left the seminary, also chose occupations that indicated higher aspirations than those open to their fathers. The many professional careers pursued by the Slovaks of Bridgeport is a particularly good example of the ease with which this ethnic minority moved into prestigious career options. For all its able children, then, upward mobility seemed to be a distinct possibility. Only careers among the business and political elite remained outside the realm of possibilities for either Irish or non-Irish Catholics during the period 1897-1921.

In the final analysis, the intangible factor of vocation must speak for itself. The motivations for choosing the priesthood were based on reasons that, at least on the conscious level, were not directly related to socioeconomic considerations.

Apart from ethnicity and class, the nativity of the seminarians has also been computed (*See,* Table 4). The rationale for separately classifying six of Connecticut's cities has already been mentioned; the tallies for smaller cities have been combined for purposes of brevity. Included among the small cities and towns are such commercial-industrial localities as Stamford, Norwalk, South Norwalk, and Danbury in western Connecticut; Ansonia, Derby, Naugatuck, Bristol, and Torrington in the central part of the state; and New London, Middletown, Norwich, Jewett City, and Willimantic in eastern Connecticut. It is important to caution the reader with regard to one factor: the reason the number of seminarians from Hartford amounted to approximately twice the number of seminarians from any other areas of the diocese is economic. Because the seminary could provide the boys of the Hartford area with a fine education without the added expenses of boarding school, it became traditional for Hartford boys to consider obtaining a high school education at St. Thomas. Thus, while still in doubt concerning their call to the priesthood, some students could take advantage of the excellent education they were able to obtain at the seminary. Thus, at least initially, the names of more Hartford boys appear in seminary lists.

TABLE 4
Geographic Background of Seminarians, Old and New Immigrants, by Time Periods

Place of Origin	Period I 1897-1902 Number/Percentage		Period II 1903-1908 Number/Percentage		Period III 1909-1914 Number/Percentage		Period IV 1915-1921 Number/Percentage		Total Number/Percentage	
Big Cities										
Hartford										
Old	20	16.4	26	15.2	45	19.1	64	23.3	155	19.3
New	—	—	—	—	6	2.5	9	3.3	15	1.9
Total	20	16.4	26	15.2	51	21.6	73	26.5	170	21.1
Bridgeport										
Old	3	2.4	14	8.2	20	8.5	26	9.5	63	7.8
New	—	—	5	2.9	2	.8	13	4.7	20	2.5
Total	3	2.4	19	11.1	22	9.3	39	14.2	83	10.3
New Haven										
Old	11	9.0	8	4.7	18	7.6	34	12.4	71	8.8
New	—	—	—	—	—	—	3	1.1	3	.4
Total	11	9.0	8	4.7	18	7.6	37	13.5	74	9.2
Waterbury										
Old	3	2.4	12	7.0	26	11.0	16	5.8	57	7.1
New	—	—	—	—	—	—	2	.7	2	.2
Total	3	2.4	12	7.0	26	11.0	18	6.5	59	7.3

TABLE 4 (Continued)
GEOGRAPHIC BACKGROUND OF SEMINARIANS, OLD AND NEW IMMIGRANTS, BY TIME PERIODS

Place of Origin	Period I 1897-1902		Period II 1903-1908		Period III 1909-1914		Period IV 1915-1921		Total	
	Number	Percentage	Number	Percentage	Number	Percentage	Number	Percentage	Number	Percentage
Meriden										
Old	6	4.9	5	2.9	7	2.9	7	2.5	25	3.1
New	1	.8	1	.6	3	1.3	2	.7	7	.9
Total	7	5.7	6	3.5	10	4.2	9	3.2	32	4.0
New Britain										
Old	9	7.4	13	7.6	16	6.8	22	8.0	60	7.5
New	1	.8	—	—	3	1.3	9	3.3	13	1.6
Total	10	8.2	13	7.6	19	8.1	31	11.3	73	9.1
Total Big Cities										
Old	52	42.6	78	45.6	132	55.9	169	61.5	431	53.6
New	2	1.6	6	3.5	14	5.9	38	13.8	60	7.5
Total	54	44.2	84	49.1	146	61.8	207	75.3	491	61.1
Small Cities and Other										
Small Cities										
Old	46	37.7	59	34.5	52	22.0	41	14.9	198	24.6
New	1	.8	2	1.2	6	2.5	3	1.1	12	1.5
Total	47	38.5	61	35.7	58	24.6	44	16.0	210	26.1
Rural										
Old	7	5.7	2	1.2	9	3.8	8	2.9	26	3.2
New	1	.8	—	—	1	.4	2	.7	4	.5
Total	8	6.5	2	1.2	10	4.2	10	3.6	30	3.7

TABLE 4 (Continued)
Geographic Background of Seminarians, Old and New Immigrants, by Time Periods

Place of Origin	Period I 1897-1902 Number/Percentage		Period II 1903-1908 Number/Percentage		Period III 1909-1914 Number/Percentage		Period IV 1915-1921 Number/Percentage		Total Number/Percentage	
Ireland	3	2.4	2	1.2	4	1.7	1	.4	10	1.2
Canada	1	.8	1	.6	—	—	—	—	2	.2
Central Europe	1	.8	5	2.9	4	1.7	1	.4	11	1.4
Out-of-State										
Old	4	3.3	9	5.3	6	2.5	3	1.1	22	2.7
New	1	.8	3	1.7	2	.8	—	—	6	.7
Total	5	4.1	12	7.0	8	3.4	3	1.1	28	3.5
Undetermined										
Old	3	2.4	4	2.3	6	2.5	9	3.3	22	2.7
New	—	—	—	—	—	—	—	—	—	—
Total Small Cities and Other										
Old	64	52.4	77	45.0	77	32.6	62	22.5	280	34.8
New	4	3.3	10	5.9	13	5.5	6	2.2	33	4.1
Total	68	55.4	87	50.9	90	38.1	68	24.7	313	38.9

TABLE 5

OLD IMMIGRANT AND NEW IMMIGRANT SEMINARIANS, BY TIME PERIODS AND PLACE OF ORIGIN

Period I, 1897-1902

Category	Big Cities Number/Percentage		Small Cities, Other Number/Percentage	
Old	52	42.6	64	52.4
New	2	1.6	4	3.3
Total	54	44.2	68	55.4

Period II, 1903-1908

Category	Big Cities Number/Percentage		Small Cities, Other Number/Percentage	
Old	78	45.6	77	45.0
New	6	3.5	10	5.9
Total	84	49.1	87	50.9

Period III, 1909-1914

Category	Big Cities Number/Percentage		Small Cities, Other Number/Percentage	
Old	132	55.9	77	32.6
New	14	5.9	13	5.5
Total	146	61.8	90	38.1

Period IV, 1915-1921

Category	Big Cities Number/Percentage		Small Cities, Other Number/Percentage	
Old	169	61.5	62	22.5
New	38	13.8	6	2.5
Total	207	75.3	68	24.7

Total

Category	Big Cities Number/Percentage		Small Cities, Other Number/Percentage	
Old	431	53.6	250	34.8
New	60	7.5	33	4.1
Total	491	61.1	313	38.9

From a review of Table 4, it becomes apparent that the majority of the seminarians (61.1%) did derive from the larger urban areas of the diocese. Especially interesting is the change that takes place over time. Whereas in the first two time periods (1897-1908) large urban and smaller settlements sent approximately equal numbers to the seminary, by the fourth period, three-fourths (75.3%) of the vocations derive from the state's six largest cities. Even over the four time periods, the big cities predominate. For example, Hartford alone accounts for 21.1 percent of all students enrolled from 1897-1921, Bridgeport's candidates represent 10.3 percent, and New Haven's represent 9.2 percent. Even though Waterbury and New Britain had much smaller populations than these thriving cities, they also sent larger proportions of candidates than cities of comparable size (7.3 and 9.1%, respectively).

This high incidence of vocations from certain large cities and the higher incidence of vocations from urban areas as they increase in size indicate some practical realities. City parishes in general attracted the more accomplished clergy; moreover, more than one priest was needed to administer them. Impressionable urban youth had more of an opportunity to observe the priestly life at its most challenging moments. The new immigrant registrations were also urban vocations largely because most of the national parishes in 1921 were in urban communities. Of the first-generation new immigrant vocations, 82.6 percent came from among the six cities listed in Table 4. Of that number, Bridgeport, New Britain, and Hartford sent the largest number of new immigrant candidates to the seminary. An interesting exception to this rule occurs with regard to Waterbury and New Haven, however. Although these cities were also considered cosmopolitan cities, more of their candidates continued to come from old immigrant stock.

Several reasons can be adduced for the differences in urban patterns among Connecticut's immigrant vocations. In the first place, New Haven's new immigrant population consisted of an extraordinarily large number of Italian immigrants, where vocations to the priesthood remained low. Moreover, both the Italian and Polish parishes in New Haven were under the direction of religious orders (the Scalabrinians and the Polish Vincentians respectively). Thus, potential candidates of Italian and Slovak background would have been directed toward entering the religious communities that staffed the parishes rather than to St. Thomas. Like New Haven, Waterbury also lagged with respect to new immigrant vocations; it also had a larger Italian population than other major cities of the state. Moreover, Waterbury lacked large numbers of Polish or Slovak Catholics from which a considerable number of the new immigrant seminarians derived. Despite these factors, however, Waterbury was not to be outdone. What the Catholic community of Waterbury was unable to provide with respect to new immigrant vocations, it made up for with respect to its Irish constituency. In fact, as late as the 1970s, Waterbury was still considered the historic cradle of vocations for the Diocese of Hartford. For this religious phenomenon, no adequate studies have yet been made. Surely it is a subject that invites sociological and psychological analyses.

What, then, can the ethnic, socioeconomic, and geographic profile of the seminarians who attended St. Thomas between the years 1897-1921 tell concerning the Catholic constituency of Connecticut at that time? To begin with, the study verifies much of the data already accepted as part of the oral tradition of the diocese. Not only does it highlight the basic reality, namely, that the Diocese of Hartford's original Catholics were, for the most part, Irish immigrants and their descendants, but it also indicates that the ethnic change that occurred mostly after 1890 found expression in the ethnic makeup of the students enrolled at its diocesan seminary. Moreover, the statistics also reflect the change in ethnic constituency during the years of the study. That increasing numbers of new immigrants and their children began to attend St. Thomas rather than to seek out seminaries that were specifically designed for the preparation of priests for national parishes seems to indicate that members of ethnic minorities viewed the diocesan seminary in a sufficiently positive manner. The choice of St. Thomas also reflects a desire on the part of ethnic minority members to become integral parts of the "establishment". Whatever the dominant reason, priests serving in national parishes persisted in the practice of recommending candidates for the seminary, while seminarians of recent immigrant background tended to find St. Thomas even more conducive for the nurture of their vocations than did candidates among the old immigrant groups.

The study also confirms that, even as late as the 1920s, many Catholics with sons in the seminary still held lower income jobs and more menial occupations than native Americans. Only the Irish majority within the Church were beginning to demonstrate that immigrants could move into higher income and more strategic occupations and professions. Even in this case, job opportunities apparently did not affect the vocational options of their children. If almost all the fathers of Irish students in the first time periods belonged to the blue-collar working class, this socioeconomic pattern would not duplicate itself in the latter two periods. By the first decades of the twentieth century, the fathers of Irish American seminarians reflected the improved status of all Irish Americans, qualifying among white-collar or skilled blue-collar occupations as well as among lower income brackets. Not only did all but three of the fifty-nine fathers classified in white-collar jobs during the period 1909-1914 bear Irish names, but even during the fourth period (1915-1921) over 80 percent were also Irish Americans. Whether employed as physicians, owners of small businesses, fire inspectors, or factory superintendents, however, they continued the practice of encouraging priestly vocations among their sons. New immigrant fathers followed a similar pattern as the incidence of small-business owners among new immigrant fathers indicates. If a rise in affluence had a negative impact upon vocations, it simply did not manifest itself in vocation statistics. The predominance of Irish Americans among seminarians in later periods and increasing numbers of vocations among children of the new immigrants continued even after the climb up the socioeconomic ladder had taken place.

Finally, the study highlights another well-known phenomenon: certain urban areas seem to encourage vocations. Clearly, the vast majority of vocations came from the cities, but the cities did not perform this function evenly. Apart from the sociologically nonmeasurable "faith-dimension" factor, the urban statistics seem to suggest that the aspect of vocation alluded to above, namely, that community support enhances the individual call to the priesthood, must also be taken seriously by those interested in the future development of the diocese. Where there was an active parish life with meaningful liturgical and paraliturgical programs, and educational, welfare, and recreational organizations, the parish environment was especially conducive and supportive; in this special environment that fostered role models, such as priests, members of religious communities, and lay leaders, vocations to the religious life seem to be particularly evident.

While, for the most part, this statistical analysis seems merely to add further proof to many assumptions already implicit within Catholic circles and commented upon impressionistically, it does help confirm the underlying truths behind these beliefs. In particular, it underscores certain aspects of diocesan policy that were apparently such an integral part of the Catholic Church in Connecticut since the turn of the century that they have literally been taken for granted. As will be pointed out consistently throughout this study, given the delicate situation that existed in the diocese at the turn of the century because of disruptive ethnic and socioeconomic changes in membership, the Diocese of Hartford performed remarkably well. It both inaugurated and sustained a seminary environment that drew upon and showed appreciation for the multi-ethnic aspects of the Catholic population of the diocese.

Perhaps one of the reasons that the diocese succeeded as smoothly as it did had much to do with what, at face value, seemed somewhat insignificant—that is, the establishment of a minor seminary in 1897. On the basis of the statistics gathered with respect to its candidates, one can argue that the establishment of St. Thomas Seminary was one of the best decisions ever made by Bishop Tierney. The seminary's overall interest in its multi-ethnic constituency as well as its consistent provision for future ethnic minority leadership set an enduring pattern. Undoubtedly the Diocese of Hartford would have been very different had Bishop Tierney not seen fit to establish his minor seminary at this crucial turning point of the diocese's history or had his philosophy with regard to the training of future priests not been ratified by his successors. From the turn of the century, St. Thomas Seminary provided a priceless opportunity for future Catholic leaders to come to appreciate the variety of talents and gifts that peoples of different ethnic backgrounds have to offer. This understanding would not only serve individual leaders of the diocese but would also contribute to the smooth transition of the Church as it moved from a largely Irish American to a multi-ethnic constituency by the early twentieth century.

4 Accommodation and Accord: The Prevailing Pattern of Interaction Between the Diocese of Hartford and European Immigrants

By tracing the careers of the bishops of Hartford, especially after the return of Bishop McFarland from Providence to permanent residence in Hartford in 1872, it has been possible to illustrate the degree to which the Catholic Church in Connecticut committed itself to the concept of the development of a "catholic" Church made up of many nations within the diocese (*See,* Shaughnessy, 1925). Composed from the start of an ethnic majority of Irish immigrants and their descendants, the Catholic Church in Connecticut manifested a general pattern of accord and accommodation that was remarkably flexible. The record of accord and accommodation was not only substantially alike from bishop to bishop but was reinforced in each succeeding episcopate. Only the manner and the degree to which cooperation was achieved differed, depending upon the external conditions of time and place as well as upon the cast of characters who interacted within the local setting.

In particular, cooperative accommodation occurred wherever the quality of local leadership, either clerical or lay, was exceptionally strong and committed, but it also developed wherever the leaders within the ethnic minority failed to be convincing in their attempts to defend grounds for dissent. Whether accord or discord existed in the short term, moreover, good will between immigrants and the Catholic Church usually emerged over time. The eventual reconciliation probably resulted from the fact that ethnic conflict within the diocese was, as historian Victor Greene (1966) has observed, not so much a case of Irish leadership conducting a "running warfare" with minorities as much as it was of Irish leaders' becoming unwitting third parties to conflict among the people themselves. When the nature of this conflict finally became clear in the minds of the dissenting participants, solutions satisfactory to both Church and ethnic community could be amicably reached — if the proper circumstances existed. It was because both diocesan and ethnic leaders continued to seek arrangements within the context of the episcopal authority of the Diocese of Hartford that the more complex web of internecine struggle that affected the immigrant population as a whole was slowly disentangled. From national parish to national parish, at least in the early period of their development, this pattern prevailed. In this chapter, emphasis will be given to the rhetoric of accommodation that would form the basis for the reconciling of differences, and to some specific examples where accord and cooperation were readily achieved.

The specific attitudes of accommodation to which the leadership of the Diocese of Hartford formally ascribed found ample expression in the pages of the *Connecticut Catholic* and, after 1896, its successor *The Catholic Transcript*. Aware of the ethnic character that had literally been created because of the diocese's Irish majority, Church leaders were fully prepared to portray their "Irish" distinctiveness through the medium of the press. Consequently, from the first editions of *The Connecticut Catholic* in 1876, allusions to the national background of the Catholics of the diocese were both direct and frequent. For example, not only did the lay editors in the early years of the newspaper urge the Irish majority to aspire to distinction as Irishmen within Connecticut society, they also encouraged them to support the causes of their native land. The early editors strove to support the same feelings of ethnic pride among the German and French minorities in the diocese. A distinct bias for news about Irish people and events were skillfully counterbalanced with special features on the achievements in the predominantly French parishes of eastern Connecticut. For a short while, efforts were even made to attract interest in producing a French edition of *The Connecticut Catholic* to emphasize the value of the French contribution to the diocese.

Moreover, the official position of the paper continued to be both pro-Irish and pro-immigrant throughout the last quarter of the nineteenth century. Even after the newspaper came under the more direct influence of the diocese, under the title *The Catholic Transcript*, an appreciation of the various national cultures within the diocese was manifested. In countless articles, Monsignor Thomas S. Duggan, its editor from 1896, dwelt upon the enrichment of the diocese because of the addition of so many "self-sacrificing", "industrious", "public spirited", and "prosperous" newcomers. With the exception of one relatively brief interlude, when certain reservations about the future development of the diocese were voiced (*See*, Chapter II), this theme would find expression well into the twentieth century.

The Catholic Transcript unhesitatingly came to the defense of the immigrant. When local units of the American Protective Association were being organized in the major cities of the state in the 1890s or when "nameless" promoters of the Ku Klux Klan or other bigoted organizations attempted unsuccessfully during the first decades of the twentieth century to turn Connecticut citizens against the immigrant, it spoke out in behalf of the aggrieved parties. A resurgence of fear-inspired literature, spawned by attempts to legislate restriction of immigration, which occurred in the last years of the century and continued until restrictive laws appeared in the 1920s, also became the focus of comment. An editorial warned, when a House bill restricting illiterates was being popularized, that

> our country was built by these. We cannot accept the reasoning[of the Exclusion Act]. The problem is taking advantage of these (newcomers). Here all enmity between races was to be broken down — all to be American... (Dec. 25, 1896).

Year after year, Monsignor Duggan continued to remind his readers that the restriction of Europeans contradicted the dream of the founding fathers, who wished to transplant the ideals of Western civilization in order to sustain them.

The efforts of the immigrants who had begun to establish national parishes within the diocese were lauded by Duggan. Singling out parishes that had been able to build churches and other institutions, he indicated that these new enterprises also had the endorsement and support of diocesan leaders. Of new Polish communities in the diocese, for example, the following comments were typical:

> The 'Rockville Poles' are beginning to build a $10,000 church. The parishioners' spirit of charity and sacrifice may be seen clearly in their decision to contribute two days pay a month for six months, one day per month for a year to the fund already raised for the same purpose. (July 6, 1905)

> In Derby, St. Michael's Polish parish which has no wealthy members will build a church estimated to cost $40,000. The immigrants Poland sends us edify us...by their attachment to the faith and by their marvelous self-sacrifice for the upholding of the material edification of religion. (July 11, 1907)

Often editorial comment declared that a bond of unity already existed between the more established members of the Church and the newcomers. The following remarks are representative of views enunciated during the later stages of rapid immigration:

> It matters not to you or to us whether the blood which courses through their veins is Celtic or Slavic or Teutonic or Latin so long as their lives are in harmony with the faith which they profess...(June 18, 1908)

> We hope — almost against hope — that the day will come when it will not be asked whether we are Irish Catholics or French Catholics or Polish Catholics or German Catholics or Lithuanian Catholics or Greek Catholics but whether we are Catholics worthy of our birthright both as members of the Church of Christ and as citizens of the American Republic....(June 18, 1908)

Furthermore, wherever cooperation between immigrants and other Americans was detected, it was quickly noted. For example, when Charles Smith, president of the State Board of Education, was guest speaker at the blessing of the Polish Catholic School in New Britain, *The Catholic Transcript* (Sept. 9, 1910) reported the ceremony and ran the text of Smith's address, part of which read: "It is touching to see how fondly each of the different races that have peopled the United States cling to the language, customs, and traditions (of their background)."

In recurrent articles throughout the early decades of the twentieth century, Duggan added still another dimension to the diocese's defense of national groups striving to retain ethnic identity. By intensifying his criticism of some "Americanizers" who were divisive or who were interested in the "indoctrinization" of the immigrant, he declared himself against rapid assimilation or any other "ill-conceived and executive fakements (*sic¿*)" "of our professional Americanizers" (Feb. 6, 1919). As he had decades earlier, he expressed his concern that the "law-abiding Catholic Poles" were running into disfavor among Connecticut's Yankees because they accepted low wages. Duggan seemed consistently conscious of the fact that the economic threat that the Poles posed would only delay their acceptance within the state. Throughout his discussions of the Polish immigrant Duggan repeated the same theme, namely, that the Poles inexperience in the art of being "politically aggressive" should not be construed as a defect. Converting them into

Americans too rapidly by depriving them—or any other immigrants—of their precious ethnic identity, he argued, would not solve the "immigrant problem" (Sept. 18, 1902).

In the first decade of the twentieth century, Duggan seemed aware that, in some cases, the immigrant was actually being bullied by some of his own people. In the pages of the Catholic press, his concerns in this regard were aired. Strife in ethnic communities, he observed, seemed less an indication of civic or religious leaders attempting to Americanize the immigrants than it was the work of "designing men...irresponsible men, ecclesiastics, too, if you please". It was the ambition of these unscrupulous men who spread "seeds of disunion" over "fancied ecclesiastical inequalities" that was more to blame for ethnic unrest than any other factor. (Sept. 8, 1902) His conclusion that immigrants were often objects of disdain on the part of outside observers because of their leaders self-seeking conduct was largely ignored; ethnic historians still underrate the internal dimensions of this kind of Church conflict. Despite this, Duggan often reverted to this argument and, in some cases, made it a point to warn immigrants that they were the targets of the manipulations of their fellow countrymen. For example, when "bogus" priests attempted to divert certain Polish and Lithuanian communities, Duggan reported these schemes and advised their followers to sever connections with them.

Duggan was especially sensitive to criticism apparently directed against the "simpler" members of a minority—regardless of the purported validity of the source. An example of this kind of response occurred in 1905, when Archbishop Francis Symon, on official visitation to the United States from Poland, was reported to have remarked that American Poles were "good, pious, God-fearing people but they are not the brains of our nation" (Catholic Transcriber, Aug. 17, 1905). Expressing his concern about the implications of this statement among the Poles of Connecticut, Duggan asked about its potentially adverse effects and added the following complimentary remarks:

> The spirit of faith displayed by the Polish Catholics in America makes it abundantly evident that their sufferings for conscience sake have proved at once wholesome and fruitful. They are as ready to build their churches as were the Irish immigrants of forty and fifty years ago. If they betray, now and again, a spirit of restiveness under the ecclesiastical reign of their adopted country, it is but the defect of their qualities and something not entirely chargeable to themselves. (Catholic Transcript, Aug. 17, 1905)

According to Duggan, it was the uncritical loyalty of the Poles to such unsympathetic leaders as Archbishop Symon that was more the source of their American difficulties and discontents than their alleged intellectual inadequacies. In this case *The Catholic Transcript's* sympathies remained with the Polish people of the diocese; in other instances, the editor sided with other immigrants at the mercy of their own unscrupulous leaders.

There are other ways by which the Catholic Church in Connecticut demonstrated its interest in immigrants seeking admission into the diocese with increasing frequency after the 1890s. Besides spokesmen like Duggan, whose support of the immigrant could find expression in the written word, there were priests, sisters and laity who manifested a similar spirit of acceptance and accommodation in their daily lives and actions. The aid and encouragement given by these Catholics to the projects initiated by immigrants were often even more dramatic proofs of sincerity than the official rhetoric aired in the diocesan press. As symbolic of the sentiments of diocesan leaders, they constituted a crucial factor toward the development of the overall ethnic philosophy of the diocese. Perhaps almost overlooked during the critical years of rapid immigration, these cooperative reactions to specific needs of the immigrant communities take on an even greater significance in any observation of attitudes conveyed by Catholic leaders during this transitional period. For this reason, they are included in the present description of the role of the Diocese of Hartford with regard to the immigrant.

Throughout the decades in which the flow of immigrants continued uninterrupted, many efforts were made not only to render praise for the good work being done within the newly created national parishes of the diocese, but also to provide support and assistance to those ethnic groups that were experiencing the greatest numerical growth. For example, when the Reverend Lucyan Bojnowski, the brash young pastor of the Polish congregation in New Britain, celebrated the laying of the cornerstone for a new church in July of 1896 as well as the dedication of the completed wooden structure later that same year, it was not only the Polish community that gathered for the ceremonies (Buczek, 1974). According to the diocesan report, not only did Bishop Tierney and "distinguished members of the Chancery" attend, but the pastors of the two so-called Irish parishes in town, numerous priests, parish society members, and onlookers all testified to the approval offered by the diocese as a whole. A similar scene occurred when the parishioners of St. Stanislaus, the oldest Polish congregation in Connecticut, celebrated the laying of the cornerstone for the new stone structure in Meriden in

1907. Then, according to a news article, a great gathering of Poles, Irish, Germans, and other national groups representing three local units of the Ancient Order of the Hibernians, two councils of the Knights of Columbus, the Knights of St. Mary of Czestochowa, as well as the local German societies of nearby St. Mary's, Meriden, took part in the joyous festivities and listened to the approving comments of such visiting notables as Bishop Tierney and other high-ranking clergy. As *The Catholic Transcript* (Oct. 10, 1907) observed, the "mingling of Catholics of varied races was in itself an object lesson in the assimilative power of the Catholic Church".

Similarly, festal days commemorating the Slovak, Hungarian, Lithuanian, and Italian churches were publicized. Accounts of the visitations of dignitaries and enthusiastic stories of great achievements testified to the manifestations of interest shown by Church and civil authorities in the accomplishments of the recent immigrants. Without exception, the message was clearly transmitted: bishop, clergy, religious, and laity all confirmed the official approval given these ventures and conveyed a sense of Catholic brotherhood. From a reading of the diocesan papers, it become evident that, in the opinion of Church leaders, the overall work of the Catholic Church in Connecticut was advancing largely because of its openness to growth. What others would have presumed would be a stumbling block caused by the differences in nationality and language had been turned into an opportunity for good. Duggan wrote:

> ...The immigrant hears the tongue of his forefathers...in the confessional and before the altar....Every consideration is meted out to the foreigner who comes to our shores. His national customs are respected, his laudable ambitions and aspirations fostered....(Feb. 22, 1906)

He went on to suggest that the spirit of cooperation that prevailed among the Catholics in Connecticut was unsurpassed by any other Christian leadership in the state.

The Church's pro-immigrant policy, stated in daily relationships, were worked out on the local level, where pastors, priests, religious women, and laity either shared parish facilities with immigrant groups or worked to help immigrants feel a sense of identity within the territorial parish community itself. From parish histories, accounts in *The Catholic Transcript* written during this period or the recollections of contemporaries, there is much evidence to suggest that generally a sense of good feeling did exist on the local level both among various immigrant groups and between the ethnic majority and the minorities.

Exceptions to this pattern did, however, occur. For example, one factor that caused trouble between the Irish parish and its immigrant parishioners was the problem of finances. Since some Irish pastors wanted to retain on their books every contributing member in order to acquire funds either to build or maintain parish buildings, they sometimes tried to prevent the establishment of national parishes. Assumption Parish, Ansonia, under the direction of Reverend Joseph Synott from 1886 to 1926, can be considered one example of this pattern. To erect a magnificent church (it was a two-thirds model of the Hartford cathedral), Father Synott blocked the creation of both the Lithuanian and Italian parishes because these allegedly would have deprived him of what he calculated as necessary revenue.

A similar case occurred in Derby, where the pastor of St. Mary's allowed the Poles, who were in the process of collecting funds for their own parish, to use the basement of his church but requested in exchange one-half of Sunday's income. Incensed, the Polish congregation leased a hall at lower rent. Wherever such restrictions were imposed, the ethnic minority usually reacted as did Derby's Poles. Despite such unfortunate situations, in which financial consideration prevented the proper accommodation of Catholic immigrants or temporarily disturbed the previous good will that had prevailed when mixed congregations worked together, the more typical pattern of local leaders mirrored the episcopal example.

Numerous examples of sympathetic concern on the part of the various diocesan leaders have already been cited. Just as in the first decade of the twentieth century when Father Farrel Martin in Waterbury had acquired a halting, self-taught acquaintance with the Polish language in order to convey to his Polish parishioners a sense of acceptance at St. Cecelia's (German) Church and had also recruited Polish-speaking priests to assist him in conferring the sacraments, so, too, in succeeding decades had other priests used similar means to assist immigrants in those semi-rural parishes in eastern Connecticut where either insufficient numbers or funds rendered it difficult to establish separate national parishes. Moreover, many eastern Connecticut parishes began to emphasize the language, customs, and traditions of the majority of their membership without disturbing the previous, more cosmopolitan, or Irish American atmosphere. Thus French Canadian priests were assigned to St. Joseph's (Dayville) after 1910, to Sacred Heart (Wauregan) from 1906, to Sacred Heart (Taftville) after 1915, and to other parishes that had become predominantly French Canadian.

For the most part, the flexibility of the diocesan clergy (Irish and non-Irish alike) and their ability to respond to the needs of various ethnic groups became a ministerial quality often acknowledged by

Catholics of other dioceses and proudly commented upon by diocesan officials. Only occasionally did the policy of accommodation to the new immigrant work to the confusion of diocesan or parochial leaders. In the long run, the years of service that these versatile priests served in the many mixed-ethnic parishes provided the most eloquent, solid testimony to both diocesan policy and the personal success of the clergy involved.

In the more populous cities and towns of the state where national parishes for the Polish, Italian and other eastern European Catholics had been established, however, diocesan leaders indicated even more clearly their commitment to the newest immigrants. In some cases this resulted in a gradual assimilation of the newer ethnics within the large, urban "territorial" parish structure; in others, it meant either accommodating the newcomers within the parish facility for religious functions or allowing them to establish national parishes within the same territorial limits. Finally, it sometimes even meant the willingness on the part of certain Irish priests to take over the leadership of parishes where national priests had been unable to succeed. Regardless of the final outcome, the general results of the various decisions proved to be remarkably harmonious for the Diocese of Hartford. For the purpose of distinguishing the various ways in which cooperation was achieved, a summary of the history of ethnic interaction within some well-established urban parishes follows.

One of the most striking examples of a parish that readjusted constantly to provide for each new wave of immigrants was that of St. Patrick's, New Haven. From the 1890s on, as the more affluent Irish members of his parish moved to the suburban parishes of St. Aedan, St. Brendan and St. Rita, the Reverend John Russell recognized that his duty to St. Patrick's remained the same. Even though French, Italian, German, and Portuguese parishioners had replaced his once exclusively Celtic flock, Father Russell did not lose sight of his primary responsibility to the new membership, nor did he find it difficult to transmit this attitude to his parishioners. According to historical accounts written by some of the newer immigrants, Father Russell welcomed the Italians to his parish and "many times comforted them"; furthermore, he assisted the newly gathered French congregation, offering the use of his school for religious services and providing other courtesies. Later, when both groups were ready to begin their own parishes, Father Russell helped them set up parishes, within the very shadows of St. Patrick's. This attitude of interest and concern continued to manifest itself. At St. Patrick's school, the Sisters of Mercy encouraged Italian, French, and Irish children of immigrants alike. Not until well past the Second World War was this school — the only surviving remnant of a curious arrangement mutually agreed upon during the 1860s by local public school officials and the Diocese of Hartford — phased out to make way for urban renewal.

In other large cities of the diocese the same kind of accommodation took place. In Bridgeport, St. Mary's earned the title of "mother of seven daughters", as several parishes, some comprising new ethnic constituencies, were organized from the original congregation. The Slovaks, who had been gathered together to form St. John Nepomucene Parish by Father Formanek in 1889, were the first ethnic minority to use St. Mary's; services were conducted in the basement of the church until their own first basement church was completed in 1891. The Italians, who were formed into a parish in 1903 under the Reverend Gaetano Ceruti of the Congregation of St. Charles Borromeo, also used St. Mary's school as well as facilities at St. Augustine's and Sacred Heart parishes years after their organization.

Following the example of St. Mary's, St. John Nepomucene took its turn as host parish. Thus, until the Polish people were able to form their own parish, they worshipped at St. John's. Only after they were granted autonomy did negotiations begin with St. Mary's for the use of one of that parish's outmoded buildings for their own services. When, finally, the Poles decided that the building, situated as it was on a tiny triangle of property directly adjacent to the railroad tracks, was not to their liking, they transferred rights to the property to still another ethnic group and prepared to build at a preferred location in Bridgeport's east side. The next owners of the property were Slovaks who, as former parishioners of St. John's, had asked for separate status on the basis of increasing numbers. Thus, in rather rapid succession, one small building lot was used first by St. Mary's, then in turn by two other national parishes. Moreover, the same neighborhood, once adequately served only by St. Mary's, saw the addition of four other Roman Catholic congregations: two Slovak, one Italian, and one Polish — all within the territorial limits of the same so-called "Irish" parish.

St. Mary's continued to be the parish for all who elected to remain within its midst. Under Father John Murphy, pastor from 1902 until 1917, and his successor the Reverend Matthew Traynor, St. Mary's was characterized by its continued spirit of charity toward the poor and needy, but most especially for its provision for the faithful of many nations. The continued vitality of St. Mary's Parish was a tribute to the "indefatigable zeal" of its Irish pastors, whose cooperation with so many different ethnic groups had actually enabled many to move on to the creation of new parishes, while others remained to share in the thriving multi-ethnic atmosphere of the mother Church (Duggan, 1930:420-422).

The only minority people who did not seem to fit into the harmonious eastside Catholic setting were the Hungarians. Yet even these later arrivals to the city eventually moved away from East Bridgeport not because of ill treatment on the part of the more established Irish or because of the bishop's disinterest toward their petitions in particular, but rather their reestablishment in the west end was a matter of their own choosing, probably initiated because of a certain "clanishness" that prevented them from joining with other groups. Perhaps this occurred because the Slovaks, whom the Hungarians traditionally considered socially and culturally inferior (their European political dominance over the Slovaks had preconditioned this attitude), had preceded them in the establishment of a national parish in East Bridgeport. In a totally undeveloped area of west-end Bridgeport, the Hungarians bought land, cleared the woods, built homes, and developed new farms. Within a relatively short period of time, not only had they located a priest and established a church, but they had also organized businesses, banks, and other social, religious, and economic institutions and societies. In this enclave, they continued to exert a certain neighborhood leadership under the direction of the Reverend George Csaba, who became a pastor of St. Stephen's Hungarian Catholic Church in 1897. Following the pattern of their former Irish and Slovak eastside neighbors, they supplied a model for Ruthenian, Croatian, and other Latin and Eastern Rite Catholic minorities. Given the history of the development of Bridgeport's Catholic Churches (by 1920 nine of the fifteen churches were national parishes), it appears that the cosmopolitan spirit that first informed the city's parishes contributed, at least to some degree, to Bridgeport's continued receptive environment.

Other cities with similar patterns of friendly cooperation among Catholic ethnic groups were Torrington and Wallingford. There Irish parishes developed such cordial relations with their newer members that plans to establish separate Hungarian parishes were initiated but never formalized, and Polish parishes were only late developments. Similar delayed patterns in the establishment of national parishes throughout the diocese indicated a certain lack of consensus on the part of sometimes aggressive minorities as to whether or not it would be necessary to duplicate Catholic efforts in smaller communities.

Once an ethnic group expressed the strong desire to form its own national parish, however, there seemed to be few obstacles preventing action, provided the petitioning group followed a procedure in effect for decades, first informally outlined by Bishop McMahon in a letter to the Slovaks of Bridgeport. First, the petitioners sought the approval of the bishop, indicating that they had a sufficiently large congregation and could support a new parish financially. Upon the bishop's approval, details concerning the acquisition of property or its transfer to the diocese were worked out, again with the concurrence of diocesan officials. Next, a legal corporation consisting of the bishop, the vicar-general, the pastor, and two lay members of the parish was duly organized in accordance with the statutes of the State of Connecticut (Duggan, 1933). From that point on, the responsibility for the development of the parish was shared by the bishop, who had to provide priests to relate culturally to the needs of the parish and to continue the work of its first pastor, and the parishioners, who had to prove themselves able to support a worthy parish complex.

Sometimes the bishop would intercede on behalf of an ethnic community experiencing difficulty in fulfilling its obligations, as illustrated by Bishop Tierney's recruitment of a Polish Franciscan community to insure economic as well as parochial stability for the newly founded St. Michael's Parish in Bridgeport. Established under the direction of the Reverend Witold Becker, a popular young pastor who had originally been recruited from Louvain, Belgium, St. Michael's had just purchased property and was in the process of constructing a new church when Father Becker was suddenly stricken with ptomaine poisoning. Even while the thirty-five year old pastor lay dying, the chancellor of the diocese began the process of persuading a newly organized Polish Franscisan community, with headquarters in Buffalo, New York, to assume permanent charge of the parish. In correspondence with the Very Reverend Hyacinth Fudzinski in June, 1906, the chancellor spoke of the Bridgeport priest's hopeless condition and of the future prospects of the new parish, located in "the most prosperous and rapidly growing city in the Diocese" in order to encourage the Franciscans to consider their overtures most seriously.

Fortunately for the parish, the Franciscans proved receptive. Although it took two years before the settlement was complete, the contract between the Franciscans and Bishop Tierney was finally sealed with the words: *"In perpetuum curam tradimus Ordini Tuo...pro necessitatibus Polonorum adlaborat"* (For all time we hand it over to your Order so that you can labor on behalf of the needs of the Polish people). In the interim, for the bereft parishioners of St. Michael's, it must have seemed as if their need for a Polish priest was not being addressed. What they never learned — nor apparently are they aware of to the present day — was that the negotiations for the transfer of the parish to a religious community had been the first order of episcopal business as soon as it became clear to diocesan officials that their first pastor was dying.

For the most part, the later bishops continued the policies begun by the first bishop of Hartford. As more and more priests, fluent in speaking French, German, Italian, and Slavic languages, were needed by the turn of the twentieth century, priests were recruited from European seminaries, from the Polish seminary in Detroit, and eventually from the diocesan seminary, where native born children of immigrants were encouraged to pursue the priestly career.

Regarding the exceptionally large Italian Catholic community, however, both Bishops Tierney and Nilan experienced more than the average difficulties in acquiring a sufficient number of priests to administer national parishes. While this problem was considered characteristic of every Catholic diocese into which these newer immigrants had come in large numbers, diocesan leaders did not allow this excuse to prevent them from finding means of meeting the challenge. From the time of Bishop McMahon, attempts had been made to supply Italian priests especially for the large numbers of Italians who had begun to settle in New Haven and Hartford. Although Bishop McMahon procured the services of the Scalabrinians, whose first missionaries came to New Haven only two years after they had been organized in Piacenza, Italy, their coming to Connecticut did not settle the problems of efficient administration or the need for additional priests. Therefore, when it became possible to find suitable Italian priests to replace the first pastors of Italian parishes as well as to find priests for other thriving Italian communities, subsequent bishops resorted to assigning non-Italian priests (albeit priests versed in both the Italian language and customs) to take charge of Italian national parishes in the capacity of pastors.

In Hartford, Bridgeport, and Meriden, priests with Irish surnames, such as Kelly or Kelley, Gleason, and Sullivan, took over sometimes faltering parishes and worked to win the hearts of their parishioners, while at the same time they strove to build churches, schools, and, most importantly, to emulate the kind of fiscal soundness that other immigrant groups seemed more able to achieve. According to the assessment of Giovanni Schiavo, author of *Italian-American History: The Italian Contribution to the Catholic Church in America* (1949), this was a pattern utilized in other dioceses as well. In his words: "To give credit where credit is due, the Italian Americans owe a great debt of gratitude to quite a few American priests, mostly Irish, with a sprinkling of German,..."who spared no efforts to help the immigrant both in his religious and civic life" (p.477).

Explanations for the unique pattern of interaction between the American Catholic Church and the Italian immigrant have been offered in historical and sociological studies since the difference between the level of achievement acquired by Italians as opposed to that of other immigrants was first perceived. Often referred to as the "Italian problem", the reasons cited by some authors for the difficulties encountered by Italians in establishing national parishes on solid bases have run the gamut of blame concerning the failures of Italian leaders to that of incrimination over the intransigence and neglect exhibited by the American Catholic hierarchy. One viewpoint enjoying widespread popularity is that proposed by historian Sam Bass Warner in *The Urban Wilderness* (1972): the Old World religious traditions of Italians constituted not only the first but perhaps the strongest barriers, preventing them from becoming full-fledged members of the Catholic Church once they had decided to settle in the United States. Because most of the early Italian immigrants were unaccustomed to supporting their Church (in most sections of Italy, Catholic institutions received state funding) and because they were strongly anticlerical as a consequence of their recent, negative political experiences in Italy, Warner argues that they simply did not feel any urgency to become committed to a Church that would require their hard-earned dollars and their loyalty as well. In his writings on Italian immigrant communities in the United States, Rudolph Vecoli (1969) has repeated the same factors as contributing causes to the strained relationships between the Italian immigrants and the American Catholic Church. Whether accepting these particular views or not, most historians at least maintain that Italian immigrants simply did not have the same motivation as Irish, German, or Slavic peoples, whose personal reasons for immigrating included a strong desire for freedom to worship as Roman Catholics.

There is evidence to support the view that the motivation that led Italian Catholics to emigrate and their subsequent New World experiences did differ from those of other immigrants. For example, during his visit to the United States in the first years of the twentieth century, Bishop Scalabrini had been among the first to propose the distinctiveness of the European experiences to help explain the poor response of Italian immigrants to the building of churches in the Diocese of Hartford and in other sections of the country. The Reverend Philip Rose, a pastor of the First Italian Congregation Church in Hartford, used the same explanation in his monograph *The Italians in America* (1975) to supply a rationalization for the Protestant evangelization of Italian immigrants. Moreover, it was a theme readily assumed by historians of the Catholic Church, such as Henry Browne, who used the assumption to explain Italian defections in his article "The Italian Problem in the Catholic Church of the United States, 1880-1900" (1946). However, the evidence of recent painstaking studies, such as those undertaken by John Briggs (1974) on Italian communities in St. Paul, Minnesota, as well as Utica and Rochester, New York, indicate that even this popular explanation may be too easily arrived at and uncritically accepted. According to Briggs, "No evidence of extreme manifestations of such sentiments" (*i.e.*, indifference, hostility, or anticlericalism) surfaced in the three communities studied; furthermore, it was only in much larger Italian colonies, such as Chicago or New York City, where vocal anticlericalism enjoyed any real strength — and that, most probably, because of the numbers of socialists among the ranks of the professionals and intellectuals who could popularize the notion.

Another argument advanced even in the newspapers of the period to explain the defection from the Church of Italians in their American setting centered around the quality of the Italian clergy called upon to lead in the organization of national parishes in the United States. It was most difficult for Italian priests to get permission to settle in the United States; for this reason immigrants were all too often bereft of clergy. Even the Scalabrinians were hampered by disciplinary restrictions within Italy. Moreover, by being allowed only a five-year assignment in the American apostolate, they were sometimes prevented from developing any lasting and constructive ties to their missionary endeavors.

Another aspect of the same problem was the question of the calibre of many Italian priests who were able to make their way to the United States from the auspices of religious congregations. Some clergymen who had legitimately been assigned to the United States proved to be so inadequate to their calling that Pope Leo had to issue a warning both to Italian and American bishops in an effort to prevent other unscrupulous candidates from entering the United States. Despite this, some Italian priests managed to immigrate, arriving on these shores without proper canonical credentials of any kind. As the secretary for the American bishops who were gathered for the Baltimore Council of 1884 suggested in this letter to Pope Leo, "It is a very delicate matter to tell the Sovereign Pontiff how utterly faithless the specimens of his country coming here are", and how "sadly remiss in their duty" were some of the Italian clergy who accompanied them. Apostate priests, especially in New York, as well as Protestant missionaries who realized the possibilities of attracting large numbers of seemingly unattached immigrants, only caused further confusion for a people who admittedly had been poorly educated and sorely neglected by their pastors even before they came to the United States. Thus it was argued that Italian immigrants, bereft of good leadership, were at a distinct disadvantage. Furthermore, they suffered from odious comparisons since other immigrants seemed to be enjoying the services of the kinds of dedicated missionaries that the Italian immigrants longed to procure.

There were many other complicating factors that altered the manner by which Italian immigrants related to American Catholicism. For example, as Frank Femminella pointed out in "The Impact of Italian

Migration and American Catholicism" (1964), a number of problems that disturbed Italians were probably due to certain attitudes about religion per se that Italians brought from their native land. According to Femminella, Italians attached more importance to warm personal relationships with God and the saints than to creedal tenets and were more devoted to socially oriented religious celebrations than to such liturgical requirements as Sunday attendance at mass—a perspective that decidedly set them apart from most German, Slavic, and Lithuanian Catholics, whose adherence to Church law and practice seemed far more strictly observed. Moreover, Italians seemed to prefer that their pastors exhibit qualities of warmth and compassion rather than display the administrative or financial skills that strong leadership characterized—another departure from the preferences of other immigrant groups. Such differing attitudes moderated their response to the Catholic Church of the United States. On the other hand, there is also evidence that even these religious biases were subject to change if exposed to more favorable situations; moreover, the vestiges of disinterest, nonconformity, disobedience, even hostility, often vanished in the presence of committed Catholic leaders.

Thus, a kind of dilemma often emerged with respect to the proper care of the so-called "neglected Italians". As has been mentioned, Bishop Tierney and his successors chose to approach the problem on the basis that good leadership was the key to better relations between Italians and the Catholic Church. Assuming that the spiritual plight of the Italians as well as the foundation for their anticlericalism were the result of the lack of good leaders, Bishop Tierney searched for exemplary priests to administer Italian parishes. Unable to acquire a sufficient number of Italian priests, he was willing to try his own novel approach to the problem. Although he had not assigned any Irish priests to other national parishes, he began—cautiously at first—to place some of the priests who received seminary training in Italy, in Italian parishes. Once the bishop was assured that these pioneering priests were well received, he began to assign still more of his clergy—especially Irish Americans—to Italian parishes. Seldom did his efforts in this regard meet with any real resistance or dissatisfaction. In fact, his approach to the situation was often applauded and encouraged by Italian parishioners themselves. Bishop Nilan followed the same practice, enlisting the aid of his own well-trained clergy and anticipating the same patience and cooperation that previous Italian congregations had given his predecessor. To a great extent, the assignment of Irish priests to those Italian parishes in need of good leadership proved to be highly successful.

Among the Irish American priests who contributed so much to the early development of the parish was Father John J. Kelley, who became the inspiration of the Italian people and the founder of the Sacred Heart Church. Because of Father Kelley, the Italian families united together and approached the pastor of the "Irish" church in June of 1920, requesting that an Italian parish be established and that Father Kelley be allowed to help them reach their goal. With the encouragement of Father O'Brien, the approval of Bishop John J. Nilan, and the aid of Father John J. Kelley, money was collected with the express purpose of planning for the building of a church. Not surprisingly, the priest chosen to be first pastor of the Sacred Heart Parish, once it was formally incorporated, was their beloved Father John Kelley.

Other Italian immigrant communities in the 1910s and 1920s often turned to Irish or Irish American pastors to help in the establishment and good management of their parishes. In Bridgeport, two pastors, the Reverends Michael Keating and Thomas Sullivan were given credit by their Italian parishioners for putting Holy Rosary Parish on a more solid financial footing than had been the case under its first two eager but unsuccessful Italian pastors. In Hartford, achievements of the ethnically Irish pastors were even more dramatic than those of their Italian predecessors. After the Reverend Angelo Chiariglione and several Scalabrinians had manifested great difficulty in managing the affairs of St. Anthony's, the Reverends Edward Flannery, pastor from 1895 to 1898, Denis Gleason, 1898-1907, and John McLaughlin, 1907-1913, contributed toward setting the foundations for a strong parish organization. Under them, a church was purchased, dedicated in 1898, and legally incorporated. Although the parish was briefly put under the direction of Father Francis Bonforti and his successor, Father Felix Scoglio, it was not long before another Irish American priest, the highly cultured and dynamic Reverend Andrew Kelley, was called upon to take over direction of the parish. During his brilliant pastorate of several decades, the parish became the focus of pride both for its parishioners and the diocese as well, while he earned the highest praise from his devoted Italian parishioners.

To provide for the tens of thousands of Italians in the New Haven area, several additional Italian parishes were created after the turn of the century. Here, too, interesting solutions to the problem of assigning suitable pastors were developed. Bishop Tierney was no longer convinced that the Scalabrinians were effective administrators. In a letter to the apostolic delegate written in December of 1904, he wrote:

> Recently, I explained to Father Novati, superior of the congregation of St. Charles in this country, that if the Fathers

found it impossible to maintain discipline in the parish, I
could put diocesan priests in charge, as there are twenty of
the diocesan clergy who speak Italian. Father Novati is at
present in Europe and we expect more explicit information
from him upon his return. (Episcopal Papers, Dec. 21, 1904)

Although the Scalabrinians remained at the head of the parish, it became evident that Bishop Nilan had alternatives in mind for the other
Italian parishes of New Haven and the diocese. As Bishop Tierney had
suggested in his letter to the apostolic delegate, Bishop Nilan also indicated that he believed some priests who had been trained in Piacenza
would actually provide as adequate leadership in Italian parishes as was
accomplished by some Italian priests. For this reason, he decided to
depart even further from diocesan policy and appoint Father Charles
Kelly to head St. Donato's Italian parish in New Haven as its first
pastor; soon afterward, he also assigned the Reverend John B. Malley
as assistant to Kelly. An unprecedented move among New Haven's Italians, the appointment proved more than adequate.

Another Italian linguist and first Catholic chaplain at Yale University, the Reverend Lawrason Riggs, was next commissioned to assist in
the establishment of a separate parish for Italians in the Foxon Park
section of East Haven. So, too, were the Reverends Michael Reagan
and Joseph Joyce called upon to help the Italians of St. Vincent de Paul
Parish, East Haven. The ability of these priests to speak Italian enabled
them to relate well to their constituents. Similarly, the warmth and
ability of Reverend Michael Lynch so favorably impressed the Italians
of Waterbury that the parish of Our Lady of Mt. Carmel became the
second Italian parish to be established in that city. Thus, in the urban
areas where tens of thousands of Italians settled after the turn of the
century, non-Italian priests became the means by which Italian Catholics found leadership within the diocesan structure, succeeding far beyond the expectations of Irish and non-Irish Catholics alike.

To a remarkable degree, this pattern had answered the needs of the
"most neglected" of the diocese's immigrants in a manner usually found
satisfying to Catholic leaders and Italian parishioners. Whether fully
conscious of what they had actually achieved by their experiment, diocesan leaders were at least aware that they had found a workable solution to a problem that had plagued most dioceses of the United States.
Indeed, so amicable was this particular accord that good will between
the Italian community and the diocese became one of the most distinctive characteristics of the Church in Hartford during the first half of
the twentieth century. Not until the 1950s, when certain Italians displayed a feeling that members of their nationality were not being given

precedence in Church promotions and that Italian parishes did not receive as much consideration as Irish parishes, were the rumblings of Italian dissatisfaction distinctly and widely heard.

Indeed, if the plan of assigning Italian speaking Irish priests to Italian congregations had failed, or if capable Italian immigrant priests were available to satisfy the need for priests in all the Italian parishes of the diocese, undoubtedly the official policy with regard to the Italian minority of the diocese would have been the same as that followed with regard to the other ethnic groups. However, this altered practice of calling upon non-Italians to serve Italian parishes had a beneficial effect for the Church of Connecticut as a whole. Not only were the particular and immediate problems of filling vacancies among the Italian constituency of the diocese solved, but some opportunities for successful mixed-ethnic integration were rendered possible, thus setting the example for other ethnic communities within the diocese. In terms of the Italian congregations, it avoided many of the conditions that led to the division and dissension within other dioceses. More importantly, it illustrated that perceiving Italian congregations solely on the basis that they were the Church's "greatest problem" may indeed have resulted in missing one of their most unique contributions to the Church.

Contrary to what occurred with respect to other new immigrant groups who appeared more anxious to retain their ties with the Catholic Church from the start, the Italians were the only group to demonstrate that an ethnic minority could accommodate itself if the right conditions for that spirit to develop also existed. In other words, the group often cited as the most capable of failing the test of integration into the American Catholic Church had, in the long run, managed to make the transition into the diocesan structure more effortlessly and to accommodate the kinds of traditions that American Catholics had developed better than those Catholic immigrants whose loyalty to the Church seemed more apparent. Perhaps it was because no other Catholic ethnic minority in the United States understood the universality of the Church as clearly as did the Italian immigrant that Italian Catholics in America were able to resist nationalistic tendencies that would have worked against their proper and gradual assimilation into the American Catholic Church.

With far more than minimal success the Diocese of Hartford had related well to the problems of the pressing throngs of new immigrants who had begun spilling into Connecticut's cities and towns during the decades immediately preceding and following the turn of the twentieth century and who were seeking membership within the only institution familiar to most of them: the Roman Catholic Church. Contrary to the view of a number of historians and critics who have argued that "...the

Catholic hierarchy of America, many of whom were of Irish origin, were opposed to any attempt to organize national parishes which they regarded as a threat to the church's essential unity" (Jones, 1960) there is no evidence that this was true or, moreover, that the allegation concerning ethnic struggles within the Catholic parishes of the Diocese of Hartford can be traced to the biases of its bishops. Instead, a review of national parishes in the diocese from the time when the new immigration began to accelerate indicates that Hartford's bishops utilized many means of assisting both old and new immigrant groups to find their place in the diocese. In a number of ways they demonstrated their concern for Catholic immigrants. Not only did officials of the diocese protect a distinctive pro-immigrant image through the medium of the press, they also encouraged dedicated personnel to serve as models of this image. Furthermore, the bishop and most clergy supported the efforts of immigrants to acquire their own priests and to establish parishes. Only when immigrant congregations encountered difficulties in finding appropriate leaders did the bishop offer the services of priests recruited from or trained in European seminaries. Nowhere did this practice work more successfully than with respect to the Italian congregations of the diocese.

At all times, a pattern of open communication between the bishop, priests, and people was evident. Almost without exception, the delays and difficulties were not a part of any deliberate effort on the part of diocesan officials to discourage ethnic communities; rather they simply resulted from the unavailability of proper personnel or other practical concerns. The evidence clearly indicates that delays resulted from exactly what the diocese always claimed to be the case. If troubles did occur after national parishes had been established, they developed because of internal problems between factions within the congregation that eventually pitted the pastor against the bishop, or the pastor against his own congregation. While often blaming the bishop, participants and complainants tended to overlook the degree to which their personal ambitions had occasioned the controversies and how their bickering had blocked effective decision making on the part of the bishop. Considering the potential for discord, it is even more remarkable that a spirit of good will was as prevalent in the diocese as it proved to be. That it did not exist during a critical period of diocesan development is a major factor in the Diocese of Hartford's continued growth in numbers over the decades, as well as for the solid reputation that the Catholic Church enjoys among the citizens of the state to the present day.

5 Trials of a Multi-Ethnic Church: Episodes of Discord in Polish and French Canadian Catholic Parishes

For a diocese that had experienced the tremendous influx of Slavic, Italian, and other European immigrants, especially during the period 1890-1920, Hartford had fared remarkably well in its accommodation to new members. Tens of thousands of newcomers had become full-fledged members of national parishes in key cities and towns in the state. After overcoming some relatively minor problems, an impressive number of parishes flourished. Churches, schools and other parish facilities had been built and societies organized — all in witness of the strong religious faith, good will, and common sense of people only recently settled on American soil.

However, some conflict marred this process of becoming part of the American Catholic Church. Although an overall spirit of accommodation prevailed in the diocese, some controversies briefly disturbed the Church leaders. There were also a number of situations so charged with emotion and so capable of causing long-lasting and irreconcilable differences that their eventual settlement must be considered another notable achievement of the Diocese of Hartford. With regard to these more enduring conflicts within ethnic communities, certain necessary ingredients fed the fires of dissatisfaction and set the stage for prolonged confrontations. One characteristic, evident in every episode that disturbed the diocese, was reluctance on the part of the lay leaders of ethnic communities to submit to authority except on their own terms. Often the power struggle that emerged as a result was clothed in the rhetoric of defending nationalism against the encroachments of the official representatives of the Catholic Church. In reality it was often an offensive launched by ambitious laymen hoping not only to maintain the authority that they believed was theirs but, moreover, to superimpose that leadership upon the power structure of the American Catholic Church. In another sense, the earlier phenomenon of lay trusteeism recurred in these latter days of the nineteenth century; once again the desire for lay leadership threatened to alter the accepted pattern of clerical leadership within the American Catholic Church.

Within the Diocese of Hartford, abrasive local controversies among ethnic minorities developed during these years. They were particularly evident among the French Canadian and Polish constituencies. As was true when lay trusteeism first disturbed the Church, these conflicts were perceived by outside observers as failures on the part of the official Church leadership to understand and to accommodate to the national aspirations of the recent immigrants. More often, they reflected power maneuvers either between ethnic priests or between factions within the parish membership itself. When the bishop of Hartford did not respond immediately to demands of French Canadian or Polish lay leaders to replace unpopular pastors or to organize new national parishes, his hesitation was construed as a deliberate policy of discrimination. Upon analysis, however, one discovers that the reactions of diocesan leaders to requests were usually not the central issue in disputes; internal factionalism, instead, lay at the heart of the problem.

Thus, regardless of the bishop's response to particular requests of either the French Canadians or the Poles, discord invariably occurred, sometimes disrupting the parish involved, sometimes even preventing — at least temporarily — the establishment of a parish. Whatever the case, the dilemma of having to choose between competing factions on the basis of loyalty either to Church or to nationality triggered much needless suffering and guilt; in its heyday, it even affected the well-being of the entire diocese for extended periods. In every case the leadership of the bishop or of his representatives eventually had to be acknowledged by those who had opposed his authority. Only then could the proper link to the American Catholic Church and Hartford's Catholic leadership be permanently forged. Perhaps because of the more consistent and enlightened policies pursued within the Diocese of Hartford, which had helped other immigrant groups facilitate their transition, these disputes did not escalate to the degree that they afflicted other dioceses. Nevertheless, because of their vitriolic nature, and because of what they reveal about the nature and circumstances of ethnic conflict within the American Catholic Church, a review of dissensions within French Canadian and Polish Catholic communities in Connecticut will be the first topic of discussion.

Perhaps the most dramatic and most publicized example of parish revolt within the Diocese of Hartford during this period occurred among the French Canadians, one of the oldest Catholic immigrant groups to settle in sizable numbers in Connecticut and, ironically, the ethnic group that could also acknowledge continued preference and status within the diocese.

As early as the 1860s, when a personable and highly talented Belgian priest had been recruited by Bishop McFarland to take charge of the thousands of temporary residents from the province of Quebec, the diocese had manifested serious interest in its French Canadian minority. With the coming of Reverend Florimond DeBruycker as resident pastor of Willimantic in 1863, and before the end of the same decade the acquisition of three other native Belgians, Fathers J.G. Van Laar, Eugene Vygen, and James A. Princen, for parochial work in, respectively, Baltic, Putnam, and Danielson, the commitment of the diocese was further sealed. Under these and other pioneer priests, permanent French Canadian communities developed in mixed ethnic parishes throughout eastern Connecticut, and Canadian migrants in numbers began to take up residence in the "Little Canadas" of the state's mill towns and rural areas.

The achievements of these early priests and parishioners were undisputed; moreover, they were a source of pride that often became the subject of comment in the newspapers of the period. Throughout the 1870s and 1880s, these thriving communities in the diocese were a source of interest to many an onlooker. Thus, when Father DeBruycker celebrated his twenty-fifth anniversary of ordination to the priesthood in 1881, he was accorded homage generally reserved only for the most esteemed. According to the *Catholic Review* (Jan. 7, 1898), the whole community had joined in the celebration: "This beautiful and prosperous New England village has, during the past few days, found its busy tide of traffic interrupted, and its toilers in mills and factories pausing to unite in the prayer of thanksgiving..." It added, "Amongst all classes of this town the pastor of Willimantic is loved; among both Catholics and non-Catholics he is highly respected". Similar remarks would be made of other French priests and sisters who labored among the French Canadians and Irish during these formative years.

During the administration of Bishop McMahon, interest in the needs of French Canadians of rural eastern Connecticut continued unabated. For the first time, too, as French immigrants were drawn to urban industrial occupations, special provisions were made for their spiritual care in the diocese's major cities. By the end of Bishop McMahon's episcopate in 1893, French national parishes stood in Meriden, Hartford, Waterbury, New Haven, and Bridgeport. While Bishop Mc-Farland had acknowledged the need to recruit French priests, it was Bishop McMahon who would make more substantial progress toward conveying the diocese's concern for the proper spiritual care of the Canadians. Despite the fact that a spirit of dissatisfaction had clouded the previous accord acknowledged by French Canadians, McMahon managed to maintain good will between himself and his French constituency.

Relatively early in his career, McMahon passed the first cross-examination of members of a Canadian nationalist group. His success at that time enabled him to become free of controversy during the remainder of his administration. In 1887, members of the Congress of French Canadians of Connecticut, a group that had been organized only the preceeding year, demanded an interview with McMahon for the purpose of determining the reasons for alleged prejudicial treatment of their people. At the meeting, he immediately disarmed the group not only by conversing with them in French, but also by delivering a tribute to the beauty of the French language. According to the account of the meeting published in *Le Travailleur* (Dolbec, *et al*, Sept. 9, 1887) of Worcester, Massachusetts, the bishop contradicted the rumor that he had publicly opposed the acquisition of French Canadian clergy for assignment in Connecticut. Instead, he argued his policy had actually been the opposite. When the three member committee pressed him to prove his allegiance to the concept of educating a French Canadian clergy for service in the United States, he did not decline the challenge. Rather, he pointed out the advantages of such an educational system. Would it be better, he suggested, for French American seminarians to study in Canadian seminaries, where they could learn both the language and the customs of Canada, so that upon their return to the United States they could better minister to their own people? Lest he be misinterpreted, however, Bishop McMahon went on to say:

> Send them to me...That they are Canadian, Irish, or German makes no difference to me...I am the father of all. Send me your children...poor and intelligent...who have the disposition to the priesthood and I will take charge of their education. But, if you decide after serious deliberations, to build a college...be certain that you will receive all possible encouragement from me. (Dolbec, *et al.*, 1887.)

Finding it difficult to find fault with a bishop who told them, in no uncertain terms, "I love the Canadians...I am ready to do for them everything possible to ameliorate their social or religious condition", the committee concluded its interview and filed the report.

Another test of Bishop McMahon's conviction would occur before the Canadians of the Diocese of Hartford were sufficiently convinced that their chief pastor was unquestionably sympathetic to their cause. Approximately the same time that Bishop McMahon received the committee of French nationalists, he also received a petition sent by a small but vocal group of French parishioners in Taftville. This group wanted the right to name their own priest. McMahon's reaction was similar to that at the meeting with the French nationalist group. Reviewing the history of Sacred Heart, Taftville, he explained, in fluent French, that Irish and French Catholics had made up the original membership of the parish. Moreover, he reminded them that the parish *"n'est pas une paroisse exclusivement Canadienne"*, since the Irish had done their part in constructing the church and were still supporting the parish. Besides, he asked the parishioners, did they not have a French speaking priest assigned them? Could they not be satisfied with this arrangement as long as they continued to share the parish facility with Irish parishioners? Once again, the bishop's straightforward remarks were perceived as credible. For two more years, the status quo in Taftville continued unquestioned.

In 1889, Nos Enfants Canadiens de Taftville, Connecticut, sent a second petition to Bishop McMahon. On the basis of numbers (almost two hundred signatures appeared on this petition), they asked him to establish a separate parish for French Canadians. Although no record exists of his response, McMahon apparently chose to reject this request. Shortly afterward, however, he assigned to the parish Reverend James Cartier, who had been ordained in Montreal and who had been an assistant pastor in the Diocese of Portland. From then on, the parish was served by French Canadian or French speaking clergy. The bishop also attempted to provide a Canadian community to staff the parish school. When the Marianite Sisters of the Cross were unable to accept his offer to teach there, the Belgian Sisters of Charity took charge in 1888. According to the Diocesan School Report of 1890, there were 396 children registered at Sacred Heart School; French was the principal language for instruction. Taftville's Canadians were apparently satisfied with these accommodations; after 1890 they made no other demands of the bishop of Hartford.

However, the day of reckoning was not over. Throughout New England since the 1870s, French Canadians were involved in repatriation associations and other Canadian nationalist movements. Although ultimately unsuccessful in sustaining their efforts, such associations had more than a subtle impact upon the Canadian immigrants in the United States. In particular, they gave courage to a number of the more outspoken ones, enabling them to make their own anxieties over issues involving *survivance* (a word specifically coined by them to express their concerns over the loss of national identity because of mistreatment or misunderstanding at the hands of civil or religious leaders in the United States). Among the chief complaints of these Franco Americans were those that centered around the neglect of French children in public and parochial schools, as well as the alleged disregard shown the faith of French Catholics. In 1892, a document entitled *"Memoire sur la Situation des Canadiens Français aux Etats Unis de l'Amerique du Nord"*, especially aimed at conveying the sense of degradation and hardship felt by Canadian immigrants to the United States, was prepared by Antoine Racine, the Bishop of Sherbrooke, Quebec, for presentation to Church officials in Rome. In Connecticut, the influence of this document, coupled with the growing stridency of Canadian nationalism, contributed to an even more tense relationship between French Canadians and the Diocese of Hartford by the 1890s.

The *cause célèbre* of French Canadian dissension in the diocese occurred in St. James Parish, Danielson, a small mill town in eastern Connecticut, a few years after accord had apparently been achieved among other French Canadians in the state. St. James was founded to serve Irish immigrants, but after the 1870s became a primarily French congregation. Its pastor, Father Thomas J. Preston, a curate in the parish since 1877 and pastor from 1883 until 1895, attempted to accommodate to the changing complexion of his parish by introducing French speaking sisters to teach in the parish school, and by sharing some of his pastoral duties with French Canadian priests. One might have expected that despite apparent differences no rebellion would develop during his pastorate. But the temper of the times was as unavoidable in Danielson as it had been in Taftville. Father Preston's leadership became seriously threatened after 1892.

Some French Canadians of St. James who had been influenced by a fellow parishioner, the "ardent patriot" and well-educated Dr. Charles Leclaire, began to argue that their pastor failed them in a number of ways. Not only, they said, had Preston demonstrated that he did not respect their culture (rumor had it that he had once suggested that his Canadian parishioners were capable of little more than procreation), but he had reneged on promises. Specifically, they believed that he had deliberately mislead them at the time of the construction of a parish school, pledging that the school would be bilingual. Yet, once the school opened, they claimed, *"adieu la promesse"*. That Preston acted in good faith when he asked the Sisters of St. Joseph of Chambery, France, to staff the school was beyond their belief. By their perception, European based religious communities might send personnel fluent in French but they could not supply educators who could identify with French Canadians in terms of either nationality or customs.

Armed with these complaints and suspicions, Dr. Leclaire's committee went to Bishop McMahon in 1892 and insisted that he send them a French Canadian pastor to replace Preston. Furthermore, they demanded that the bishop review the school situation. As McMahon had done several years before in Taftville, he responded to the Danielson committee by assigning a Canadian native, the Reverend Louis Dusablon, an assistant to Preston; however, he made no change with respect to the school.

For the next two years Dusablon remained at St. James. From the start, his ministry was hardly neutral. Under the influence of the young assistant, the nationalistic spirit of the parish waxed stronger. By the time Bishop Tierney succeeded Bishop McMahon as head of the diocese in April of 1894, relations between pastor and assistant had so deteriorated that episcopal intervention seemed essential. Hoping to gain the momentum, Leclaire's group insisted upon an early appointment with Tierney in a renewed effort to achieve their aims. In the course of the proposed meeting, the committee again stressed that it would not be satisfied until a French Canadian priest replaced Preston. Moreover, they repeated their grievances about the school situation, insisting that at least two hours of French be taught daily. Hearing them out, Bishop Tierney intimated that he would do his best to honor their requests. Heartened by this news, the committee returned to Danielson.

But no change was forthcoming. Thus, when the Congress of French Canadians assembled for its annual meeting in Taftville in September, 1894, Leclaire took the occasion to forge a spirit of rebellion and to gather extraparochial support. Sensing how easily dissatisfaction might spread to other French Canadian communities, Father Florimond DeBruycker, the senior pastor at the convention, attempted to restrain the dissidents by warning that socialistic or revolutionary tactics might be easily introduced. He urged restraint and continued loyalty to the bishop. Although somewhat curbed by these monitions, dissent continued to run high, and lines became drawn between clerical and lay leadership. In the last analysis, the people would have to decide whether Leclaire or DeBruycker had the stronger case.

Encouraged by the support shown by some French Canadians, Leclaire and his followers embarked on a course that would be repeated at one time or another by almost every dissatisfied ethnic minority that attempted to organize a separate national parish within the Diocese of Hartford. Claiming that they had been wronged by both their bishop and his representatives, and believing that they were justified in their course of action, the Danielson dissidents decided to appeal to higher Church authority. Aware that there was a newly established office of the apostolic delegate in Washington, D.C., organized to receive complaints or grievances, they planned to contact it. If this office gave them no satisfaction, they were prepared to move on to the Sacred Congregation of the Propagation of the Faith Office in Rome and, if need be, to the Pope. Somewhere along the way, they fully expected their concept of authority within the Church would be vindicated and their demands heard.

The Leclaire group addressed their first formal petition to the apostolic delegate, Archbishop Francesco Satolli, in March of 1895. Within a month they received a reply from his office. Expressing sympathy with such efforts to protect their language and customs, he nevertheless explained that they had overstepped their bounds in the pursuit of this goal. "To insist on having your own way after your Bishop has prudently decided that it is not feasible", the delegate suggested, "is to act in a spirit which is not laudable in those who wish to be considered good Catholics". In conclusion, Satolli remarked:

> I find that the Bishop has always done all that was possible to him to provide for all the real needs of your congregation, and that he has never left you without a priest who could speak French sufficiently well to attend to all your religious necessities. More than this could not reasonably be expected from him. (Archives of the Archdiocese of Hartford)

Undaunted by Archbishop Satolli's rejection of their claim, the committee took their complaints to the Propagation of the Faith Office in Rome. But the congregation ignored their petition; instead the prefect wrote to Bishop Tierney, vindicating him just as Satolli had done.

Smarting from these defeats, the dissidents still remained unconvinced that their cause was completely lost. Thus began the second phase of their campaign. In Danielson they threatened outright schism and managed to persuade most of their fellow countrymen to stay away from all religious services in the parish. Moreover, through regional meetings they attempted to convince an ever widening audience of French Canadians throughout Connecticut of the justice of their claim.

However, from this point on, they were to meet with stronger opposition. When the Reverend Paul Roy, the highly respected pastor of St. Ann's, Hartford, was approached by them, he declined to give them support; his abstention undermined the credibility of the dissent. For a brief moment, however, their cause seemed to be given new life. Although Father Bourret, then pastor of St. Ann's, Waterbury, also cautioned them to submit, he hinted that their complaints had brought results. "In two months you will have a Canadian pastor", he told them;

furthermore, he suggested that he expected Father Roy to be the priest chosen by their bishop as the next pastor. Bourret's advice quickly reversed the drive toward schism.

Believing, for the second time, that Bishop Tierney was about to answer their specific demands, the French Canadians returned to Church services in the summer of 1895. Although convinced that they were "under the laughing eyes of the Irish", they persevered, anxiously awaiting the appointment of the French Canadian pastor. But, as the months passed and Father Roy continued as pastor in Hartford, the dissidents began to feel betrayed by both Father Bourret and their bishop. Finally, in December of 1895, Father Preston was transferred. Yet instead of a French Canadian, Preston's replacement was a French European, the Reverend Clovis Socquet, a member of the LaSalette community from Grenoble, France; henceforth, the parish was to be under the direction of the LaSalette community. News of the appointment of French European priests to head their parish was a veritable last straw. To the minds of the dissidents, this kind of French leadership was as much a capitulation to Americanization and assimilation as the continuance of the Irish leadership of the diocese. Nothing the bishop could say from this time on could in any way make this latest appointment acceptable to the Canadian dissidents of St. James.

On the basis of this new evidence of episcopal insensitivity to their spiritual needs, Leclaire and his supporters embarked upon a third phase of their continuing warfare with the Diocese of Hartford. Without clarifying whom the bishop had recently assigned to their parish they sent a second series of complaints to both the apostolic delegate and to the Roman Propagation Office, citing the recent decision of the bishop as proof positive of the mistreatment of an ethnic minority that was clinging to the last vestiges of ethnic *survivance*. On March 31, 1896, their letter to the apostolic delegate was mailed; barely a month later Cardinal Satolli's reply was in their hands. Again, Satolli repeated the essence of the argument he had set forth in his previous letter. Despite the group's legitimate attachment to their religion and to their native language, as well as their right to present grievances to the Bishop, their present methods were "far from commendable, and little in keeping with your character as Catholic Christians". Furthermore, he informed them that he knew that Tierney had taken pains to locate priests whom he believed able to identify with the language and culture of the Canadians, and concluded his remarks in the following strong terms:

> Your obstinate opposition in this provision causes the suspicion that you are not in good faith, but have in view some other end than that expressed in your original complaint. I

can only say that, if you really desire the religious welfare of yourselves and your children, it is your duty now to show yourselves good Catholics and submit to the government of your bishop, who has shown the most fatherly spirit in his treatment of you. Do not any longer lend an ear to those who, either ecclesiastics or laymen, may be attempting to sow seeds of discord and discontent...(*Hartford Times*, May 4, 1896)

As Cardinal Satolli had suggested in his earlier letter, it seemed as if Leclaire's committee was really pursuing the satisfaction of having their own way even after their bishop had decided it was not feasible. If that were the case, Church leaders would have no way to correct the situation short of surrender to the demands of the dissidents; to this solution neither he nor the bishop of Hartford would resort.

Similarly, when the Propagation Office was consulted for the second time by the dissidents, its response also indicated that Vatican officials had been close observers of the case, and that they had also concluded that the dissidents were not sincere. According to Rome's sources, the complainants had withheld information and misrepresented their case from the start. What the dissidents did not know was that the Roman office had attempted to ascertain the truth of the original charges, even to the extent of questioning Bishop Tierney in correspondence and through a personal review. As a result of their investigation, the Propagation Office once again sent a message of support to the bishop on his course of action.

Incredibly, even these rebuffs, did not deter the Danielson dissidents from their course. Though they had been, they said, "bullied by their bishop", and "blamed by the Apostolic Delegate and the Pope", they still believed that their cause would be vindicated if only the Pope could hear their complaints (Rumilly, 1958). Accordingly, the committee began a search for a representative who could personally bring their cause to the Holy Pontiff. The co-author of the Canadian memorial of 1892, the Reverend Jean Baptiste Proulx, was consulted. After several negotiating sessions, he agreed to represent their cause in Rome. As the official delegate of the petitioners, Proulx first attempted to negotiate with Bishop Tierney. Unable to reach an acceptable compromise (only the bishop's representative would meet with him), Proulx traveled to Rome, his expenses largely paid for by the French Canadians of Danielson.

However, instead of explaining the grievances of the tiny Connecticut parish, the Canadian priest spent most of his time taking up another cause of far greater significance to him — the alleged failures of the bishops of Quebec and Manitoba. Once the Canadian bishops became aware of Proulx' attack on them, they reacted so strongly that Proulx was immediately put on the defensive. In the process of retreating, he lost sight of his original purpose, neglecting the advance of any arguments on behalf of the Danielson French Canadians. By the end of 1896, Proulx was back in the United States with little to report to the people of Danielson except that they should expect nothing more from him, their bishop, or from Rome. With Proulx's debacle came the end of the Danielson affair.

In time, a degree of reconciliation was effected within the parish. Although a French Canadian schismatic church was established under the inspiring influence of Leclaire, a number of French Canadians returned to St. James, and the LaSalette Fathers remained in charge of the parish. A legal suit, brought by several members of the parish who claimed to be the duly elected trustees of the parish and conducted during the heyday of the controversy, was finally judged in error by the Supreme Court of Connecticut and subsequently clarified by an amendment to the Catholic Church's incorporation act.

The greatest victory, in the long run, was Bishop Tierney's. From the beginning of his episcopate he had been embroiled in the unpleasant business of parish discord. Although even before he was named bishop he had been well aware of the weakness of the complainants' case, and the political maneuvers of the French Canadian priest assigned to the parish, it had fallen to him to find a satisfactory solution to an issue that steadfastly defied settlement — cxcept, of course, according to the terms demanded by the strong-willed minority. In a letter that Bishop Tierney wrote to Rome in April, 1896, in his own defense, he explained that he had always viewed the problems as a question of "nationality" rather than one of "religion". Yet, for two long years he had been forced to answer the complaints of Leclaire and his supporters as if the complaints pertained directly to religion and spiritual concerns. Cross-examined by his people and his superiors as well, he could not always count on the support of his fellow bishops, some of whom seemed unsympathetic to his efforts for conciliation. Not only had Archbishop Williams of Boston told him that he had already gone "too far", but Bishop James Healy of Portland, had informed him that he should simply "stand to [sic] your guns and let them rave". His discouragement must have reached its nadir when his appointment of the LaSalette Fathers was greeted with hostility. Seen by the Danielson community as a last straw, it sought to effect the kind of compromise worked out successfully by the LaSalette community and the French Canadians in the neighboring Diocese of Springfield. Left with no alternative but to persist in his attempts to follow the safe procedures outlined by the Propagation Office with regard to national parishes and to continue to respond fairly to the demands of ethnic minorities, Bishop Tierney had relied on the LaSalette priests to help return the parish to its previous pattern of ethnic coexistence. For all too long, his position remained a lonely one.

Thus, when the news of the second vindication by the apostolic delegate and by the Rome office was received, it was Bishop Tierney who must have felt the greatest sense of relief. For the first time he would learn that his conduct during the two year ordeal had not gone completely unnoticed. Days after word arrived from the apostolic delegate, the news spread throughout the diocese, in both civic and religious circles. *The Hartford Courant* (May 24, 1896) editorialized on "Satolli's Sharp Words" to the Canadians and his attitude distinctly supportive of the bishop. *The Morning Union* (May 24, 1896) announced that Satolli "has apparently heard enough of the Danielson French-Canadians" and "has advised them to heed the counsel of their bishop". Other religious and civic leaders acknowledged their admiration for the bishop's patient endeavors during the Danielson crisis. For the first time in his episcopal career, Bishop Tierney had found public support as well as the confirmation of his superiors. Throughout the remainder of his career, he would rely upon the final settlement of this case as a guide to the policies he would pursue with respect to the demands of other ethnic minorities. For the most part, his patience and consistency prevented any subsequent problem from attaining the dimensions of the Danielson affair. Undaunted by the unpleasantness of the situation, moreover, Bishop Tierney would spend much of his episcopate in developing a complex policy relative to immigrants; only one aspect of this would be a continued commitment to their need for parishes established in a manner satisfactory to all concerned.

The Danielson case was to fit the classic mold of many other ethnic disputes that occurred in the Diocese of Hartford after 1890, reflecting elements indicative of how closely the issues of nationality and religion were entwined. Not that every sign of unrest that occurred can be attributed to comparable circumstances in which troubles could be so easily assigned to self-seeking involvement in parish affairs for the sake of promoting national interests. But just as an outside observer was able to note in the Danielson case that "...the people, therefore, were, to a certain extent, under the influences of designing men who sought the advancement of self, and who, therefore, endeavored to curtail the power of the priest with his people, and sometimes to destroy it altogether", (O'Donnell, 1900:434) so too in the early years of a number of national parishes throughout the diocese were there isolated examples of similar activities on the part of unscrupulous priests or popular lay leaders who organized groups around causes highlighting national or personal interests, though with alarming repercussions with regard to the unity of the Church. Probably because the Roman Catholic Church was the one American institution capable of attracting so many of the recent immigrants from Canada and Europe, it inadvertently became the appropriate forum for varied ethnic responses. When Church authorities attempted to orchestrate these differences within the American Catholic Church, a power struggle often resulted, similar to the one that developed in Danielson, the parish becoming the battleground of the dispute. Conflicting loyalties — one nationalistic (or political), the other Church oriented (or religious) — separated the congregation into incompatible groups. One followed either a self-appointed committee or a priest of their own choosing, while the other remained zealously on the side of the legitimate authority of the Church as vested in the person of the bishop.

Some variations occurred, but the phenomenon itself remained constant, especially from the 1890s on. This kind of attack against the authority of the bishop of Hartford became even more prevalent among the Polish communities of the diocese, where intraparish factions emerged, gathered momentum in the isolation imposed upon them by a suspicious host society, and disrupted entire parishes in their drive for prestige or power. Although peace was usually restored to the parish where the troubles occurred, in some cases independent national churches were established by the insurgents, in close proximity to the parent organization. However, for the most part, the accusations of the detractors usually became dulled and proved ineffective not only because of the strength of Church authorities, but also because of the weakness of the complaints raised against the particular church, pastor, or bishop. As the dissenters of Danielson had been reminded by Archbishop Satolli in 1895:

> ...You must remember that you have left the country in which the use of that language is universal and have voluntarily come to another in which a different tongue is spoken. You must not then expect that here all the same provisions can be made with the same perfection for the propagation and continued use of your own language...(Archives of the Archbishop of Hartford)

Thus, their future as Roman Catholics, loyal to the American Catholic Church as well as the universal Church with its center at Rome, depended upon their appreciation and understanding of the ties that bound them to the Church as a whole. Furthermore, their undeniable right to complain was contingent upon what the Church could do for them in their new setting. Representatives of other dissident groups would also become familiar with the same kind of defense of the Church's policy with respect to new immigrant parishes.

Troubles within Polish parishes of the Diocese of Hartford during the period 1880-1920 exemplified the true nature of the conflicts often mistakenly considered to have been directly inspired by intransigent insensitivity on the part of Church authorities. Like the Italians, Polish immigrants had also been attracted by Connecticut's industrial promise after the 1880s. Even by 1910, the Polish community of Connecticut numbered approximately 120,000, and accounted for 13 percent of all immigrants who had taken up residence in the state. More than three-quarters of these new immigrants, who derived mostly from the Australian and Russian partitions of Poland, entered the country as members of the Roman Catholic Church. Once in the United States, they quickly manifested a strong desire to maintain that same allegiance in their new Protestant-oriented setting.

In many ways, their initial response to the American Catholic Church leadership corresponded closely with that of the French Canadian model. In the first place, wherever the Poles settled, they sought to establish a "Polish kind of faith" (Greene, 1966:447). Although most Poles eventually became content with the American Catholic Church as they found it, a small vocal minority often expressed dissatisfaction over real or imagined injustices perpetuated against them by "unsympathetic" or "misguided" bishops who appointed pastors who did not satisfy their needs and who attempted to interfere with other aspects of their parish life. As a result, two camps often emerged within Polish Catholic communities in the United States: the majority element supported their own priests and the diocese, but a highly visible minority verbalized their criticisms of what they perceived to be an autocratic and biased Catholic hierarchy. Thus, it was not so much the Polish people's distaste for American Catholicism that often caused episodes of discord within Catholic communities as much as it was a reluctance on the part of some Poles to give their allegiance to any American institution that they could not identify as according a primacy to their own ethnic needs.

This inability to submit themselves to "outside" agents of authority — whether secular or religious — was to have serious ramifications for the more than three million Poles who had entered the United States by 1910. It was at the heart of the separatist movements and the setting up of the independent national churches in Chicago, Buffalo, and Scranton, and it had plagued many Polish priests and members of the laity who could not identify with its strong-willed attachment to national ties at the expense of loyalty to the Roman Catholic Church. It was, in some way, also part of every dispute that emerged within the Polish Catholic communities of the Diocese of Hartford.

The bishops of Hartford as well as the clergy of the diocese were well aware of the sources of discord and dissension that could be utilized by Polish malcontents. Indeed, they had seen them manifested in the first Polish communities to establish parishes in the diocese — those of Meriden and New Britain. Perhaps it was for this reason that the official Catholic newspapers of the diocese consistently sought to indicate approval of the Polish minority, made a point of reporting the establishment of Polish churches, schools, and other institutions, and made every effort to sympathize publicly with the problems Poles encountered. On one occasion, for example, *The Catholic Transcript* claimed that these Central Europeans were being victimized by "designing men" who could easily start rebellions based on "fancied ecclesiastical inequalities" (Sept. 18, 1902).

Beyond this rhetorical stance and other normal measures, Church officials seemed at a loss to find ways to convince the Polish people that their interests were also being taken as seriously as were the needs of other Catholics in the diocese. Thus, the same kinds of conflicts that had created tensions in the early days of both the Meriden and New Britain parishes continued to recur as new Polish communities in Connecticut — from Derby to Rockville, Southington to New London, Terryville to Thompsonville — sought to establish their own parishes. Indeed, a closer look at the disputes that emerged within Polish communities of the Diocese of Hartford confirms the thesis proposed by Victor Greene (1975), that the bickering and dissatisfaction in Polish parishes were caused by national and regional differences among members of the parish and not by substantive religious issues or the legitimacy of authority. It also reveals the same pattern earlier evidenced in the Danielson case, namely, that the disputes that did arise occurred despite honest attempts by Church officials to forestall them. If, indeed, fewer troubles were encountered in the Diocese of Hartford than in other dioceses where large numbers of Polish immigrants had also settled, this happened because, to a great extent, the fears, anxieties, and suspicions of early Polish immigrants were greatly understood and responded to in that diocese. Despite accusations that the contrary was true, there is considerable evidence that during the crucial decades, 1890-1920, both Bishops Tierney and Nilan, as well as the priests they appointed to care for the needs of the Polish, maintained a policy that aimed at the promotion of the best interests of the Polish minority in the diocese.

Examples of the infighting that was endemic to the local Polish communities abound. One episode that best demonstrates the complexity
of the reasons behind the discord that surfaced in Polish communities
has been recorded in the golden jubilee booklet published in 1955, by
the St. Michael Parish of Derby. According to the Reverend Stanislaus
Konieczny, first pastor of St. Michael's and author of its early history,
the Polish immigrants who had settled in the small manufacturing town
(its total population during this period was approximately eleven thousand) had been bedeviled by problems even before the parish was
formed.

Father Konieczny described the status differences that basically divided the Polish immigrants of the area. According to Konieczny, because most of the Poles who lived in Derby immigrated from two regions of Austrian Poland, where the terrain alone had dictated differing
cultural and economic styles of life (the village of Kolbuszowa as opposed to the more urban Tarnow), they had little in common even
before they emigrated. Once in the United States, these newcomers
settled in a community where Irish Catholics had established themselves as early as the 1850s, but which by 1900 had also attracted many
of the most recent immigrants from eastern and southern Europe. In
this setting, the dissimilarities among the Poles, resulting from their
diverse backgrounds, seemed to become all the more pronounced and
divisive. To compound their problems, these strangers in the land were
also subjected to the usual prevailing forms of discrimination, as they
sought the lowest-paying unskilled jobs in the brass and metal goods
factories in Derby, or otherwise attempted to become part of the social
or economic milieu. As a result, economic competition occurred between the Kolbuszowa and Tarnow groups, and jealousy quickly deteriorated into threats of physical violence when the Kolbuszowa people
resorted to calling their Tarnow associates *mioflarze* or "broom-makers",
and were, in turn, ridiculed as *mariarze* or "grease-makers" by the hu-
miliated workers from Tarnow. When enough wine and beer flowed,
these harmless terms were perceived as especially abrasive, and hard
feelings and physical confrontations resulted. This competitiveness,
bordering precariously upon even more serious conflict in an environment that effectively short-circuited social and economic mobility,
proved stronger than either the national or religious ties that might
have united the Poles. Caught up in these rivalries, Connecticut's Poles
projected the cause of their troubles, blaming their plight on economic,
political, or religious forces outside themselves.

Thus, when Francis Stochmal, who had been among the first Polish
families to settle in Derby in the late 1870s, attempted to bring Poles

together in 1896 for the express purpose of establishing a Polish parish, he found that the factionalism that was already well developed would deter his efforts. For example, when Ansonia's Poles, who had derived from the Russian controlled city of Warsaw, were consulted in terms of a possible merger, they proved resistant. Until 1903, Stochmal tried to convince the two communities to collaborate. Steadfastly Ansonia's Poles refused to consider the probability that the parish would be located in Derby, where the vast majority of the area's Polish population lived. The dispute over location and other petty problems effectively prevented any common action by the Poles of Ansonia and Derby.

In 1903, Stochmal reorganized the parish society, retitling it the Parish Society of St. Michael the Archangel in Derby, Connecticut. By stating the location of the proposed parish and by enlarging its base membership to include other Poles of Seymour and Orange, he hoped to avoid one argument and forestall the easy two-way division that had blocked the development of his original organization. This aspect of his plan succeeded. Unfortunately, other extraneous problems interfered with his master plan.

Mindful of the needs of the constantly increasing Polish population of Connecticut (by mid-decade there would be at least ten thousand Poles in the diocese), Bishop Tierney visited Poland in the same year that Stochmal revised his plans, attempting to find Polish priests to staff a number of proposed Polish parishes in the diocese. In the fall of 1903 Tierney returned to Hartford with the word that the Polish bishops were painting a very gloomy picture concerning clerical prospects. Claiming that there was a great shortage of priests in Poland, all Polish bishops whom he visited indicated reluctance to release their clergy to do missionary work in the United States. However, the Polish Vincentians had responded favorably. Encouraged by the prospect that there would soon be a community of Polish priests upon whom he could rely for the organization of needed Polish parishes, Bishop Tierney asked Stochmal to wait until he could complete his transactions with the Vincentians. In the meantime, he organized the first parish to be staffed by the Polish community in New Haven, undoubtedly with a view toward observing the extent of their initial success, and attempted to relieve the disappointment of Derby's Poles by asking the Vincentians to visit Derby on a regular basis. He even implied that, if the Polish committee were able to locate a priest, he would allow the Poles to establish a parish.

This "refusal" on the part of Tierney to act immediately on the Polish committee's behalf was to provide a new basis for discord among the members of the Derby Polish community. Somehow the combined efforts of Stochmal and the bishop to prepare for a future parish were rejected; hurt feelings were expressed in the form of strong accusations against the Catholic leadership. Some former members of the St. Michael Society rallied around an unauthorized priest from Poland, the Reverend Walter Stec. With him, a new committee traveled to Hartford to make demands. Joining a protest staged by a local Polish Catholic Congress meeting in Union City in 1903, the members of the committee also signed petitions against the bishop, complaining about his response to the Derby community. While some Poles continued to give allegiance to the bishop and to worship at the "Irish" church, St. Mary's in Derby, the dissidents backed Father Stec's efforts to establish a parish. For two years, while protests against the bishop were addressed to the apostolic delegate, and while other complaints and criticisms lingered on, some members of the Polish Catholic community continued to worship at St. Mary's, where the Polish Vincentian priests, stationed in nearby New Haven, visited on a regular basis. Unable to gain the full support of the Poles, Father Stec finally decided to leave Derby in 1904 and Stochmal's persistent entreaties to Bishop Tierney were rewarded. Apparently satisfied that the religious community of Polish Vincentians could provide the kind of strong leadership needed, Bishop Tierney commissioned this congregation to formally organize a parish in Derby.

In November of 1905, Father Konieczny assumed duties as first pastor of St. Michael's; the Reverend Paul Waszko was named as his assistant. Despite a temporary setback sustained when Father Konieczny was transferred in the spring of 1906 and replaced by Father Waszko, the parish continued to develop on a sound basis.

Finally united under the leadership of Fathers Konieczny and Waszko, the Poles improved their parish plant to include a rectory, convent, and school, and paid off the entire debt on their church — all within the first ten years of the parish's corporate existence. Under Father Waszko, the parish displayed the strength and unity that had eluded it during its formative years.

Although colorful and somewhat more complex than other intraparish conflicts that developed in Polish Catholic communities, the Derby situation was by no means unique within the Diocese of Hartford. In the areas where the first Polish churches were established, Meriden and New Britain, the same kind of factionalism was also typical from the beginning. Both cities, as major centers for the production of metal goods, had experienced rapid increases in population after 1880. By 1920, the population of Meriden had doubled, while that of New Britain was five times its earlier count. Among the Polish immigrants attracted to the unskilled factory work available in both areas were the same kind of hard-working, but potentially troublesome laborers who had also chosen to settle in Derby. Immediately, these intruders into Yankee society sensed their imposed alienation from most of the social and economic positions of any importance. For this reason, they sought recognition within the general Polish community and acceptance within the Catholic Church, the only American institution with which they could feel a sense of identity. The conflicts that resulted from the clash of personal ambitions can be discerned from the early histories of both St. Stanislaus, Meriden, and Sacred Heart, New Britain.

The infighting that unsettled the first Polish Catholic community in the diocese (St. Stanislaus, Meriden, 1891) has been well chronicled in a series of reports and letters appended to the first financial statements sent to the bishop by the parish. From these pastoral reports, all dated 1893, a dismal picture of an already well-developed intramural dispute becomes clear. In fact, from the first entry of the parish's financial statement, the atmosphere of parish discord is apparent. According to the Reverend Anthony Klawiter, first pastor of St. Stanislaus, his work had been undermined from the beginning by those whose aim was to destroy his credibility in order to procure their own selfish ends. Thus, although he and his cashier had worked to correct the deficiencies and irresponsibilities of previous collectors, Father Klawiter feared that the future development of the parish was in doubt. How was he, he asked in his first report to the bishop, to clear his own reputation when these "conspirators" accused him of "thievishness"; to prevent "faithless men" from convoking meetings, and taking up Sunday collections; to disallow elections of trustees after his own already had been chosen, and to correct disrespectful attitudes towards the authority of the Church, which had led them to reject the incorporation of the parish as he repeatedly proposed? Unless some corrective action were taken, Father Klawiter warned the bishop, these troublemakers — abetted as they were by outside sympathizers or instigators — would soon undermine the efforts of good Catholics to fulfill their obligations as members in good standing of the Diocese of Hartford.

As Father Klawiter suggested in his report to Bishop McMahon, the dissidents claimed that the true nature of the troubles within the parish centered on the question of ownership of property, of financial control, and of means as to how these two aspects of parish administration could be reconciled within the structure of the American Catholic Church. Because some of his parishioners needed guidance in understanding how American Catholic parishes should operate, he appealed to the bishop to assist in clarifying these functions of authority so that he could move forward with the business of establishing the parish. Despite this appeal, however, no action was taken and the parish remained unreconciled. Within weeks, follow-up entries indicated that Father

Klawiter's hold on the parish was weakening. In a "Statement and Appeal" written by some of the collectors deputized by Father Klawiter, a tone of respect for the "Reverend Rector" as well as for the bishop of Hartford was sustained, although the suffering of those who supported Klawiter was also detectable. Harassed by their opponents and even threatened with being arrested if they pursued their "collections" within the parish, those who supported the authority of their pastor began to tire of the battle.

Intensifying their drive to take over financial control of the parish organization, the dissenters collected funds in the name of the St. Stanislaus Society. Moreover, they took steps to force both the pastor and his collectors to turn over funds previously obtained, declaring that they had received the permission of the Reverend Paul McAlenney, pastor of St. Rose, Meriden, to function as collectors. The final scenario was replete with dramatic confrontation; the insurgents disrupted liturgies conducted by Father Klawiter and attempted to take up their own collections while services were in progress. Not long after, the broken-spirited pastor parted from Meriden; the last financial statement bearing his signature was dated June 11, 1893.

The following month, the Reverend Francis Havey, a young curate from St. Joseph Cathedral Parish in Hartford, arrived to administer to the needs of the Polish parishioners of Meriden as their temporary pastor. Fluent in Polish, and nicknamed "Father Haveski" by his friends, Havey restored a semblance of peace and order to the troubled parish, remaining in charge until another Polish priest could be located to replace him. The departure of Father Klawiter brought relief to the troubled parish; Father Havey's arrival contributed to the calm. The two camps dispersed and no new challenges were immediately forthcoming. For the time being, the Polish community was less concerned over the threat of Irish hegemony within the parish or the diocese than they were with the choice of an appropriate Polish pastor who could represent all their interests. This preoccupation continued for the next dozen years. From 1894 until 1906, the administration of St. Stanislaus changed hands several times in rather rapid succession. First, the Reverend Thomas Misicki, who came to the diocese bearing the strong endorsement of Ignatius Horstmann, Bishop of Cleveland, attempted to head the parish. A well-educated priest, Misicki should have been able to bring some note of harmony to the St. Stanislaus community. Instead he found himself the object of suspicions and criticisms. It was not long before Misicki was also complaining to the bishop about the treatment he received at the hands of some of his parishioners. Within two years, he, too, left the diocese, departing so abruptly that a young priest, the Reverend Lúcyan Bojnowski, who was in charge of Polish

Catholics in New Britain, had to temporarily take charge of St. Stanislaus as well. Under Bojnowski's successor, the Reverend Casimir Kucharski, the first steps toward a sense of unity were achieved and the legal incorporation of the parish was finally negotiated. But two more pastorates would pass before the affairs of the parish were finally put on a solid basis under the outstanding leadership of the Reverend John Ceppa, pastor from 1906 until his death in 1948.

It would be difficult to assign primary responsibility for the parochial disorders of this oldest Polish Catholic community to the bishops of Hartford since they had provided a Polish priest to serve the parish from the start, and had even promised initial financial support. A review of the pattern of dissatisfaction within St. Stanislaus, Meriden, from the 1890s until the second decade of the twentieth century suggests that the same kind of factionalism that had beset both the French Canadians of Danielson and the Poles of Derby was at the source of the difficulties. This factionalism, moreover, plagued the Polish community until the advent of a strong leader who could finally forge the necessary bond of unity among the various conflicting elements.

Even the history of the most celebrated Polish parish in the diocese, Sacred Heart, New Britain, reveals the same kind of initial internal divisiveness. Indeed, its pastor, the Reverend Lúcyan Bojnwoski, was the first to chronicle the kinds of bitter struggles and confrontations that preoccupied the parish in its early development. In his biography of Father Bojnowski, historian Daniel Buczek (1974) reviewed these troubled beginnings. According to Buczek, from the time the St. Michael the Archangel Society was founded in 1889 to establish a Roman Catholic Church in New Britain for Polish Catholics, a spirit of factionalism prevailed. For, even though the society had managed to secure the legal papers for the incorporation of the parish under the title of St. Casimir the Prince, it was not able to agree on the acceptable site for the parish church.

Not long after a series of unsuccessful attempts to organize a parish failed, some members of the St. Michael Society withdrew, invited in their own priest, and made plans for an independent parish. By the time the newly ordained Father Bojnowski was assigned to New Britain, there was only a remnant organization authorized to decide the future of the Polish parish. By suggesting that a new plot of land be considered for the proposed church and by reorganizing the society under the title St. Casimir, Father Bojnowski attempted to resolve the complications. Unfortunately, even after both suggestions were implemented, the "spirit of factionalism" continued to disturb the Polish Catholic community of New Britain.

Probably offended by the rapidity with which the young priest had taken charge of matters in New Britain, certain members of the new society decided to confront their new pastor in a debate on questions ranging from morality and dogma to the rights of pastors and bishops as opposed to those of parishioners. This unpleasant meeting, as well as subsequent scenes, convinced Bojnowski that the society he had formed could not be counted upon for support. Reorganizing the society again so as to include only those members agreeable to episcopal and pastoral authority, Bojnowski petitioned for a change in the name of the original Church corporation and began to work toward a stable Polish Catholic community in New Britain.

For many years, Bojnowski's goal continued to elude him. Often he grew discouraged over the lack of cooperation, as well as many evidences of personal disregard for self-improvement on the part of his own people. "To uproot evil habits, dissuade parishioners from drunkeness, debauchery, quarreling, fighting, entering into civil marriages, raising a ruckus, wasting time and money, and instead to plant Christian virtues", he wrote, were endless tasks, seldom accomplished with any sense of satisfaction (Buczek, 1974). Nor were incidents of infighting and factionalism to lessen as other direct confrontations and court suits continued to plague him during the first decade of his pastorate.

One instance of conflict occurred in 1899 when the "Legion of the Freemen of Krakus", with the help of recruits from the Meriden chapter of the Polish National Alliance, disrupted the parish and attacked Father Bojnowski's authority by mounting a weekend demonstration on "behalf of Polish nationalism and anti-clericalism". To emphasize that Father Bojnowski was the direct object of their displeasure, the Alliance members gathered at Sacred Heart Church on the final day of their meeting and disrupted services. When he rebuked them, they moved on, in a body, to the home of one of New Britain's most prominent citizens, Judge G.V. Andrews, whom they presented with a petition charging their pastor with autocratic measures. Because this course of action brought no change in their pastor's attitudes or performance, tensions persisted at Sacred Heart Parish. Neither Bojnowski nor his opponents sensed either victory or vindication.

Other self-styled Polish "nationalists" followed the Legion's example of attempting to discredit Father Bojnowski. These new campaigns finally forced Bojnowski to explain his mode of operation to the bishop of Hartford. To bolster his theory that it was the least religious among Polish Catholics who were the troublemakers, Bojnowski repeated the rumors his delegates had heard when they were attending the Meriden meeting, that "the dissidents were not even Catholics". Using this argument as proof that the discord was not primarily directed at him, Father Bojnowski suggested that future troubles could be avoided if his Polish Catholics could be organized into their own "Catholic Union". With the approval of the bishop, Father Bojnowski organized a Polish Union in 1900. Unfortunately, it would not be sufficiently strong to ward off successive blows against his authority.

The most serious crisis against Father Bojnowski's administration occurred two years later. Beginning in the summer of 1902, almost a decade after he had first assumed his pastoral duties in New Britain, Father Bojnowski's position became so threatened that he tendered his resignation to the bishop. Ironically, he had, to a certain degree, contributed to this crisis himself. The conflict, began when he decided that he needed an assistant to care for the more than 2,500 members of his congregation. What compounded his predicament was his imprudent agreement with fellow Poles that Bishop Tierney was being unnecessarily scrupulous when he insisted that no immigrant priests be permitted to serve in the diocese without proper credentials.

When the Reverend Edward Uminski, a visiting priest who claimed credentials from a Polish diocese, asked to be Bojnowski's assistant, Bojnowski prevailed upon the bishop to grant his request despite Uminski's lack of canonical documents. Because of Bojnowski's personal intercession, Bishop Tierney granted Uminski exception from the rule, and the priest assumed his duties at Sacred Heart.

Soon after Uminski's assumption of the duties of the parish, Father Bojnowski received a letter from some members of the parish that demanded, under the threat of violence, that the trustees of the parish be changed. Next, the rectory was searched in an attempt to prove that, as pastor, Father Bojnowski was guilty of improperly managing parish funds. Further, while the search was going on, other members of the dissident group milled around the rectory in an effort to intimidate the pastor. When no evidence was found to substantiate their claims against the pastor, the dissenters resorted to other means of intimidation, bringing their grievances to a series of self-initiated parish meetings. Among the complaints made at these meetings was that their pastor could not be counted upon to further their "Polish kind of faith". Even though Father Bojnowski's supporters could ridicule the insurgents for their haste in rallying around Uminski—he had, in fact, only served the parish for less than a month before the troubles began—they could not prevent the momentum of the insurgents' attack. In the face of a clear case of mutiny, Bojnowski forwarded his resignation to Bishop Tierney.

Before the situation corrected itself, and Father Bojnowski was allowed to resume his position as pastor, much ill-will surfaced, revealing the degree to which the Polish community was seriously divided. Even though the dissidents charged that both Bojnowski and his diocese were neglecting them, they only succeeded in calling attention to their pastor's deficiencies as well as their own. For it was not an Irish priest that the parishioners of Sacred Heart were willing to accuse of

> ...not performing a multitude of priestly functions; refusing to visit the sick and the dying, refusing baptism to infants, throwing penitents from the confessional, refusing Holy Communion to women dressed in summer clothing, not delivering sermons or reading the Gospel, but using the pulpit to tell stories, becoming abusive to various groups, like the choir whom he told that they would do better to sing in a brothel rather than in a church,

but it was Father Bojnowski himself (Buczek, 1974). Nor was it any Irish temperance policy that the Polish saloon keepers were resisting but the anti-saloon harangues delivered by their own Polish pastor. Finally, it was not an outside enemy whom they had charged with acting unjustly and causing them pain and grief but one of their own. The fault for much of the unhappiness that had arisen derived from an unwillingness of the Polish community to accept any authority outside itself. By rejecting Father Bojnowski on the grounds that he had made friends with Americans and Irishmen, they jeopardized their chances of finding an intermediary ground between Roman Catholicism of the Polish or American varieties. Instead of ridding themselves of outside controls, they damaged their own chance for strengthening themselves in their new setting. In the long run, the intraparish revolt against Bojnowski and the legitimate authority he represented could not maintain its original support. Within time, the New Britain Polish Catholic congregration was once again attempting to find its proper place within the Diocese of Hartford.

The lessons of the Uminski affair were well learned by both Bojnowski and parishioners who had temporarily followed Uminski. When Father Bojnowski was once again permitted to take up his duties at Sacred Heart Parish, he was sufficiently mindful of the valid criticism he had received concerning his autocratic method of dealing with his parishioners. Furthermore, when in December of 1903 a local Polish Catholic Congress met in Union City to protest Bishop Tierneys' refusal to assign them priests of their own nationality and later, when this petition was sent in the form of a memorandum to the apostolic delegate, there was no longer any possibility of enlisting Bojnowski's support. In fact, never again would Bojnowski join with critics of the bishop who questioned why authorities were so anxious to follow the direction of the Propagation Office with regard to careful selection of priests to serve in Polish parishes. As for the faithful among the Sacred Heart parishioners, there would be better days ahead as their pastor would try harder to gain the admiration and the understanding of his congregation — a final vindication of their loyalty had been well placed from the start.

With regard to the experiences that occurred in Derby, Meriden, and New Britain, there were a number of interesting parallels. For the first several years in each Polish community, regardless of whether its origins had occurred in the 1890s or the early 1900s, there were honest attempts made by committees to organize for the sake of establishing a parish united to the Roman Catholic Church. But there was also dissension in the ranks caused by differences in religious or political background, or from competition based on a number of variables. The discord, furthermore, tended to occur even when there were not only strong indications of concern on the part of Church authorities, but also evidence that the qualities of Polish leadership were of a high caliber.

To a great extent, the grievances within these parishes were also similar. They revolved around the more mundane questions of leadership and its prerogatives; for example, who was to collect funds, who would head the committees, or how the money was to be spent and for what purposes it was to be raised. Seldom were disputes initiated over the more abstract questions or ecclesiastical rights, or of matters in dogma or morals. Furthermore, it was quite easy for ambitious local leaders — either lay or clerical — to confuse a congregation and lead it according to their own designs, and yet to escape the brunt of any failures by redirecting the object of any attacks toward the common enemy — the Irish leadership of the Catholic Church. Thus, although Francis Stochmal's opponents in Derby included the Polish missionary, Father Stec, and his supporters, much of the verbalized dissatisfaction pitted the parishioners against the bishop. Likewise, although Dr. Misicki experienced more difficulty with those who met in Meriden's political and special clubs to misconstrue his aims and plot against him, it was the bishop to whom he complained that he was angry about the way he was being treated. Finally, despite the fact that Bojnowski suffered more from immigrants among his own congregation than from acts of diocesan officials or Irish pastors, Polish Alliance adherents continued to complain to "higher authority" that it was the Irish bishop of Hartford — not one of their own members — who was ignoring the most primary spiritual needs of Polish immigrants.

A memorandum sent to the apostolic delegate in 1905 by the Polish Catholic Congress of Connecticut also illustrates the degree to which Polish Catholics were willing to redirect their anger against the bishop of Hartford. Read in the context of the troubles engaged in by three parishes so far described, it says more about its composers than about the actual situation prevailing in the diocese. For, at a time when Polish parishes, headed by Polish clergy, were functioning in several key urban areas of the state where the largest numbers of Polish immigrants had settled, the authors of the memorandum still considered it appropriate to accuse Bishop Tierney of rejecting the pleas of Polish Catholics "with various excuses"; of subjecting Polish Catholics to the jurisdiction of Irish priests; and of refusing to accept Polish priests from Europe or from other American dioceses. Moreover, it charged the bishop with failing to send Polish students to Polish seminaries because he did "not have Polish parishes for them", yet with sending Irish students to Poland on the grounds that these priests "might be able to entice the Poles to Irish churches...and gradually to Americanize them...". Finally, it made four demands — all of which had already been implemented by Bishop Tierney (Buczek, 1974:36).

Considering all that the bishop had been attempting to do to assist his various ethnic constituencies throughout his administration, the contents of the memorial of 1905 must undoubtedly have disturbed him. Somehow, he seemed to understand, however, that at the heart of all the unjust charges was a general sense of frustration over inequities and the preoccupation of some participants with one crucial demand, namely the right of having Polish representatives in the American Catholic hierarchy. Realizing that little could be done to convince certain Polish leaders and their supporters of good faith, and unable to exert any influence beyond his own diocese, Bishop Tierney persisted in doing what was at least possible with regard to the proper care of immigrants. Most of the Polish clergy, following Bojnowski's lead, came to understand the episcopal predicament. Mindful of the kind of loyalty that Poles traditionally gave to Roman Catholicism, both the diocesan leadership and the Polish clergy and laity remained confident that accord would eventually be reached if mutual patience and understanding were sustained.

As the years passed and other difficulties occurred in the newer Polish congregations in the diocese, Bishops Tierney and Nilan continued to look for appropriate solutions to the new problems. When, for example, the Terryville Polish community made demands and even rejected Bishop Tierney's offer to send Polish Vincentians to take charge, the bishop heard their complaints, reversed the unpopular decision, and appointed Reverend Joseph Raniszewski to head the new parish of St. Casimir. He also located another pastor for the Poles of Stamford after their first pastor, Reverend Joseph Luczycki, retired. Furthermore, Bishop Tierney made sure that the thirteen native Polish priests and two Polish educated American priests who were serving in the diocese after 1900 were well utilized. As he told the apostolic delegate in a letter explaining his policies, he had always made every effort to influence young men of Polish nationality to enter the seminary. Because of this policy, there were currently six Polish seminarians being supported at diocesan seminaries.

Bishop Nilan also attempted to find appropriate ways to satisfy the Polish constituency of the diocese. When, for example, a Union City Polish congregation petitioned against the Reverend Ignatius Maciejewski in 1911, Bishop Nilan sent the Reverend Felix Baran, one of the most respected Polish priests in the diocese, to act as an intermediary. Only after the people continued to express dissatisfaction with Maciejewski and refused to contribute financially to the pastor's upkeep did Bishop Nilan search for another priest. In September of 1912, the recently ordained Reverend Paul Piechocki, the first Polish American native of Connecticut to be ordained, was appointed pastor of St. Hedwig's, Union City; under him, for the first time, the parish would begin visibly to prosper.

As the number of Polish immigrants settling in Connecticut continued to increase dramatically, however, and many Poles took up residence in the farming regions and small factory settlements of the state, Bishop Nilan experienced even greater difficulty in supplying priests to serve his Polish minority. As a result, in a number of smaller communities there was "much agitation and coercion from outsiders to go off on their own independently". Such incidents led to the establishment of independent Polish national churches in more than half a dozen communities in Connecticut (Mierzwinski, 1971). In each case, critics of the bishop of Hartford pointed to these splinter churches as prime examples of actions taken in response to deliberate patterns of episcopal neglect and prejudice on the part of the Roman Catholic Church. Once again, as many parish histories have also mentioned, the majority of the Poles in these communities waited out the long delay and ignored the flurry of activity directed toward them by leaders of the Polish National Church. Eventually, those who had waited patiently were rewarded, as recently ordained Polish American priests — many of whom were natives of the diocese who received their first training in St. Thomas Seminary — were appointed to organize new Polish parishes. After 1915, the Reverends Stanley Federkiewicz, George and Paul Bartlewski, John Kowalski, and William Topor, all second-generation

Connecticuters, took firm charge of the newly organized Polish parishes such as St. Adalbert's in Thompsonville, St. Stanislaus in Bristol, St. Mary's in Torrington, and St. Hedwig's in Union City.

By 1915, there were twenty Polish priests serving in seventeen Polish parishes of the diocese. Sensing their need for collaboration, these priests organized the Association of Polish Priests, which has since successfully functioned. Together with some non-Polish priests trained in Polish seminaries, these priests organized new parishes where Polish communities had settled until, by 1930, twenty-four of two hundred thirty-five parishes of the diocese were Polish national parishes. Although factionalism and troubled times would continue to befall these new Catholic communities as well (the Polish National Church actively recruited new members on the grounds of Polish nationalism), seldom was the early pattern of difficulties repeated. From the late 1920s on, under the guidance of a number of outstanding Polish priests such as Father Ceppa, Musiel, and Federkiewicz, and with the cooperation of second generation Poles who had been carefully educated and formed in the many Polish parochial schools, a strong Polish Catholic community offered both personnel and talent to the building of their own parishes and of the diocese as well.

In retrospect it seems clear that Bishop Tierney and Nilan gave sufficient attention to the needs of both the French Canadian and Polish minorities under their jurisdiction. But many internal and external factors conspired against bishops and people to impede the kind of steady advance that both minorities had envisaged. Upon analysis, it also becomes evident that much of the responsibility for the troubles that occurred in Polish and French Canadian national parishes of the Diocese of Hartford can be attributed to certain members within ethnic parishes whose ambitions for leadership, and subsequent agitation against some of their own leaders, prevented the firm establishment of their own parishes until internal crises could be resolved. Loyalties between nationality and Church became the rationale for many of these disputes. Not until the ambitions of those promoting dissension had been curtailed could the real issues of the debate be analyzed and attended to. When complaints proved reasonable, the diocesan response was appropriate. Consequently, over time, the internal conflicts that so besieged some French Canadian and Polish parishes in their early phases of settlement were resolved to such satisfaction that both minorities may boast of a strong network of national parishes throughout the diocese to the present day.

6 Episodes of Discord Within Other European National Parishes in the Diocese of Hartford, 1890-1920

Episodes of discord also occurred within Slovak, Hungarian, and Lithuanian national parishes, especially in their formative periods in the Diocese of Hartford, 1890-1920. Lacking the large numbers and the outspoken national or regional alliances that especially characterized French Canadians and Poles at the time, the Slovaks, Hungarians, and Lithuanians tended to react to perceived grievances differently, thereby emphasizing their ethnic distinctiveness. Consequently, the conflicts that engaged these eastern European immigrants in their struggle for parochial autonomy within the Diocese of Hartford merit separate investigation and evaluation.

The first interchanges between Connecticut's Slovak community and diocesan officials set this ethnic group apart from other new immigrants of the late nineteenth century. Although Connecticut's Slovaks would never numerically rival their Slavic cousins, the Poles (by 1920 the estimated Polish immigrant population in the state was 46,000 while that of the Slovaks was 6,000), they quickly developed a special ethnic identity in those industrial areas where they found factory employment and settled.

Unlike the Poles, the Slovaks saw the importance of identifying themselves as members of the Diocese of Hartford and of expecting reciprocal interest. Slovak laymen initiated formal contact with the bishop of Hartford as early as 1889. After members of a newly formed Catholic Slovak fraternal society petitioned Bishop Lawrence Mc-Mahon to establish a church in 1890, they received his permission to separate from St. Joseph (German) parish, where they had special status. Under the Reverend Joseph Formanek, they began the construction of the basement church of St. John Nepomucene in Bridgeport's east side factory district. Accenting their distinctness from the Germans, for whom St. Joseph had originally been organized, they declined to be classified as "Czech", "Bohemian", or "Hungarian". The Slovak lay founders of St. John's emphasized their uniqueness as — in their own phrase — "Slovanians". Not only were they the first eastern European immigrant arrivals in Connecticut — perhaps in the United States — to petition formally for separate ethnic status, but they became a model for other Slovak communities in New England, as well as hosts for other central and eastern European minorities in the process of establishing their own national parishes in the diocese.

Despite showing early signs of conforming with Church regulations, Bridgeport's Slovaks occasionally experienced the kind of problems with official Church leadership that typified other ethnic minorities in the diocese. Even during the first decade of their establishment at St. John's, dissension erupted among the Slovaks. Their first pastor's transfer from the diocese, implied in a letter he wrote to Bishop Tierney from his new post in Scranton, was one consequence of intramural problems. So, too, was the interdict placed upon two of St. John's parish societies, and the excommunication of their leaders by Bishop Tierney shortly after the pastor's departure. Since it was not until 1900 that the three men who were excommunicated retracted all they had said, bad feelings continued to disturb St. John's Parish during the successive pastorates of Reverend F.J. Pribyl, whose tenure lasted little more than a year, and his successor, the Reverend Joseph Kossalko.

In their struggles for separate parochial rights within the Diocese of Hartford, the Slovaks seemed to handle their presentations of grievances and their general dissatisfaction with a greater sense of propriety than did Connecticut's Poles or French Canadians. For example, the Slovaks generally used a more respectful mode of communication with diocesan officials than other minorities had employed. Further, when presented with convincing counter arguments against particular proposals, Slovak insurgents — although often fiery at some stage of reaction — seemed to acquiesce more quickly to the wishes of Church representatives. Perhaps these apparent differences in style derived from what their Bridgeport contemporaries referred to as *"Tauben Blut"*, or the "dove blood" of the Slovaks (Whelan, 1934). A pacific and predominantly rural people who had been oppressed in their homeland either by the more urbanized Czechs or by the politically dominant Hungarians, they were described by the Reverend Matthew Jankola in a letter to Bishop Tierney as a victimized people, similar to the "Irish of the Hungarian Kingdom". Apparently their subordination to the alien authority in Europe preconditioned them to a more conciliatory attitude in the face of continuing direct confrontations. At least their ability to curb first impressions of emotional resentment against authority appeared to give them an advantage in negotiating for rights and privileges.

Possibly their experiences in Europe were consciously recalled when Connecticut's Slovaks consistently gave indications of their desire to adjust to ecclesiastical authority in Connecticut. Just as, in their first correspondence with the bishop of Hartford concerning the establishment of St. John's, they had altered their tactics and complied with the bishop's recommendations, so, too, in their subsequent dealings with him would they continue to strive for the right words and the best means to achieve the goals that they believed might be denied them through a less careful and refined approach.

Correspondence between the Slovaks and Bishop Tierney concerning the establishment of a second Slovak parish in Bridgeport illustrates this mode of operations. In 1907, a group of parishioners from St. John's Church formed a new society, the SS. Cyril and Methodius Society, for the express purpose of establishing another Slovak parish. This move was deemed necessary, they explained in a letter to the bishop, because their membership had grown too large for the first tiny Bridgeport church building. But a review of their entire interchange with the bishop reveals that the real reason for wanting the new parish was dissatisfaction with the performance of the pastor of St. John's. Instead of stating their grievances against Father Kossalko or suggesting his removal, the newly formed parish society chose what they deemed a more tactful course, arguing simply that the church was too small.

Apparently recognizing that the Slovaks were expressing deeper problems than those entailing mere expansion, the bishop responded favorably to their request, and indicated that his approval would be forthcoming. He added that he thought the new parish should be located on the opposite side of the city in order to justify a duplication of Slovak parishes. Replying immediately, the Slovaks rejected the idea of relocation, explaining rather simplistically that "it is impossible for us to build a church in the West End, as we are all residing in the East Side...". At the same time they strongly reaffirmed the need for the new parish and added: "We have enough for a new church...and you are asking us too many questions which keep us back. We think we gave you a plain census no one can give you no better....We are also loosing [sic] hope in you because you delay this matter." Their letter ended on a submissive note:

> Of course we know only well that Right Reverend Bishop
> has to meet with the wishes of some priests here but we can

not help to ask of you again and again for a parish....
I did not mean to say that we are loosing [sic] confidence
exactly. We also have the full confidence that the Right Reverend Bishop will consider our request which is already four
months old.

Sometime during the period of correspondence with the bishop,
Father Kossalko had finally learned of SS. Cyril and Methodius Society
and of their acknowledged intent to form a second parish. In June,
1907, the irate pastor addressed his first letter to Bishop Tierney on this
subject: "There are in my Congregation, as there are everywhere in
our parishes of immigrants — some troublesome and turbulent men,
who without any visible, or reasonable cause, are discontent with the
incumbent priest, and avail themselves of every opportunity to mortify,
to torment, and to worry out their priest, and to foment the discord
among the parishioners".

These troublemakers, Kossalko continued, seized "every occasion to
harass, and to humiliate" their pastor. But what bothered Kossalko even
more than their attitude toward him was the rumor that his parishioners were actually seeking permission to establish a new parish in the
neighborhood. If this plan were being seriously considered, Kossalko
declared that he was against it, he warned..."It is better to have ONE
flourishing parish, than two BEGGAR parishes...". Clearly angry,
Kossalko asked the bishop this pointed question: "Have those people
the permission of the Ordinary to establish a new Slovak parish, and
to build a new Church?".

Perhaps because their plan had come to Kossalko's attention, the
spokesmen for the society finally revealed to the bishop their disapproval of their pastor. In a letter detailing their continued attempts to
assist in the process of finding an acceptable priest, the Slovak petitioners admitted for the first time:

> We also cannot stay in this small church and with only one
> old deaf priest. We hear that his assistant is going to leave
> him. You see yourself that no priest will stay with him. If he
> remains himself again he cannot supply our needs as he stays
> on the farm all week and comes in the city on Saturday to
> unite marriages and on Sunday to say mass.

At this point, another aspect of the problems concerning Kossalko's
management of the parish came to light. Several months before the
request for a second parish had been made, sources apprised the bishop
that reservations were being raised in other circles concerning the con-

duct of the pastor of St. John's. For example, in a letter he received from the apostolic delegate in January of 1907, Tierney was questioned about Kossalko's activities in Slovak national affairs. Of particular concern to the apostolic delegate was a 1906 circular letter written to the American bishops by Kossalko in which the Bridgeport pastor criticized the spiritual care given the Slovak community throughout the United States. The delegate also expressed displeasure over Kossalko's announced plan to boycott a Slovak Congress approved by the American hierarchy and soon to be held in Scranton.

Already considered a troublemaker by the apostolic delegate, Kossalko had thus come to Bishop Tierney's attention even before being implicated in the petition for a new Slovak parish in Bridgeport. In fact, the delegate's observations about Kossalko's misconduct had probably been a major factor in the bishop's initial favorable response to the requests of the SS. Cyril and Methodius Society. With the added information concerning Kossalko's mismanagement of St. John's, Bishop Tierney was in a solid position to decide in favor of founding the new parish. Shortly after receiving the letter detailing Kossalko's neglect, the bishop established SS. Cyril and Methodius Parish in east side Bridgeport.

From 1907 on, St. John Nepomucene and SS. Cyril and Methodius Parishes coexisted within blocks of each other. Undoubtedly, the persistence of the SS. Cyril and Methodius Society was a major factor in influencing the bishop to approve this unique situation. The discord that had surfaced, moreover, had not so much indicated that the spiritual needs of the Slovaks had been ignored by diocesan officials and it pointed to Slovak dissatisfaction over their own priest and his failure to respond to their more pressing, daily concerns.

During the second decade of the twentieth century, Bridgeport's two Slovak parishes made great strides under the direction of competent pastors. By 1911, the Reverend Andrew Komara, the first ethnic Slovak graduate of St. Thomas Seminary, was named pastor of St. John's. Under him, the parent church finally began to gain the prominence and prestige that had eluded it. In similar fashion, SS. Cyril and Methodius progressed under the leadership of an equally energetic and gifted administrator, the Reverend Matthew Jankola. Only nine years after he became pastor, however, Father Jankola succumbed of a stroke; in his short years as pastor he had done much to bring the newer parish citywide attention for the outstanding contributions of its membership.

The unexpected illness and death of Father Jankola would once again accent the factionalism that could easily develop in the Slovak community. As Father Jankola lay dying, unrest became so evident in the parish that Bishop Nilan moved with uncharacteristic haste to assign a new pastor, the Reverend Gaspar Panik, who had been for a relatively short time pastor of Sacred Heart (Slovak) Parish in Torrington. Acknowledging that he realized the impact of the transfer upon the Torrington parish, the bishop said he had to take the risk of upsetting Torrington's Slovaks because of the greater need in Bridgeport.

This extraordinary means of calming a troubled community failed to prevent a display of ill-will in Bridgeport only two weeks after Father Panik's arrival. On May 25, 1916, a front-page story, headlined "Women Rioters with Babes Spent Night in Jail After Attack on Church Rectory", appeared in *The Bridgeport Telegram*. The news story explained that, since Father Panik's arrival, dissension within the parish increased to the degree that delegations were sent to the bishop asking for the new pastor's removal. When no replacement was made, the situation became more tense. Finally, on May 24, a group of women — at least seventy-five — seized the initiative. Supported by about five hundred parishioners, they met at 8:30 a.m. and "armed with eggs, some stale, others fresh, and with bricks and stones", they rang the front doorbell of the rectory. At the time, Panik had several house guests, including his brother (just married), a sister, and members of the wedding party. Sensing serious trouble, Panik slammed the door, refusing them entry. But they broke in, proceeding to run through the house, hurling missiles and breaking furniture and appointments. Anxious for the safety of his guests and himself, Panik retreated to the attic and set up barricades. Police, summoned by the frightened priest before he retreated, responded by arresting the women leading the attack. Four were charged with injury to property, nine with breach of the peace; all thirteen refused to accept bail. In a somewhat elated mood, the women — most of them in their twenties and married — spent the night in jail "singing, laughing, telling humorous stories...nursing babies", and partaking of the food brought in by families and friends. Throughout it all, the newspaper reported, a "sort of carnival spirit" prevailed.

During the ensuing trial, the women remained uncooperative. Pleading not guilty, they claimed they had been provoked to act by misconduct on the part of the new pastor. This charge seemed to stem from the fact that Panik's relatives and members of his brother's wedding party had lodged overnight at the rectory following the wedding ceremony. Four of the guests had been women: not only Panik's sister and niece but also the bride and a non-relative, who was, presumably, the maid of honor. This might have been viewed an unbecoming and compromising situation for a youthful priest; *The Bridgeport Telegram's* reference to it in the context of the riot suggests that some notice, at least, was given the overnight visit.

The women also alleged that they were upset because changes had been made by the new pastor "with regard to the distribution and care of the collection money". They explained that whereas during the previous administration, parish money was held by certain church members, it was now under the direct control of the pastor. Thus, the women felt impelled to remove their pastor — even bodily — from the parish.

Other more pertinent reasons for the women's overreaction were hinted at in Father Panik's assessment of the problem also reported in *The Bridgeport Telegram*. "The grievances are imaginary ones", he maintained in his public statement. Dismissing the allegations against him, he suggested instead that the women had been "incited by male members of their families" to the point of violence. Had he not himself heard one of the women remark, "Let's drive him out. If he don't go we will kill him"? Father Panik admitted to reporters he was warned by some of his former Torrington parishioners, who had been alerted to the parish troubles that preceded his assignment to SS. Cyril and Methodius, not to accept the appointment. According to Panik,

> One of the chief causes of this morning's outbreak...is my sincere regard for Father Kamora [sic], pastor of St. John's in this city. The deceased priest of Saints Cyril and Methodius was not on friendly terms with Father Kamora and it is my belief that the congregation became imbued with the attitude of their pastor towards him.

Father Kamora, hospitalized with pneumonia at the time of the incident, was also asked to comment. They are "fanatical agitators", he told reporters, people craving "excitement and novelties...They do not represent the majority of Slovak Roman Catholics...Slavonian Catholics...are known for their respect for the lawfully constituted ecclesiastic [sic] authorities...".

Perhaps *The Torrington Register's* (May 26, 1916) report of the Bridgeport disturbance was as close to the mark as any. The subheadline over its story read: "Not Satisfactory to One Faction". The report suggested that even before Panik's appointment there was bitter rivalry among the groups within the parish. Despite the bishop's swift action of appointing a new pastor after Jankola's death, one faction remained discontented, complaining about the new pastor's method of selecting "persons who were to perform specified duties about the church". Believing that they might have a justifiable reason for demanding a hearing from either civil or religious authority if they could only present their charges against the pastor, a few women parishioners decided to take this matter into their own hands. Caught up in the excitement of the moment — and perhaps believing that the young priest was, at the very least, indiscreet — they vented their resentment to the fullest.

When the women were brought to trial on the charges of injury to property and breach of peace, they were found guilty, fined, and severely reprimanded by the judge, who warned them not to repeat such riotous behavior. With the sentencing of the women, this dramatic episode of discord came to an abrupt end. Contrary to the contention that it was insensitivity of Church officials that had precipitated the conflict, the difficulty of explaining the outbreak, as well as subsequent discord in the parish, suggests that it emerged within a community that was seriously fragmented. If the conflict had been a good example of "lay initiative" againt the alleged unyielding and oppressive Church authority, one must ask why the charges were not pursued during the calm aftermath of the episode, and why the pastor was not transferred. Instead, all traces of accusation and insinuation vanished, even from the folklore of the parish. After his vindication by the bishop and by civil authorities, Father Panik remained at SS. Cyril and Methodius, where he quickly acquired a reputation as one of the most capable Catholic pastors in the city's history. Such a turnabout among the people would hardly have been possible if the women had a just complaint. Undoubtedly, the internecine rivalry that had divided other Slavic minorities had brought the SS. Cyril and Methodius Parish in Bridgeport to humiliating public attention.

When, after almost twenty years of uninterrupted and highly acclaimed service to the parish and to the community at large, Panik died, the Bridgeport community in general mourned his passing. To *The Bridgeport Times Star* (Jan. 20, 1933) Father Panik had been a model for the Slovak people, and an outstanding example of resourcefulness and loyalty that all Bridgeport citizens might emulate. Other newspapers commended the Slovak priest for his continued ability to interpret American life and ideals for his people, his organizational talents, and his abilities as a public speaker. So thoroughly had he been accepted by both parishioners and the city, that it came as no surprise that his cousin, the Reverend Stephen Panik, was chosen to succeed him. To this day, the contributions of both Paniks are still remembered; health and welfare urban projects bear their names.

Hungarian Catholics represented another ethnic minority that addressed itself to the problem of separate identity within the Roman Catholic Church of the Diocese of Hartford. Although the Hungarians had gained numerical superiority over the Slovaks in other dioceses, they remained consistently second to the Slovaks in their early development as a Catholic community in the diocese. For example, in Bridgeport — the one enclave in Connecticut where large numbers of

Hungarians had settled early and where they would eventually develop their largest Catholic community in northeastern United States — they did not establish a national parish until 1897. Furthermore, it would be almost another decade before the Hungarians would organize a second parish, this one encompassing the Norwalk-South Norwalk area. Despite the fact that there were several small Hungarian communities in various other industrial cities and towns, no other Hungarian national parishes were established in the diocese during the years 1890-1920. Thus, in New Haven, Wallingford, and Torrington, where Hungarian communities were sufficiently large to support independent parishes (one apparent exception: a mission was begun in New Haven during Bishop Nilan's administration), Hungarians chose to continue worshipping in local Irish parishes, and to accept the leadership of the Irish priests trained in European seminaries in order to work among them. For this reason, Hungarian adaptation to Catholic parish life seemed to reflect more the attitude that had made for amicable relations between the Italian immigrants and the Irish Church than it did the pattern set by the Slavic people of the diocese. There is, moreover, no evidence to suggest that either the Hungarians or the diocesan officials who assigned Hungarian speaking priests viewed this accommodation as conferring second class status on the diocese's Hungarian minority. Although some Hungarians continued to anticipate the time that they would form their own national parishes, most of the Hungarian minority seemed satisfied with the diocesan commitment to their spiritual needs.

There were some obvious reasons as to why the Hungarians adapted differently from other ethnic groups to both the Connecticut environment and the Diocese of Hartford. Late arrivals in the state, they found it difficult to first establish themselves. In search of work as molders' apprentices or carpenters, they were often turned down for employment and discouraged from settling permanently. Had not Bridgeport's booming steel and textile mills, metal works shops, and foundries continued to demand immigrant labor, it is very possible that the Hungarians in the state would soon have moved to Cleveland or other midwestern cities, as the majority of their relatives did. For those who remained in Bridgeport, a number of obstacles barred social acceptance. Disadvantaged by their small numbers, Hungarian Catholics worshipped for a while at St. Mary's, where a Hungarian speaking priest assisted immigrants. Once they had migrated to the city's west end, however, they felt compelled to work toward organization of their own parish. Their first efforts to locate a Hungarian Roman Catholic pastor miscarried as their choice, the Reverend Joseph Formanek, chose to work instead among the city's more established Slovaks. Only with the establishment in 1897 of St. Stephen's Hungarian Catholic Church in Bridgeport's west end did the Hungarian Catholics achieve religious solidarity as a group.

Other factors interfered with the progress of the Hungarians, further distinguishing them from earlier immigrants to Connecticut. The troubled beginnings of their first two parishes in Bridgeport and South Norwalk forced some to rethink their need to establish separate parishes among the smaller communities of the state. Moreover, the fact that, as an ethnic group, only a little more than half were members of the Roman Catholic or Eastern Rite churches prevented them from developing an assertiveness that might have prompted a greater sense of unity. Nevertheless, in a manner that at times appeared very similar to the pattern of other immigrants, they found their way of adapting to their new environment and of relating to the Diocese of Hartford.

Not surprisingly, factionalism was an integral feature in this accommodation. The same kind of discord that fragmented other European immigrant communities plagued the Hungarians from their beginnings in the diocese. Thus, even though St. Stephen's had prospered during the administration of its first pastor, the Reverend George Csaba (1897-1906), it soon fell heir to dissension after his death. Despite all of Csaba's effort to build an impressive parish (under his direction a church, rectory, convent, and school had been completed), St. Stephen's became so troubled after 1906 that its chances for survival almost seemed in doubt. Anxiety to this effect was expressed by Bishop Nilan, who feared that the Hungarian parish was undergoing such a difficult period that he fully believed more than half of its parishioners could be lost to the Church.

Since the situation could hardly have been brought about because of neglect on the part of the bishop (almost immediately after Csaba's death Bishop Nilan had appointed another Hungarian, the Reverend John Madar, to succeed him), one had to conclude that the problems lay within the confines of the parish community. There is sufficient evidence to support this conclusion; Father Madar's return to Europe "out of homesickness" being but one sign of the alienation that divided pastor from his congregation. Madar's successor, the Reverend Edmund Neurihrer, seemed no more content as pastor of St. Stephen's. Despite his being personally recommended for the position by some members of the parish, Neurihrer was unable to manage the affairs of St. Stephen's either more efficiently or more sympathetically than his predecessor. In fact, the Hungarians were so dissatisfied with his method of handling parish matters that they sent several complaints to the bishop.

According to one petition asking for Neurihrer's removal, the parishioners maintained that their pastor was not only guilty of dispensing "harsh treatment", of insulting remarks, and of unorthodox financial policies but, he was, they said, determined to belittle and betray them by emphasizing his German rather than his Hungarian heritage. By 1913, the Bridgeport Hungarian community could no longer tolerate their mistreatment under a pastor they had once enthusiastically espoused. Formally refusing to accept the annual financial report, the parish trustees served notice to the bishop that they would no longer support Neurihrer. When Nilan realized that he could not conciliate all elements, he sent Neurihrer the following advice: "I am convinced that in the interests of peace and progress a change of management is imperative and that the parish spirit of the Hungarians of Bridgeport may thrive under another spiritual guide...I request you, therefore, to seek another field of labor".

A month after Neurihrer severance from St. Stephen's, Bishop Nilan took a more positive step toward improving the climate of the parish. Anticipating that his action would not disrupt St. Ladislaus Parish in South Norwalk, he transferred the Reverend Stephen Chernitzky from that parish to St. Stephen's. With far greater success than ordinarily accompanied such drastic moves, Father Chernitzky won the loyalty of the troubled community. As pastor of St. Stephen's from 1914 until his death in 1948, Chernitzky helped the parish recover its former prestige, bringing it national prominence in Hungarian circles as the most progressive Hungarian parish in the northeastern United States. So skillful a leader was Chernitzky, that his contributions to St. Stephen's in Bridgeport did not adversely prejudice the growth of the other Hungarian parish in South Norwalk. From 1914 on, both parishes developed as vital centers of Hungarian Catholic activity within the Diocese of Hartford; from them other key Hungarian Catholic communities in the diocese derived both direction and inspiration.

The continued vitality of St. Ladislaus is all the more impressive when one considers that, even from its origins, it had encountered great difficulties. In fact, its establishment was due to demonstrations by the "Huns" (as the Reverend William Maher, pastor of St. Mary's, the Irish church in Norwalk, had described them). Suspecting that the Hungarians of his parish were being strongly influenced by an immigrant priest, Father Francis Gross, who wanted to be their pastor and whose pastoral competence he questioned, Maher first tried to reason with them about the need to use appropriate channels to obtain their goals. Frustrated by their persistence, and fearful of violence, he finally recommended to Bishop Tierney "that the church of the Hungarian Catholics of South Norwalk be given to [their own priest] Father Gross.

The bishop commissioned him to organize St. Ladislaus Hungarian Catholic Church in 1907. Surprised by the positive diocesan response, Gross wrote to the bishop, "...Maher is sincerely kind to myself and my congregation, and I want [to] be to him all time a good friend and a stady [sic] help".

It was longer, however, before Maher's original judgment about Gross proved true. When troubles mounted over the question of the choice of trustees for St. Ladislaus, new decisions about Gross's competence had to be made. It was at this point that Father Chernitzky first entered the Connecticut scene. Anxious to become established in the East after work as both a missionary in West Virginia and a newspaper editor in Ohio, Chernitzky saw in the challenge of the Norwalk community an opportunity to prove his pastoral ability. Within five years, the talented young priest managed to so improve the climate of St. Ladislaus and so shape its character that even his later transfer to St. Stephen's in 1914 would not disturb the South Norwalk parish. Under Chernitzky's successor, the Reverend John Szobo, who was pastor for three years, and for the next twelve years under the guidance of the Budapest-trained priest, the Reverend Joseph Degnan, St. Ladislaus progressed without further incidents of unrest.

After Chernitzky's assignment as pastor of St. Stephen's Parish in 1914, the cohesiveness and solidarity of the Hungarian Catholic community within the Diocese of Hartford became a reality. It also seems that the "satellite" aspect of other Hungarian communities in New Haven, Torrington, and Wallingford dates from this period: as long as Chernitzky kept up a peripatetic pattern, visiting all of these communities or somehow overseeing their efforts, the Hungarians remained satisfied with existing conditions, assured that their religious traditions within the Diocese of Hartford were being respected. It is even possible that it was because of Chernitzky's approval of Father Degnan as pastor of South Norwalk's St. Ladislaus Parish that the Hungarian people were able to accept Irish priests as their pastors. For whatever reason, the acceptance of Degnan and other non-Hungarians as pastors, as well as the gradual assimilation of Hungarians into other mixed-ethnic parishes, typified the unusual pattern developed by Connecticut's Hungarians while Chernitzky remained their Catholic leader at St. Stephen's. Only when native born Hungarians, such as the Reverends James Lengen, Vincent Bodnar, and Zoltan Kish, began serving in the Hungarian parishes by the 1930s would the next phase of Hungarian leadership within the Diocese of Hartford begin.

One final observation could be made regarding the character of the Hungarian Catholic commitment to the Diocese of Hartford. To a greater extent than any other immigrant group, the Hungarian people had been swayed from allegiance to Roman Catholicism by the prose-lytizing efforts of Protestant Reformational Churches. The prospect of losses to Hungarian Reformed Churches may have served to keep Hungarian Roman Catholic leaders alert to the need to exhibit loyalty to the Catholic Church. In some way, such a defensive reaction on the part of Hungarian Catholics may have sealed the pattern of coopera-tion between the Hungarian Catholic community and the Catholic Di-ocese of Hartford (Souders, 1922).

The Lithuanians also had identity problems. Perhaps certain social ties with other immigrants in Meriden and New Britain first led Lith-uanians to look for jobs in Connecticut's factory cities or towns, and to settle in the state. By the mid-1890s sufficiently large numbers of Cath-olic Lithuanians were living and working in the brass and hardware factory communities of Waterbury, Union City, and New Britain (over a hundred families) as to warrant diocesan concern for their spiritual welfare. By 1920, when the Lithuanian immigrants would number eleven thousand, this concern had resulted in the establishment of six Lithuanian national parishes.

The first priest to take a serious interest in the early Lithuanian immigrants of Connecticut was the Reverend Joseph Zebris, an immi-grant whose first work in the United States was as a missionary to Lithuanians in Pennsylvania and New Jersey. By 1893, Zebris was ready to lead the Waterbury Lithuanians in petitioning for the establishment of a parish. His request apparently received the attention of diocesan officials, but was tabled after the death of Bishop McMahon. With the consecration of Bishop Tierney the following year, Zebris was author-ized to work toward the establishment of the first Lithuanian parish in New England — St. Joseph, Waterbury.

Regardless of some cultural ties to other eastern European immi-grants (especially Poles), Connecticut's Lithuanians made no attempt to create a bond of religious fellowship with other immigrant groups. Nor did diocesan officials attempt to impose ethnic coexistence within the same national parish (as was sometimes the case in other dioceses). In a manner similar to the one that gained the Slovacs of Connecticut their distinctiveness as an ethnic qroup, Catholic Lithuanians were able to create a separate identity for themselves in the industrial areas where they first came in search of jobs. The Lithuanians, like the Slovacs, were guided toward this goal by inspired leaders. Yet, while the Slovacs could rely upon a number of outstanding priests, such as Father Jan-kola, Komara, and the Paniks, and could, moreover, count on the sup-port of some exceptional laymen, the Lithuanians seemed to rally around one key pastor, the Reverend Joseph Zebris, in their attempt to acquire religious and ethnic solidarity. Had it not been that Zebris was influenced by political and economic ideas that were sharply divergent from the capitalistic American consensus, he might have proved to have been as successful a leader among the Lithuanians as were the Slovak clergy.

More like Chernitzky in his desire to maintain the solidarity of his people, Zebris perceived himself as an organizer, innovator, and religious civic leader. Not only would he be instrumental in the formation of every Lithuanian parish in the state, he would also use his creative talents in a number of enterprising projects. Unlike Chernitzky, though, Zebris wanted to introduce new ways of enhancing the life of his parishioners and he experimented with ideas that went far beyond the scope of religious leadership. What ultimately thwarted his designs was an inability to marshal others into his ranks. Despite a certain cohesiveness that he inspired in the Lithuanian community, Zebris eventually became a sign of contradiction among his people. Especially during his early years of directing the Lithuanian community in Connecticut, dramatic discord surfaced.

From the first years of Zebris' career as pastor of St. Joseph's, Waterbury, a web of dissension and resistance typical of early Lithuanian parishes was evident. In existence since March of 1894 — it was the first national parish approved by Bishop Tierney — St. Joseph's seemed, initially, to make rapid progress. Yet, by 1898, Zebris had become the object of so much controversy that the bishop was forced to transfer him. Although his parishioners at St. Joseph's had cooperated with Zebris in completing the parish church, a spirit of resistance soon developed regarding other proposed projects. It was one thing, the parishioners apparently argued, to raise money for the building of a church, quite another to support business schemes. Thus, their pastor's launching of a cooperative grocery, bakery, and farm, and his publication of a foreign-language newspaper were perceived as a kind of secular involvement that many of the untutored members of the parish could neither understand nor support.

The cooperatives that Zebris wanted his parishioners to develop involved a greater commitment than immigrant mutual and fraternal aid societies usually required. Thus, soon after the opening of the third venture, the cooperative bakery, in 1896, Father Zebris' non-priestly pursuits became a major source of divisiveness among his parishioners. Some were embarassed about their pastor's ideas; others were suspicious of his motivations, suspecting that perhaps their pastor was secretly harboring a personal desire for wealth. Heeding the warning of critics who published articles against Zebris in Lithuanian newspapers, a discontented minority gathered against him.

When he proposed that the five Lithuanian saloons of Waterbury also be combined into a cooperative to be managed by a church-affiliated society — one whose aim would be to "control the evil consequences of drink", he was perceived as overstepping his bounds. After this further intrusion in their private lives, the number of his supporters dwindled drastically. As far away as Brooklyn, New York, the editor of *Vienybe Lietuvninku* wrote of Waterbury's disenchantment with Father Zebris. So, too, did Zebris himself write of parish troubles, albeit from a different perspective. According to Zebris, a petition demanding his removal as pastor was drawn up at one particularly stormy meeting in September of 1897. Because he "spent too much of his time" in his business ventures, he should not longer be in charge. If he were not removed, the protest went on to warn, "noble men would withdraw from the bishop". Signed by twenty six parishioners, the protest was promptly sent to Bishop Tierney.

The bishop's reply to the protesters was by no means as prompt. For several months, the impasse with the parish continued. Angered by the bishop's silence, the parish committee resorted to what Zebris termed as "revengeful acts" and "threats of physical violence". In the fall of 1897, the trustees of the parish took more direct action, voting to withhold their pastor's salary. Undaunted, Father Zebris responded by dismissing the entire group and calling forth a new election of officers. With accusations of misrule and usurpation of power, the parish committee countered by bring Zebris to civil trial. When the civil court found in favor of Zebris, the parish insurgents returned to Bishop Tierney, repeating their litany of frustrations and grievances. Finally convinced that the parish conflict was irreconcilable, Bishop Tierney met with Zebris in the spring of 1898. On June 1, news of the pastor's transfer to New Britain and an interview of Zebris appeared in the *Waterbury Republican*. According to the newspaper, Zebris had accepted the bishop's decision graciously. Zebris was quoted as saying, "I consider my removal to New Britain a promotion and I am well pleased with the change...." On that abrupt note, the pastoral ties between St. Joseph Parish, Waterbury, and its first pastor ended.

Even though Zebris' successor, the Reverend Peter Saurusaitis, worked earnestly to rebuild the parish along more traditional patterns, his efforts were met with the same kind of opposition that Zebris had experienced. From the time of his appointment, both the plans and the personal life of the new pastor were severely criticized. His attempts to conduct religious missions, to start an evening school — in effect, his general management of the parish — were viewed with suspicion. Even questions concerning the propriety of his leaving his religious community (he had been a Redemptorist) in order to become pastor of St.

Joseph became topics of complaint against him. The spirit of factionalism that divided the parish during Zebris' time continued to characterize its development.

In 1902, some unsuspecting members of the congregation made what
proved to be a particularly disastrous mistake. Rallying around an exceptionally talented but unauthorized priest with a record of successful
impersonations in several seminaries and dioceses, they established an
independent parish and proceeded to build All Saints Independent
Lithuanian Catholic Church. For several years, these Lithuanians, apparently believing that they had received the bishop's approval for their
independent venture, remained separated from St. Joseph. Only after
Bishop Tierney made a public disclosure of their pastor's false claims
did those who believed that the new church was in union with Rome
concede their errors and submit to the authority of Saurusaitis and the
bishop of Hartford. After that, St. Joseph Parish was once again united.
After Saurusaitis' resignation in 1919, the parish would, for the first
time, be guided by a Lithuanian from Waterbury who was educated in
American seminaries. Under the Reverend Joseph Valantiejus, the internal discord that had so plagued the parish for many years would
finally be checked.

A review of parishes subsequently established in the Diocese of Hartford to serve the Lithuanian minority indicates that internal discord,
exacerbated by uncompromising attitudes between pastor and parishioners, was an aspect of Lithuanian parishes elsewhere in the diocese.
Thus, despite the diocese's willingness to support the effort of Lithuanian priests, dissension and discord all too often disturbed the early
period of the establishment of Connecticut's Lithuanian parishes.

The pattern of dissension during the early history of St. Andrew's,
New Britain, is an illustration of this phenomenon. Even before Zebris'
official appointment to head this church, the parishioners of St. Andrew's initiated correspondence with a priest in Lithuania for the purpose of locating a pastor, and had received a revealing reply. The response, written by one candidate for the pastorate who was residing in
Lithuania, indicates how widespread was the belief that affairs among
Lithuanians seemed tense. "Is it true", the candidate asked the New
Britain community,

> as has been rumored, that in response to what the priest says
> in the pulpit, people persecute him, fire bullets through his
> windows, submit untruthful remarks to newspapers, sever
> parishes in two? It is said that there are dishonest shrews
> who defame the priest's honor so that people flee from the
> priest and hasten with complaints to the bishops, and that

some bishops persecute those who give meager donations to
the bishop.

Zebris' appointment to St. Andrew's obviated the need to respond to
this Lithuanian priest's rather probing questions.

Whether Zebris was aware of the kinds of troubles alluded to by the
Lithuanian priest, there is little to indicate in his conduct as pastor
there that either these sobering questions or his previous experience in
Waterbury in any way altered his dealings with the Lithuanians of St.
Andrew's, New Britain. Once assigned to St. Andrew's, Zebris seemed
as determined and singleminded about the pursuit of ways to advance
that parish as he had been in Waterbury. At the same time he became
interested in a smaller group of Lithuanians in the Hartford area; these,
too, he helped toward the development of a parish. For both the New
Britain and Hartford communities he spent long hours of spiritual ministry and parish building, but his penchant for plain talking and autocratic management of financial matters still caused much hard feelings.
More often than not Zebris was in trouble, defending his practices either to his trustees or to his bishop.

Trouble between Zebris and the parishioners at St. Andrew's were a
part of his daily life in New Britain and in Hartford; misunderstand-
ings would divide him from his parishioners constantly. Indeed, until
the very end of his life, Father Zebris remained a source of controversy
among his people and within his church. Had it not been for the continued backing of Bishops Tierney and Nilan, the pioneer Lithuanian
pastor may have found himself a pastor without a parish in the Diocese
of Hartford.

But the question as to Zebris' future in Connecticut never required
resolution. On the evening of February 8, 1915, twenty years after he
had taken up his work in New Britain, a shocking event occurred in
the city. Apparently in pursuit of vast sums of money rumored to be
hidden there, two criminals forced their way into St. Andrew's rectory
and brutally murdered both Father Zebris and the parishes' housekeeper. "An unheard of report has shaken all Lithuanian colonies of America — Father Joseph Zebris is dead!...." the eulogist began his last tribute the day of the funeral. So, too, had Zebris' death shocked the entire
state, as well as every member of the Roman Catholic Church in the
Diocese of Hartford. Any lingering spirit of dissatisfaction with their
pastor was forgotten by his parishioners as they wept openly at the
elaborate and crowded funeral ceremonies. "One of the most popular
clergymen in town", as a local newspaper put it, had been killed; the
first to agree with that description of Father Zebris were the bereaved
Lithuanian Catholics in New Britain.

Some questions concerning other possible explanations for the crime occurred at the time of the murders and linger to the present. Had the murder of Father Zebris, for example, been somewhat of an anticlimax, almost a culmination to the recurring pattern of internal conflict that had kept the parish from achieving the kind of unity achieved by other ethnic communities: Had not Zebris consistently been so imprudent — his very last sermon centered around a denunciation of Lithuanian anarchists and "Black-hands" — that he had brought himself to this sorry end? What of the fact that there had been so many recent threats upon his life that one of his priest-friends had advised him to arm himself, or at least to install a telephone as a precaution against possible violence? Even while the funeral was being offered before thousands of mourners, such questions preoccupied the conversations of Lithuanians and non-Lithuanians alike — in New Britain and throughout Connecticut, indeed in every part of the nation where Lithuanian Catholic communities existed.

A month after the murder, two Lithuanian immigrants, Bernard Montvid and Peter Krakas, were approached by police in Wilmington, Delaware, as they attempted to pawn some watches and other jewelry. In their attempt to escape, the suspects killed one policeman and seriously wounded three others. The items that the two were trying to sell linked them circumstantially with the murders of Zebris and the housekeeper. In the spring and summer of 1915 the two men stood trial. Krakas was found guilty of killing the policeman and was hanged. Montvid was put on trial in Hartford for the murders of Zebris and the housekeeper. Found guilty of those crimes (still only on circumstantial evidence), as well as implicated in the killing of the policeman, Montvid was also executed.

During the trial, one of the questions that had lingered from the time of the murders was explored. Had Zebris been killed because of his bitter attacks against those whom he referred to as "radical anarchists"? Were his well-known arguments with free-thinkers, socialists, or those whose very lifecycles set them at odds with the strict Lithuanian pastor at the source of the ugly incident? From the evidence at the trial it was concluded that Zebris' murder was not a deliberate act of revenge or hatred. Instead, there was ample indication that the primary motive had been robbery. Disappointed in their expectations that Father Zebris was a wealthy man the suspects attacked their reluctant and recalcitrant captive. Ironically, though, parish discontent over Zebris did play a part in the crime. For, if the rumor that Father Zebris had appropriated and was hoarding the wealth of Lithuanian Catholics had not been heard by Montvid and Krakas in a New Britain saloon the night before the murders, they might not have chosen a rectory as their prime target for robbery. The unbroken pattern of internal discord that had plagued the parish throughout its first twenty years had, in its own strange way, finally visited the parish with this unexpected tragedy.

The effect of Zebris' tragic death upon the Lithuanian communities within the Diocese of Hartford cannot be precisely determined. Undoubtedly, it had its chastening effect. From the time of the murder, the spirit of contention and fault-finding that had for so long absorbed the conversations and embittered so many Lithuanians diminished rapidly. Three years after his death, the Lithuanian Priests' League of America finally granted Zebris the public tribute that it had not been able to render while he lived. In a reprint from the eulogy that had been first preached at the time of his burial, the league publication added its own assessment of Zebris' career. Praising the New Britain pastor, the publication commented that Zebris had "distinguished himself with great generosity for the people and labored zealously for their spiritual benefit". Not without reason, it summarized, "was he called 'Father of the New England Lithuanians'".

Under other dedicated Lithuanian priests, such as the Reverend Edward Grikis who replaced Zebris in New Britain and the Reverend John Ambot who became pastor of Holy Trinity, Hartford, in 1912, as well as under the Reverend Matthew Pankus in Bridgeport, Vincent Karkauskas in New Haven, and Vincent Bukaveckas in Ansonia, the Lithuanian national churches in the Diocese of Hartford finally developed some sense of unity and belonging. The bickering that had for so long sharply divided Lithuanian parishes seemed finally to have been displaced by the impact of the unforeseen events of 1915.

Just as serious episodes of discord rent the many French Canadian and Polish parishes in the Diocese of Hartford during the early periods of their establishment, so dissension also unsettled parishes founded for the less numerous minorities, such as the Slovaks, the Hungarians, and the Lithuanians. Despite the efforts of the bishops of Hartford to develop policies to accommodate to the needs of each ethnic minority seeking special status in the diocese, a pattern of crises often developed. Although certain common characteristics indicated that the problems faced by immigrants, regardless of nationality and cultural background, were to a large extent identical, other aspects of the incidents also suggested that ethnic differences sometimes made for a variety of unexpected responses. All too often, moreover, discord occurred where priests were in charge of parishes; thus, the discord appeared in communities that were enjoying the very privileges of strong religious leadership that the minority demanded. Seldom were the difficulties that developed in the Diocese of Hartford the immediate outgrowth of either neglect or unsympathetic treatment on the part of either bishops or clergy of the diocese even when less numerous minorities were involved. For the most part, the problems of these ethnic groups were also internal, created by bickering over who should rule or over which preferences should prevail, with factions that purported to champion religious aims battling with forces equally vociferous in protesting what they alleged to be their rights as Roman Catholics.

Perhaps because of the temptation to combine forces, a few disputes were even inter ethnic. Thus, the Polish pastor of St. Michael's, Bridgeport, contended with the Lithuanian pastor at St. George's because the Lithuanian pastor was permitting Polish speaking Lithuanians to remain as members of his parish; Polish parishioners in Waterbury demanded better treatment from the diocese because they no longer accept their alleged second class status at St. Cecilia's German national parish; and French Canadians became restless under either Irish or French pastors in eastern Connecticut's parishes unless those priests were fully conversant with French Canadian culture and customs.

In the long run, whatever the sources of the specific complaints, all were somehow influenced by immigrant insecurities concerning their place in social and economic affairs or over their appropriate status among peers and leaders. Not until jealousy or rivalry was resolved and leadership agreed upon did lasting patterns of peace occur within the national parish setting.

In the light of such data it seems difficult to concur with those who argue that patent injustices perpetuated by the Irish majority were the root causes of ethnic discord within the Roman Catholic Church with respect to the Diocese of Hartford. Rather, allegations of blame leveled against authority by minority groups must be seen in their totality, reflective as much of the specific minority's sense of inferiority and need for positive reinforcement as of the majority's desire to impose its authority over groups deemed subordinate. This is not to suggest that the bishop, clergy, or other more established Catholics of the Diocese of Hartford cannot be faulted for particular decisions prejudicial to immigrants. Nor is it to ignore the evidence of accord that at times prevents problems from developing or lessened the repercussions of some unpopular decisions. It is simply to suggest that the all too facile assignment of blame on the officials of the diocese with respect to inequities that befall ethnic minorities overlooks the complexity of the internal dynamics that may indeed have been the greatest source of parochial discord.

A review of ethnic conflict among the new immigrants of the Diocese of Hartford begins to yield a different kind of picture than the one ordinarily offered by ethnic historians and sociologists, one in which rivalries among fellow immigrants, or between immigrant leaders and their communities constantly seethed beneath the surface, where jealousy often prevented capable clergy from the proper discharge of their duties; where fault-finding and ridicule were key instruments of conflicting parties. If one can argue that the many incidents of ethnic conflict were not primarily due to the failures of officials of the Diocese of Hartford during the period 1890-1920 but were instead the result of this kind of factionalism, one final question emerges. Why have these conflicts often been perceived as having been the direct result of discriminatory policies or poor treatment initiated by the Church? Perhaps the failure of the Church historians to research the episodes of conflict explains this assumption. Without the careful investigations of historians as well as the insights of psychologists and sociologists into the factors promoting such patterns of behavior, the unanalyzed folklore of ethnic minorities will continue to be taken as the authentic record of the immigrant past.

Epilogue

Because of multi-ethnic developments, the Catholic Church of Connecticut, and of the United States as well, has been viewed as "an immigrant institution", its present numbers and organization being more the result of the waves of turn-of-the-century immigration than of indigenous growth. This designation has not been the intention of its American founders, nor can it be considered accurate if one recalls that the very establishment of the Church had occurred during the formative years of the American republic. From the start, a number of factors seemed to have militated against the Catholic Church's right to consider itself a native institution. Thus, despite early efforts to establish a Church that could be perceived as akin to other Christian Churches, the Roman Catholic Church in the United States could not shake off the "foreign" label that had clung to it since colonial times, nor could it prevent multi-ethnic layers from surrounding its American core. To further complicate matters, this image became even more firmly reinforced through immigration. Even today, the American Catholic Church may be seen as an institution singled out by a significant number of immigrants, whether they derive from Europe, Asia, the West Indies, Central America, or South America.

Given this phenomenon of constant growth from the addition of new immigrants, it would seem that a concern that should have been uppermost in the minds of the leaders of the American Catholic Church throughout its history would involve the proper accommodation of new members. However, both contemporaries and historians have observed that, despite the obvious challenges presented by immigration, the formulation of a constructive policy with respect to the proper provision for and acceptance of new immigrants was by no means a priority concern among American Catholic leaders. Certain reasons can be advanced to account for this seemingly inappropriate lack of joint episcopal response to a pressing reality. For one, so many structural problems confronted the Church in its attempt to organize provinces, archdioceses, and dioceses throughout the United States that Church leaders tended to become preoccupied with the administrative problems associated with establishing churches and health, educational, or other facilities. As a result, Church leaders struggled over more immediate local concerns. Some prelates became quickly involved in the problems of rapid growth within burgeoning industrial areas, while others labored in frontier regions concerned more with the mundane problems peculiar to the missions. Different constituencies required divergent responses.

To further intensify the separateness of diocesan response, moreover, the American Catholic Church developed no national body of bishops to acknowledge various perspectives yet somehow coordinate apostolic efforts. Despite the issuance of national pastoral letters, the American Catholic Church could not and did not speak with one voice. The Americanist controversy of the 1890s, moreover, delivered a severe blow to American Catholic unity. Since the apparent criticism of the American Church on the part of Rome had highlighted the negative consequences that national collaboration by the American hierarchy might entail, most bishops in the early decades of the twentieth century hesitated to become involved in formulating national programs or policies.

Thus, despite the fact that the problems of immigration which the larger and more urbanized dioceses were forced to address also had relevance for the American Catholic Church as a whole, each diocese fashioned its own response and developed its own way of adjusting to the new membership. As a result, some dioceses met the challenge more imaginatively than others, and the policies of the more prestigious dioceses tended to be the ones most identified with the Catholic Church as a whole. Unfortunately, this did not always work to the advantage of the American Catholic Church. Since some of the larger dioceses did not go beyond the offers of minimal assistance, or, worse, sometimes failed to meet minority challenges with sufficient insight and skill, their dubious efforts received wide publicity; while, on the other hand, the efforts of the bishops who seemed much more clearly attuned to both the demands of immigrants as well as to the opportunities new membership might bring went largely unnoticed. To this day, the more negative assessment of Catholic Church policy has lingered.

The task of assessing the policy of the American Catholic Church with respect to the immigrants of the nineteenth and early twentieth century remains a needed one. Only through investigations of each diocese and the collation and evaluation of data will the historian be able to determine more accurately the policies and practices of the American Catholic Church in this regard. On the basis of the information assembled in this study, a step in this direction has been taken.

In the midst of confusing problems and pressing needs that engaged it simultaneously in building a religious organization, establishing a respectable image in a Protestant environment, and making its own impact within the American Catholic structure, the Diocese of Hartford responded imaginatively and consistently to the problems of immigration. Policies and programs initiated during the administrations of Bishop McFarland and McMahon were extended under both Bishops Tierney and Nilan to include all "new immigrant" constituencies. Immigrant priests were not only recruited to serve in leadership capacities throughout the diocese, but they were given such freedom, within the context of orthodox religious leadership, that a number of them rose to positions of prestige among their respective ethnic groups on a national level, even while remaining pastors within the diocese. Furthermore, in a somewhat indirect manner, the laity within national parishes exercised an even stronger voice in decision making that was true of the so-called "Irish" parishes; in fact, greater autonomy generally prevailed among national parishes throughout the diocese. Together pastor and laity built impressive parish structures in every major city in the diocese and even in a number of smaller industrial communities of the state; in several cities, ethnic parishes outnumbered the more traditional and multi-ethnic parishes. New vocations nurtured in national parishes and encouraged in the diocesan seminary, gave further evidence of the good feeling that existed between the new ethnic leadership and the Catholic establishment in Connecticut. On the more official level, the Catholic press repeatedly voiced the sentiments of Connecticut's bishops as it reviewed the accomplishments of the national parishes, their pastors, and other outstanding leaders among its laity. Perhaps a concession to both bishop and Church, the press overlooked consistently the factionalism that disturbed many national parishes in the first years of their establishment; had they accentuated these problems, it is possible that little good would have been accomplished in the effort. Thus, during the most critical period in the building of national parishes, praise over the accomplishments of ethnic minorities within the Church and silence over internal dissension typified the official policy of the diocese.

Despite this and other attempts to achieve a spirit of cooperation within the diocese relative to its ethnic minorities, the good performance of the Diocese of Hartford with respect to the accommodation of immigrants has not been singled out for commendation. This is, in part, due to the fact that little attention has been given to the diocese as a whole, as well as because, previous to this study, no serious research into the policy of the diocese with respect to immigration had been undertaken. But it is also because the episodes of discord, some of which have been alluded to in detail in earlier chapters, often rendered such vivid testimony against the conduct of the Church that, regardless of the objective truth, a convincing case against the officials of the Church could most easily be made. Already oversensitive to the wrongs that the American society as a whole heaped upon them, it was not difficult for dissidents among minority Catholics to generalize this attitude to any specific example of prejudice wherever it presented itself in Catholic circles. As a result, all too often the scapegoat for problems that certain factions within ethnic minorities had brought upon themselves became the Bishop of Hartford.

In one specific regard, the Catholic leadership seemed to have done a disservice to its own position, missing its finest opportunity to prove its sincerity about accommodating to the new ethnic minorities on a solid basis of equality. Although the Church promoted ethnic minority priests by nominating some to the rank of prelates of papal honors with the title of "Monsignor", it seems evident that there were few efforts to incorporate any members of the new ethnic minority constituencies into the more influential positions of authority within the Office of the Chancery or in key administrative positions. Even to this day, the diocese within Connecticut must claim an almost exclusively Irish predominance among its leadership. Whatever the justification, the symbolism that this pattern conveys to Connecticut's multi-ethnic Catholic population stands as the single most damaging argument against an enlightened Connecticut Catholic Church policy with respect to the proper accommodation of Catholics of ethnic-minority status.

Even with respect to this noticeable failure on the part of diocesan officials to place priests of non-Irish background into more prestigious positions, certain qualifications must be pointed out. As late as the 1930s and 1940s, the overwhelming number of priests ordained for the diocese were still of Irish descent and the shortage of priests of non-Irish background in national parishes remained so acute that ethnic minority priests were simply too scarce to be sacrificed for administrative posts. This situation lasted until the 1950s, when greater numbers of second and third generation Italian and Slavic American priests finally became available. Then it appeared that they did receive equal consideration, either being assigned to parishes that were formally the domains of the Irish clergy or chosen to fill some of the key special administrative and educational positions of the diocese. That this was accomplished without complaints or antagonism is in itself an indication that a natural selection process could finally take place. In retrospect, therefore, it seems that it is the very process of establishing national parishes during the years 1890-1920 in keeping with the demands of ethnic minorities that ultimately delayed the process of assimilation of children of immigrants into the power structure of the diocese for still another generation. That being the case, ethnic minorities must accept some responsibility for their slow move upward within the diocesan structure.

Apart from assessing the strengths and weaknesses of the Catholic policy of the Diocese of Hartford, one must, finally, remember the overall effect that the creation of Connecticut's twentieth century Catholic Church with its strong ethnic minority components has had upon Connecticut society and the American Church as a whole. For, in spite of the warnings of conquest, "The Land of Steady Habits" did indeed become the haven of the immigrant, tens of thousands of newcomers choosing to remain as residents of the state. By the 1950s, Connecticut's population of over two million was a mosaic of ethnic groups, and the Catholic Church claimed 37.3 percent of this population among its membership. An institution that had begun to command respect among Connecticut's elite even by the end of the nineteenth century, the Catholic Church could by this date easily rely upon its numbers to guarantee that it would be taken seriously in the twentieth century. Because of this, the Catholic Church affected the state and even national politics and society in a variety of ways. Moreover, it substantially altered the cultural and social patterns of Connecticut life and history as it became a major force in the dismantling of the Yankee stereotype. Constantly enriched by its new population, the Catholic Church in Connecticut remains a source of religious and ethnic diversity and a sign of what good can come from ethnic Catholicism. In the person of Peter Rosazza, a Connecticut native who was ordained auxiliary bishop of Hartford in June of 1978, the challenge has once again found a firm representative. A dedicated servant of Hispanic Catholics of the diocese for years before his appointment, Bishop Rosazza combines his Italian American heritage, his seminary training in Issy, France, and his apostolic concerns for the diocese's most recent immigrants to continue the pattern begun by Connecticut's earlier bishops, ignoring, as Bishop McMahon formerly did, the "old lads" who "shake their heads and seem to think...the world is going rapidly astray" when the needs of other ethnic groups had to be seriously considered. Thus has the tradition of one diocese formed its present leaders and guided their future commitment to unity and diversity by advocating respect for the divergent nationalities and cultures of its people.

Appendix A

Parishes for Ethnic Minorities Established During the
Administration of Bishop Michael Tierney (1894-1908)*

Parishes in Larger Cities   *Parishes in Smaller Towns*

Italian Parishes

Our Lady of Mount Carmel, Meriden, 1894   St. Peter, Torrington, 1907
St. Michael, New Haven, 1895
St. Anthony, Hartford, 1898
Our Lady of Lourdes, Waterbury, 1898
Our Lady of Pompeii, (Holy Rosary), Bridgeport, 1903
St. Anthony, New Haven, 1903

Polish Parishes

St. Casimir (Sacred Heart), New Britain, 1894   Holy Name, Stamford, 1904
St. Michael, Bridgeport, 1899   St. Joseph, Rockville, 1905
St. Stanislaus, New Haven, 1902   St. Michael, Derby, 1905
SS. Cyril and Methodius, Hartford, 1902   St. Casimir, Terryville, 1906
St. Mary, Middletown, 1903
St. Hedwig, Union City, 1906

*Incorporation dates are used as criterion for establishment.

| *Parishes in Larger Cities* | *Parishes in Smaller Cities and Towns* |

Lithuanian Parishes

St. Joseph, Waterbury, 1894
St. Andrew, New Britain, 1895
Holy Trinity, Hartford, 1903 (as mission)
St. George, Bridgeport, 1907

Hungarian Parishes

St. Stephen, Bridgeport, 1899
St. Ladislaus, South Norwalk, 1907

Slovak Parishes

| SS. Cyril and Methodius, Bridgeport, 1907 | Sacred Heart, Torrington, 1905 |

French Canadian Parishes

St. Mary, Willimantic, 1905
St. Ann, Bristol, 1907

Appendix B

Parishes for Ethnic Minorities Established During the
Administration of Bishop John Nilan (1910-1934)*

Italian Parishes

Holy Rosary, Ansonia, 1909 (beginnings during *interregnum*)
St. Donato, New Haven, 1915
St. Anthony, Bristol, 1920
Sacred Heart, Stamford, 1920
St. Ann, Hamden, 1920
Our Lady of Pompeii, East Haven, 1921
Our Lady of Mt. Carmel, Waterbury, 1923
St. Lucy, Waterbury, 1926
St. Raphael, Bridgeport, 1925
St. Sebastian, Middletown, 1930

Polish Parishes

St. Stanislaus, Waterbury, 1912
St. Adalbert, Thompsonville, 1915
Our Lady of Perpetual Help, New London, 1915
Immaculate Conception, Southing, 1915
St. Joseph, Suffield, 1916
St. Stanislaus, Bristol, 1919
St. Mary, Torrington, 1919
Sacred Heart, Danbury, 1924
SS. Peter and Paul, Wallingford, 1925

*Incorporation dates are used as criterion for establishment.

St. Joseph, Ansonia, 1925
St. Anthony, Fairfield, 1927
Holy Cross, New Britain, 1927

Slovak Parishes

All Saints, New Britain, 1918
Holy Name, Stratford, 1923

Lithuanian Parishes

Holy Trinity, Hartford, 1912
St. Anthony, Ansonia, 1915

Appendix C

Urban Parishes Founded by End of Administration
of Bishop Tierney (1908)

Hartford

St. Joseph Cathedral
St. Patrick
St. Peter
St. Lawrence O'Toole
Our Lady of Sorrows
Immaculate Conception
St. Michael

St. Ann (French)
Church of the Sacred Heart (German)
St. Anthony (Italian)
SS. Cyril and Methodius (Polish)
Holy Trinity (Lithuanian)

New Haven

St. Mary
St. Patrick
St. John the Evangelist
St. Francis
Church of the Sacred Heart
St. Lawrence, West Haven
St. Joseph

St. Boniface (German)
St. Michael (Italian)
St. Louis (French)
St. Stanislaus (Polish)
St. Anthony (Italian)

Bridgeport

St. Augustine
Sacred Heart of Jesus

St. Joseph (German)
St. John Nepomucene ("Slovanian" or Slovak)

St. Patrick
St. Peter
St. Charles

St. Anthony (French)
St. Stephen (Hungarian)
St. Michael Archangel (Polish)
Holy Rosary (Italian)
St. George (Lithuanian)
SS. Cyril and Methodius (Slovak)

Meriden

St. Rose
St. Joseph

St. Laurent (French Canadian)
St. Mary (German)
St. Stanislaus (Polish)
Our Lady of Mt. Carmel (Italian)

Waterbury

Immaculate Conception
Sacred Heart
St. Francis Xavier
St. Patrick and St. Thomas

Our Lady of Lourdes (Italian)
St. Anne (French)
St. Cecelia (German)
St. Joseph (Lithuanian)

New Britain

St. Mary
St. Joseph

Sacred Heart (Polish)
St. Peter (German)
St. Andrew (Lithuanian)

Bibliography

ARCHIVES

Archives of the Archdiocese of Boston, Boston, Massachusetts.

Archives of the Archdiocese of Hartford, Hartford, Connecticut: Episcopal Papers, William F. Kearney Papers, Parish Annual Reports, Register of Clergy, Wolkovich Materials.

Archives of the Archdiocese of Philadelphia, Philadelphia, Pennsylvania.

Archives of the Catholic University of America, Washington, D.C.: Terence Powderly Papers.

Archives of the Catholic University of America, Washington, D.C.: Ellis Papers.

Archives of the Diocese of Cleveland, Cleveland, Ohio: Church and School Reports.

Archives of the Diocese of Providence, Providence, Rhode Island.

Archives of the Diocese of Springfield, Springfield, Massachusetts.

Archives of the Religious Sisters of Mercy, West Hartford, Connecticut.

Archives of St. Joseph College, West Hartford, Connecticut.

Archives of the University of Notre Dame, Notre Dame, Indiana: Bernard Smith Papers (Archives of the Monastery of St. Paul's Outside the Wall, Rome), prepared by Anton Debevec; Hartford Collections; Ludwig Mission Association Collections; Propagation of the Faith Collections; Richmond Papers.

Bridgeport (Burroughs) Public Library, Bridgeport, Connecticut: Church Files.

Connecticut State Library, Hartford, Connecticut.

New Jersey Catholic Historical Records Commission (Seton Hall University Press, 1978) Pp. 65-74.

Secretary of the State's Office, Hartford, Connecticut: Church Files, Corporation Division.

BOOKS

Abbott, E.
1926 *Historical Aspects of the Immigration Problem*. Chicago: The University of Chicago Press.

Abbott, M. and J. Gallagher
1966 *The Documents of Vatican II*. New York: Guild Press.

Abell, A.
1960 *American Catholicism and Social Action: A Search for Social Justice, 1865-1950*. Garden City, NY.: Hanover House.

Abramson, H.J.
1973 *Ethnic Diversity in Catholic America*. New York: John Wiley and Sons.

Ahlstrom, S.E.
1972 *A Religious History of the American People*. New Haven: Yale University Press.

Andrews, T.
1953 *The Polish National Catholic Church: In America and Poland*. London: Society for Promoting Christian Knowledge.

Bacigalupo, Rev. L., O.F.M.
1973 *The Franciscans and Italian Immigrants in America*. Wappinger Falls, NY.: Mount Alvernia Friary.

Bailyn, B.
1967 *The Ideological Origins of the American Revolution*. Cambridge: Harvard University Press.

Balch, E.
1910 *Our Slavic Fellow Citizens*. New York: Charities Publishing Company.

Bardin, H., *et al.*
1959 *The Hungarians in Bridgeport: A Social Survey*. Bridgeport: The University of Bridgeport.

Barry, J., O.S.B.
1953 *The Catholic Church and German Americans*. Milwaukee: The Bruce Publishing Company.

Barton, J.J.
1975 *Peasants and Strangers: Italians, Rumanians and Slovaks in an American City*. Cambridge, MA.: Harvard University Press.

Baumgartner, A.
1931 *Catholic Journalism: A Study of Its Development in the United States, 1789-1930*. New York: Columbia University Press.

Beals, C.
1951 *Our Yankee Heritage: The Making of Greater New Haven*. New Haven: Yale University Press.

Billington, R.A.
1938 *The Protestant Crusade, 1800-1860: A Study of the Origins of American Nativism*. New York: The Macmillan Company.

Bland, Sister J.
1957   *Hibernian Crusade: The Story of Catholic Total Abstinence Union.* Washington, DC.: Catholic University of America Press.

Blejwas, S., ed.
1982   *Pastor of the Poles: Polish American Essays.* New Britain, CT.: Polish Studies Program Monographs.

Blied, B.
1945   *The Catholics of the Civil War.* Milwaukee, WI.: n.p.

---------.
1944   *Austrian Aid to American Catholics.* Milwaukee, WI.: n.p.

Bojnowski, L.
1975   *History of the Establishment and Growth of the Roman Catholic Polish Parish Under the Patronage of St. Stanislaus, Bishop of Martyr, in Meriden, Connecticut.* New Britain: *The Catholic Leader*, 1908; reprinted in translation by St. Stanislaus Parish, Meriden.

1929   *The Book of Bridgeport, Connecticut: A Handbook of Civic, Industrial and Commercial Information.* Bridgeport: Bridgeport Chamber of Commerce.

Bouscaren, T. and A.C. Ellis
1947   *Canon Law, A Text and Commentary.* Milwaukee, WI.: The Bruce Publishing Company.

Brewer, D.C.
1926   *The Conquest of New England by the Immigrant.* New York: G.P. Putnam's Sons.

Brown, T.
1970   *The Irish Layman.* Part II of *The United States of America*, Vol. VI of *A History of Irish Catholicism.* Edited by P. Corish. Dublin: Gill and Macmillan, Ltd.

Browne, H.J.
1949   *The Catholic Church and the Knights of Labor.* Washington, DC.: Catholic University of America Press.

Buczek, D.S.
1974   *Immigrant Pastor: The Life of the Right Reverend Monsignor Lucyan Bojnowski of New Britain, Connecticut.* Waterbury, CT.: Heminway Corporation, Association of Polish Priests of Connecticut.

Burns, J.A.
1969   *The Growth and Development of the Catholic School System in the United States.* New York: Arno Press.

Byrne, S., O.S.D.
1969   *Irish Emigration to the United States.* New York: Arno Press.

Byrne W., W.A. Leahy, and J.H. O'Donnell
1899   *History of the Catholic Church in the New England States.* N.p.:n.p.

Cada, J.
1964   *Czech-American Catholics, 1850-1920.* Chicago: Center for Slavic Culture, Benedictine Press.

Cadden, J.P.
1944   *The Historiography of the American Catholic Church, 1785-1943.* Washington, DC.: Catholic University of America Press.

Capek, T.
1970   *The Czechs (Bohemians) in America: A Study of Their National, Cultural, Political, Social, Economic, and Religious Life.* Westport, CT.: Greenwood Press.

Carthy, Mother M.P., O.S.U.
1959   *English Influences on Early American Catholicism.* Washington, DC.: Catholic University of America Press.

Ciesluk, J.E.
1944   *National Parishes in the United States.* Washington, DC.: Catholic University of America Press.

Clark, G.L.
1914   *A History of Connecticut: Its People and Its Institutions.* New York: G.P. Putnam's Sons.

Clarke, R.H.
1872   *Lives of the Deceased Bishops of the Catholic Church in the United States.* New York: P. O'Shea Publishing Company.

Code, J.B.
1940   *Dictionary on the American Hierarchy, 1790 to 1940.* New York: The Macmillan Company.

Commons, J.R.
1907   *Races and Immigrants in America.* New York: The Macmillan Company.

Conley, P.T. and M.J. Smith
1976   *Catholicism in Rhode Island: The Formative Era.* Providence, RI.: The Diocese of Providence.

Connelly, J.F.
1960   *The Visit of Archbishop Gaetano Bedini to the United States: June 1853-February 1854.* Rome: Pontificae Univertatis Gregorianae.

Cross, R.D.
1958   *The Emergence of Liberal Catholicism in America.* Cambridge, MA.: Harvard University Press.

Curry, R.O. and T.M. Brown
1972   *Conspiracy: The Fear of Subversion in American History.* New York: Holt, Rinehart and Winston.

Dakin, W.S.
1926   *Geography of Connecticut.* Boston, MA.: Ginn and Co.

Dehey, E.T.
1930 *Religious Orders of Women in the United States: An Account of Their Origin, Works, and Most Important Institutions.* Rev. ed. Cleveland: Hammond Press.

DeMarco, W.M.
1981 *Ethnics and Enclaves: Boston's Italian North End.* Ann Arbor, MI.. University Microfilms International Research Press.

Demos, J.
1970 *A Little Commonwealth: Family Life in Plymouth Colony.* New York: Oxford University Press.

Desmond, H.J.
1912 and 1969 *The A.P.A. Movement.* Washington, DC.: The New Century Press, reprint ed., New York: Arno Press.

Dignan, P.J.
1933 *A History of the Legal Incorporation of Catholic Church Property in the United States, 1784-1932.* Washington, DC.: Catholic University Press of America.

Dolan, J.P.
1977 *Catholic Revivalism: The American Experience, 1830-1900.* Notre Dame, IN.: University of Notre Dame Press.

-------.
1975 *The Immigrant Church: New York's Irish and German Catholics, 1815-1865.* Baltimore: Johns Hopkins University Press.

Duggan, T.S.
1930 *The Catholic Church in Connecticut.* New York: The States History Company.

Dvornik, F.
1961 *Czeck Contributions to the Growth of the United States.* Washington, DC.: Dumbarton Oaks.

Dyrud, K.P., M. Novak, and R.J. Vecoli, eds.
1978 *The Other Catholics.* New York: Arno Press.

Egan, M.F., and J.B. Kennedy
1920 *The Knights of Columbus in Peace and War.* 2 Vols. New Haven: Knights of Columbus Press.

Ellis, J.T.
1965 *Catholics in Colonial America.* Baltimore: Helicon.

-------.
1962 *Documents of American Catholic History.* Milwaukee: The Bruce Publishing Company.

-------.
1956 *American Catholicism.* Chicago: The University of Chicago Press.

------.
1956 *Americans Catholics and the Intellectual Life.* Chicago: Heritage Foundation.

------.

1947   *A Select Bibliography of the History of the Catholic Church in the United States.* New York: The Declan X. McMullen Company.

1917-Present   *Encyclopedia of Biography: Representative Citizens.* 4 Vols. New York: American Historical Society, 1917-.

Fichter, J.H.
1967   *Catholic Parents and the Catholic Vocation: A Study of Parental Attitudes in a Catholic Diocese.* Washington, DC.: Center for Applied Research in the Apostolate (CARA).

Fischer, D.H.
1969   *The Revolution of American Conservatism.* New York: Harper and Row.

Fitton, Rev. J.
1872   *Sketches of the Establishment of the Church in New England.* Boston: Patrick Donahoe.

Foerster, R.F.
1919   *The Italian Emigration of Our Times.* Cambridge: Harvard University Press.

Fogarty, G.P., S.J.
1974   *The Vatican and the Americanist Crisis: Denis J. O'Connell, American Agent in Rome, 1885-1903.* Vol. 36. Rome: Miscellanea Historiae Pontificiae.

Foner, E.
1970   *The Ideology of the Republican Party Before the Civil War: Free Soil, Free Labor, Free Men.* New York: Oxford University Press.

Ford, E.E.
1912   *Notes of the Life of Noah Webster.* 2 Vols. New York: n.p.

Fox, P.
1970   *The Poles in America.* New York: Arno Press.

Gallagher, Rev. J.P.
1968   *A Century of History: The Diocese of Scranton, 1868-1968.* Scranton: The Diocese of Scranton Press.

Glaab, C.N., and A.T. Brown
1976   *A History of Urban America.* New York: The Macmillan Company.

Gleason, P., ed.
1970   *Catholicism in America.* New York: Harper and Row.

---------.ed.
1969   *Contemporary Catholicism.* Notre Dame: University of Notre Dame Press.

Grant, E.S., and M. Grant, eds.
1969   *Passbook to a Proud Past and a Promising Future, 1819-1969. 150th Anniversary of Society for Savings.* Hartford: Connecticut Printers.

Greeley, A.
1977   *The American Catholic: A Social Portrait.* New York: Basic Books.

--------.
1971   *Why Can't They Be More Like Us?: America's White Ethnic Groups.* New York: E.P. Dutton and Company.

Greene, V.R.
1975   *For God and Country: The Rise of Polish and Lithuanian Ethnic Consciousness in America, 1860-1910.* Madison: State Historical Society of Wisconsin.

----------.
1968   *The Slavic Community on Strike: Immigrant Labor in Pennsylvania Anthracite.* Notre Dame: University of Notre Dame Press.

Guignard, M.J.
1982   *La Foi-ha Langue-ha Culture: the Franco-Americans of Biddeford, Maine.* Author.

Guilday, P.
1932   *A History of the Councils of Baltimore, 1791-1884.* New York: n.p.

----------.
1923   *The National Pastorals of the American Hierarchy, 1792-1919.* Washington, DC.: National Catholic Welfare Council.

Hall, D.T., and B. Schneider
1973   *Organizational Climate and Careers, the Work Lives of Priests.* New York: New York Seminar Press.

Handlin, O.
1959   *Immigration as a Factor in American History.* Englewood Cliffs, NJ.: Prentice-Hall.

----------.
1954   *The American People in the Twentieth Century.* Cambridge: Harvard University Press.

Hansen, M.L.
1940   *The Immigrant in American History.* New York: Harper and Row.

Hareven, T., ed.
1971   *Anonymous Americans: Explorations in Nineteenth Century Social History.* Englewood Cliffs, NJ.: Prentice-Hall.

Hays, S.P.
1957   *The Response to Industrialism: 1885-1914.* Chicago: The University of Chicago Press.

Healy, K.
1973   *Francis Warde: American Foundress of the Sisters of Mercy.* New York: The Seabury Press.

Heffernan, Rev. A.J.
1936   *A History of Catholic Education in Connecticut.* Washington, DC.: Catholic University of America Press.

Hennesey, J.,S.J.
1981 *American Catholicism: A History of the Roman Catholic Church in the United States.* New York: Oxford University Press.

Herberg, W.
1955 *Protestant, Catholic, Jew: An Essay in American Religious Sociology.* Garden City, NY.: Doubleday.

Herron, Sister M.E.
1929 *The Sisters of Mercy in the United States, 1843-1928.* New York: The Macmillan Company.

Higham, J., ed.
1978 *Ethnic Leadership in America.* Baltimore: Johns Hopkins University Press.

----------.
1970 *Strangers in the Land: Patterns of American Nativism, 1860-1925.* New York: Atheneum.

Hughes, W.H.
1889 *Souvenir Volume, Three Great Events in the History of the Catholic Church in the United States.* Detroit: n.p.

Hutchinson, E.P.
1956 *Immigrants and Their Children, 1850-1950.* New York: John Wiley and Sons.

Hynes, M.J.
1953 *History of the Diocese of Cleveland: Origins and Growth, 1847-1952.* Cleveland: n.p.

Iorizzo, L.J., and S. Mondello
1971 *The Italian-Americans.* New York: Twayne Publishing Company.

Janick, H.F.
1975 *A Diverse People: Connecticut 1914 to the Present.* Chester, CT.: The Pequot Press.

Johnston, A.
1903 *Connecticut: A Study of a Commonwealth Democracy.* Rev. ed. Boston: Houghton Mifflin Company.

Jones, M.A.
1960 *American Immigration.* Chicago: The University of Chicago Press.

Kenneally, F., O.F.M., ed.
1971 *United States Documents in the Propaganda Fide Archives: A Calender 1st Series.* Washington, DC.: Academy of American Franciscan History.

Kennedy, J.F.
1964 *A Nation of Immigrants.* Rev. ed. New York: Harper and Row.

Kervick, F.W.
1953 *Charles Patrick Keely, Architect: His Life and Works.* South Bend, IN.: n.p.

Kinzer, D.L.
1964   *An Episode in Anti-Catholicism: The American Protective Association.* Seattle: University of Washington Press.

Koenig, S.
1938   *Immigrant Settlements in Connecticut: Their Growth and Character.* Federal Writers Project for the State of Connecticut. Hartford: Connecticut State Department of Education, Works Progress Administration.

Kolko, G.
1963   *The Triumph of Conservatism.* Chicago: Quadrangle Books.

Linkh, R.M.
1975   *American Catholicism and European Immigrants, 1900-1924.* Staten Island, NY.: Center for Migration Studies.

Lopata, H.Z.
1976   *Polish Americans: Status and Competition in an Ethnic Community.* Englewood Cliffs, NJ.: Prentice-Hall.

Lord, R.H., J.E. Sexton, and E.T. Harrington
1944   *History of the Archdiocese of Boston: In the Various Stages of the Development, 1604-1943.* 3 Vols. New York: Sheed and Ward.

McAvoy, T.T., C.S.C.
1970   *The Irish Clergyman.* Part I of *The United States of America*, Vol. VI of *A History of Irish Catholicism.* Edited by P. Corish. Dublin: Gill and Macmillan, Ltd.

---------.
1969   *A History of the Catholic Church in the United States.* Notre Dame: University of Notre Dame Press.

---------.
1960   *Roman Catholicism and the American Way of Life.* Notre Dame: University of Notre Dame Press.

---------.
1957   *The Great Crisis in American Catholic History, 1895-1900.* Chicago: Henry Regnery Company.

MacDonald, F., C.P.
1946   *The Catholic Church and the Secret Societies in the United States.* Edited by T.J. McMahon. New York: The United States Catholic Historical Society.

McGee, T.D.
1852   *A History of the Irish Settlers in the Irish Settlements in North America, From the Earliest Period to the Census of 1850.* Boston: Patrick Donahue.

McGuire, C.E., ed.
1923   *Catholic Builders of the Nation.* Vol. I: *Catholicism in the Building of the Nation.* Boston: Continental Press. Vol II: *Catholicism and the Nation's Social Development.* Boston: Continental Press.

McGuire, J.F.
1876   *The Irish in America.* New York: D.J. Sadlier Company.

McSeveney, S.T.
1972   *The Politics of Depression: Political Behavior in the Northeast, 1893-1896.* New York: Oxford University Press.

Mann, A.
1954   *Yankee Reformers in the Urban Age.* Cambridge: Harvard University Press.

Mason, M.P.
1953   *Church-State Relationships in Education in Connecticut, 1633-1953.* Washington, DC.: The Catholic University of America Press.

May, E.C.
1947   *Century of Silver, 1847-1947.* New York: n.p.

Maynard, T.
1941   *The Story of American Catholicism.* New York: The Macmillan Company.

Melville, A.
1955   *John Carroll of Baltimore: Founder of the American Catholic Hierarchy.* New York: Charles Scribner's Sons.

Merwick, D.
1973   *Boston Priests, 1848-1910: A Study of Social and Intellectual Changes.* Cambridge: Harvard University Press.

Milkey, J.
1950   *New Britain: The Hardware City of the World.* New Britain: n.p.

Miller, R., and T. Marzik, eds.
1977   *Immigrants and Religion in Urban America.* Philadelphia: Temple University Press.

Mohl, R.A., and J.F. Richardson
1973   *The Urban Experience: Themes in American History.* Belmont, CA.: The Wadsworth Publishing Company.

Morse, J.M.
1933   *A Neglected Period of Connecticut History, 1818-1850.* New Haven: Yale University Press.

Myers, G.
1943   *The History of Bigotry in the United States.* New York: Random House.

Nevins, A.J., M.M.
1973   *Our American Catholic Heritage.* 2d. ed, rev. Huntington, IN.: Our Sunday Visitor.

1967   *The New Catholic Encyclopedia.* 15 Vols. New York: McGraw-Hill.

1978   *New Jersey Catholic Historical Records Commission.* Seton Hall University Press.

Noonan, C.
1938   *Nativism in Connecticut, 1829-1850.* Washington, DC.: Catholic University of America Press.

Novak, M.
1972   *The Rise of the Unmeltable Ethnics.* New York: The Macmillan Company.

O'Brien, D.
1968   *American Catholics and Social Reform: The New Deal Years.* New York: Oxford University Press.

O'Donnell, Rev. J.H.
1900   *History of the Diocese of Hartford.* Boston: D.H. Hurd Company.

O'Grady, J.
1930   *Catholic Charities in the United States: History and Problems.* Washington, DC.: National Council of Churches.

Osborn, N.G.
1925   *History of Connecticut.* 5 Vols. New York: The States History Company.

Osterweis, R.
1953   *Three Centuries of New Haven, 1638-1938.* New Haven: Yale University Press.

Pallen, C.B., ed.
1916   *A Memorial of Andrew Shipman, His Life and Writings.* New York: Encyclopedia Press.

Pawlowski, R.E., *et al.*
1973   *How the Other Half Lived: An Ethnic History of the Old East Side and South End of Hartford.* West Hartford: Robert E. Pawlowski, Northwest Catholic High School.

Pospishil, V.J., J.C.D.
1960   *Code of Oriental Canon Law, the Law on Persons.* Ford City, PA.: St. Mary's Ukrainian Church.

Ray, Sister M.A., B.V.M.
1974   *American Opinion of Roman Catholicism in the 18th Century.* No. 416: *Studies in History Economics and Public Law.* Edited by the Faculty of Political Science Columbia University. Reprint ed. New York: Octagon Books.

Rice, M.H.
1964   *American Catholic Opinion in the Slave Controversy.* Gloucester, MA.: Peter Smith.

Riley, A.J.
1936   *Catholicism in New England to 1788.* Washington, DC.: Catholic University of America Press.

Rischin, M., ed.
1976   *Immigrants and the American Tradition.* Indianapolis, IN.: Bobbs-Merrill Company.

Roemer, T., O.F.M.
1950   *The Catholic Church in the United States.* St. Louis, MO.: B. Herder Book Company.

Rooney, J.
1877   *The Connecticut Catholic Yearbook, Being An Epitome of the History of the Church in the Diocese of Hartford From April 1876 to May 1877.* Hartford: The Connecticut Catholic Publishing Company.

Rose, P.M.
1922 and 1975   *The Italians in America.* New York: n.p. reprint ed., New York: Arno Press.

Rumilly, R.
1958   *Histoire des Franco-Americains.* Lazard, Montreal: n.p.

Schaff, P.
1961   *America: A Sketch of Its Political, Social and Religious Character.* Edited by P. Miller. Cambridge: Harvard University Press.

Schiavo, G.
1949   *Italian-American History.* Vol. II: *The Italian Contribution to the Catholic Church in America.* New York: Vigo Press.

Sears, C.H.
1922   *The Czechoslovaks in America.* New York: n.p.

Sexton, J.E., and A.J. Riley
1945   *History of St. John's Seminary, Brighton.* Boston: Roman Catholic Archbishop of Boston.

Shanabruch, C.
1981   *Chicago's Catholics: The Evolution of an American Identity.* Notre Dame: University of Notre Dame Press.

Shea, J.G.
1886-1892   *History of the Catholic Church in the United States.* 4 Vols. New York: n.p.

Shearer, D.C.
1933   *Pontificia Americana: A Documentary History of the Catholic Church in the United States, 1784-1884.* Washington, DC.: Catholic University of America.

Shields, C.
1958   *Democracy and Catholicism in America.* New York: McGraw-Hill.

Shuster, G.N.
1927   *The Catholic Spirit in America.* New York: L. MacVeagh, The Dial Press.

Smith, H.S., R.T. Handy, and L.A. Loetscher
1960   *American Christianity: An Historical Interpretation with Representative Documents.* Vol I: *1607-1820.* New York: Charles Scribners's Sons.

Solomon, B.
1956   *Ancestors and Immigrants: A Changed New England Tradition.* Cambridge: Harvard University Press.

Souders, D.A.
1922   *The Magyars in America.* New York: George H. Doran.

1892   *Souvenir of the Consecration of St. Joseph's Cathedral, May 8, 1892.* Hartford, CT.: Fowler and
        Miller.

Sweet, W.W.
1930   *The Story of Religious America.* New York: Harper and Brothers.

Taylor, G.
1890   *Religious Census.* Hartford: Connecticut Bible Society.

Thernstrom, S.
1973   *The Other Bostonians: Poverty and Progress in the American Metropolis, 1880-1970.* Cambridge:
        Harvard University Press.

Thomas, W.F., and F. Znaniecki
1958   *The Polish Peasant in Europe and America.* 2 Vols. New York: Dover Publications.

Thwaites, R.G., ed.
1959   *Jesuit Relations and Allied Documents.* 72 Vols. New York: Paegeant Book Company.

Tomasi, S.M.
1975   *Piety and Power: The Role of the Italian Parishes in the New York Metropolitan Area 1880-1930.*
        Staten Island, NY.: Center for Migration Studies.

---------and M.H. Engels, eds.
1975   *The Italian Experience in the United States.* Staten Island, NY.: Center for Migration Studies.

Trumbull, J.H., ed.
1886   *The Memorial History of Hartford, Connecticut.* 2 Vols. Boston: n.p.

Van Dusen, A.E.
1961   *Connecticut.* New York: Random House.

Vollmar, E.R.
1956   *The Catholic Church in America: An Historical Bibliography.* New Brunswick, NJ.: Scarecrow
        Press.

Yinger, J.M.
1963   *Sociology Looks at Religion.* New York: The Macmillan Company.

Wakin, E., and Father J.F. Scheuer
1966   *The Romanization of the American Catholic Church.* New York: The Macmillan Company.

Walburg, A.
1889   *The Question of Nationality in Its Relation to the Catholic Church in the United States.* Cincinnati:
        Herder and Company.

Waldo, G.C., Jr.
1917   *History of Bridgeport and Vicinity.* Vol I. New York: The S.J. Clarke Publishing Company.

Warner, S.B.
1972   *The Urban Wilderness.* New York: Harper and Row.

Warner. W.L., and L. Scrole
1945   *The Social Systems of American Ethnic Groups.* New Haven: Yale University Press.

Whalen, W.J.
1981   *Minority Religions in America.* New York: Alba House. rev. ed.

Wolkovich-Valkavicius, Rev. W.
        Bay State "Blue Laws" and Bimba. Brockton, MA.: Forum Press. n.d.

Woodham-Smith, C.B.
1963   *The Great Hunger: Ireland 1845-49.* New York: Harper and Row.

Wueste, A.E.
1968   *Abilities, Traits, and Interests of Minor Seminarians: A Pilot Study.* Washington, DC.: Center
        for Applied Research in the Apostolate (CARA).

ARTICLES

Abell, A.
1952   "The Catholic Factor in Urban Welfare: The Early Period, 1850-1880", *Review of Politics*,
        14:289-325. July.

Agnew, W.H.
1913   "Pastoral Care of Italian Children in America", *American Ecclesiastical Review*, 48:265-283.
        March.

Agonito, J.
1976   "Ecumenical Stirrings: Catholic-Protestant Relations during the Episcopacy of John Car-
        roll", *Church History*, 45:358-373. Sept.

1903   "American Bishops and the Polish Catholic Church", *American Ecclesiastical Review*, 29:347-
        352. Oct.

Barry, C.J.
1958   "Some Roots of American Nativism", *Catholic Historical Review*, 44:137-146.

Bern, Sister M.A.
1948   "St. John's Polish College", *Polish American Studies*, 5:85-97. July-Dec.

Brennan, Rev. T.C.
1920   "America's Welcome to Cardinal Mercier", *Records of the American Catholic Historical Society of
        Philadelphia*, 31:43-92.

Browne, H.J.
1957   "American Catholic History: A Progress Report on Research and Study", *Church History*, 26:372-380. Dec.

---------.

1946   "The Italian Problem in the Catholic Church in the United States, 1880-1900", *Historical Records and Studies of the United States Catholic Historical Society of New York*, 35:46-72.

Clancy, R., C.S.C.
1937   "American Prelates in the Vatican Council", *Historical Records and Studies of the United States Catholic Historical Society of New York*, 28:7-135.

Cross, R.D.
1973   "How Historians Have Looked at Immigrants to the United States", *International Migration Review*, 7:4-13. Spring.

---------.

1962   "The Changing Image of the City Among American Catholics", *Catholic Historical Review*, 48:33-52. April.

Cullen, T.F.
1937   "William Barber-Tyler, 1806-49, First Bishop of Hartford", *Catholic Historical Review*, 23:17-30. April.

Cygan, M.
1983   "Ethnic Parish As Compromise: The Spheres of Clerical and Lay Authority in a Polish American Parish, 1911-1930". Working Papers Series, CUSHWA Center, University of Notre Dame, Series 13, No. 1. Spring.

Dorn, J.
1973   "Religion and the City". In *The Urban Experience*. Edited by R.A. Mohl and J.F. Richardson. Belmont, CA.: Wadsworth Publishing Company.

Femminella, F.
1962   "The Impact of Italian Migration of American Catholicism", *International Migration Review*, 22:21-24.

Galush, W.
1984   "Both Polish and Catholic: Immigrant Clergy in the American Church", *American Catholic Historical Review*, 70(3):407-427.

----------.

1972   "The Polish National Catholic Church: A Survey of Its Origins, Development and Missions", *Records of the American Catholic Historical Society of Philadelphia*, 83:131-149.

Greene, V.
1966   "For God and Country: The Origins of Slavic Catholic Self-Consciousness in America", *Church History*, 25:446-460. Dec.

Hennesey, J., S.J.
1966   "The Distinctive Tradition of American Catholicism", *Records of the American Catholic Historical Society of Philadelphia*, 77:175-189. Sept.

Hersher, Father I.
1943 "St. Bonaventure College and Seminary", *Historical Records and Studies of the United States Catholic Historical Society of New York*, 33:77-100.

Higham, J.
1958 "Another Look at Nativism", *Catholic Historical Review*, 44:147-157. July.

Kane, J.J.
1955 "The Social Structure of American Catholicism", *American Catholic Sociological Review*, 16:23-40. March.

Kulik, E.
1967 "Polish-American Roman Catholic Bishops", *Polish American Studies*, 24:27-32. Jan.-June.

Lannie, V.
1970 "Alienation in America: The Immigrant Catholics and Public Education in Pre-Civil War America", *Review of Politics*, 32:503-521. Oct.

LeProhon, E.P., A.M.
1895 "Memorial of the Rev. William Tyler, First Bishop of Hartford, Connecticut", translated by J.M. Toohey, C.S.C., *American Catholic Historical Researches*, 12:2-9.

1889 "Leo XIII and the Italian Catholic in the United States", *American Ecclesiastical Review*, 1:43-45. Feb.

Liptak, D.Q.
     "Connecticut". In *The New Catholic Encyclopedia*, 4:177-180. n.d.

McAvoy, T.T.
1966 "The Catholic Minority and Contemporary Society", *Records of the American Catholic Historical Society of Philadelphia*, 77:99-107. June.

----------.
1966 "Public Schools vs. Catholic Schools and James McMaster", *Review of Politics*, 28:19-46. Jan.

----------.
1959 "The Catholic Minority After the Amercianist Controversy, 1899-1917: A Survey", *Review of Politics*, 21:53-82. Jan.

----------.
1953 "The American Catholic Minority in the Later Nineteenth Century", *Review of Politics*, 15:275-302. June.

----------.
1950 "Bishop John Lancaster Spalding and the Catholic Minority", *Review of Politics*, 12:3-19. June.

----------.
1948 "The Formation of the Catholic Minority in the United States", *Review of Politics*, 10:13-34. Jan.

McKeown, E.
1974   "Apologia for an American Catholicism: The Petition and Report of the National Catholic
       Welfare Council and Pius XI, April 25, 1922", *Church History*, 43:514-528. Dec.

McSeveney, S.T.
1973   "Ethnic Groups, Ethnic Conflicts, and Recent Quantitative Research in American Political
       History", *International Migration Review*, 7:14-33. Spring.

Marty, M.
1972   "Ethnicity: The Skeleton of Religion in America", *Church History*, 41:5-21. March.

Middleton, Rev. T.
1893   "A List of Catholic Periodicals in the United States", *Records of the American Catholic Historical
       Society of Philadelphia*, 4:213-242.

Monzill, T.I., *et al.*
1969   "The Catholic Church and the Americanization of the Polish Immigrant", *Polish American
       Studies*, 26:34-58. Jan.-June.

O'Connor, T.F.
1946   "Catholic Archives of the United States", *Catholic Historical Review*, 31:31-50. Jan.

O'Reilly, B. (of Hartford, Connecticut)
1902   Letter to Mr. Frenaye, May 15, 1854. *Records of the American Catholic Historical Society of
       Philadelphia*, 13:483-484.

Parton, J.
1868   "Our Roman Catholic Brethren", *Atlantic Monthly*, 21:432-451. Apr.

Pekari, M.A.
1925   "The German Catholics in the United States of America", *Records of the American Catholic
       Historical Society of Philadelphia*, 36:305-358. Dec.

Podea, I.S.
1950   "Quebec to 'Little Canada': The Coming of the French Canadians to New England in the
       Nineteenth Century", *New England Quarterly*, 23:365-380. Sept.

Procko, B.P.
1973   "Soter Ortynsky: The First Ruthenian Bishop in the United States, 1907-1916", *Catholic
       Historical Review*, 58:513-533. Jan.

Purcell, R.J.
1942   "Missionaries from All Hollows (Dublin) in the United States, 1842-64". *Records of the Amer-
       ican Catholic Historical Society of Philadelphia*, 53:204-249. Dec.

Reher, M.M.
1973   "Leo XIII and Americanism", *Theological Studies*, 34:679-689. Dec.

Rischin, M.
1972   "The New American Catholic History", *Church History*, 41:225-229. June.

Rooney, J.
1915   "Early Times in the Diocese of Hartford, Connecticut, 1829-1873." *Catholic Historical Review*
       1:148-163. June.

Sedgwick, H.D., Jr.
1899   "The United States and Rome", *Atlantic Monthly* 84:445-458. Oct.

Senner, J.H.
1896   "Immigration from Italy", *North American Review,* 162:652-687. June.

Shahan, T.J.
1889   "Early Catholics in Connecticut", *The United States Catholic Magazine* 2:274-294. March.

--------.

1890   "The Catholic Church in Connecticut", *The United States Catholic Magazine,* 3:16-25.

Sheedy, Rev. M., L.L.D.
1916   "History of the Catholic Summer School of America", *Records of the American Catholic Histor-
       ical Society of Philadelphia,* 27:287-295. Dec.

Silvia, P.T., Jr.
1979   "The 'Flint Affair': French Canadian Struggle for *Survivance*", *American Catholic Historical
       Review,* 65:414-435. July.

Smith, T.
1969   *Immigrant Social Aspirations and American Education, 1880-1930",* American Quarterly* 21:523-
       543. Fall.

Stolarik, M.M.
1978   "Building Slovak Communities in America". In *The Other Catholics.* Edited by K.P. Dyrud,
       M. Novak and R.J. Vecoli. New York: Arno Press, Pp.69-109.

----------.

1976   From Field to Factory: The Historiography of Slovak Immigration to the United States",
       International Migration Review, 10:81-102. Spring.

----------.

1972   "Lay Initiative in American Slovak Parishes: 1880-1930", *Records of the American Catholic
       Historical Society of Philadelphia* 83:151-158. Sept.

Thomas, S.J.
1976   "The American Periodical Press and the Apostolic Letter, *Testem Benevolentiae*", *Catholic His-
       torical Review,* 62:408-423. July.

Tollino, J.W.
1939   "The Church in America and the Italian Problem", *American Ecclesiastical Review,* 100:22-
       32. Jan.

Vecoli, R.
1969   "Prelates and Peasants: Italian Immigrants and Catholic Church", *Journal of Social History,*
       1:217-268. Sept.

Wade, M.
1950   "The French Parish and Survivance in Nineteenth Century New England", *Catholic Historical Review*, 36:163-189. June.

Walsh, J.J.
1918   "An Apostle of the Italians", *Catholic World*, 106:64-71. Apr.

Weber, N.A.
1916   "The Rise of the National Church in the United States", *Catholic Historical Review* 10:422-434. Jan.

Willging, E.P., and H. Hatzfield
1954-1956   "Catholic Serials in the Nineteenth Century in the United States: A Bibliographical Survey and a Union List". Part I, *Records of the American Catholic Historical Society of Philadelphia*, 65:158-175; Part II, 66:156-173; Part III 66:222-238; Part IV, 67:31-50.

Wolkovich-Valkavicius, W.
1983   "Religious Separatism among Lithuanians Immigrants", *Polish American Studies*, 40(2).

Woodcock-Tentler, L.
1983   "Who Is The Church? Conflict in a Polish Immigrant Parish in Late Nineteenth Century Detroit", *Society for the Comparative Study of Society and History*, 241-276.

PUBLIC DOCUMENTS

1897   *The Atlantic Reporter*. Vol. 37: *Containing All the Decisions of the Supreme Courts of Maine, New Hampshire, Vermont, Rhode Island, Connecticut and Pennsylvania, May 5-August 25, 1897*. St. Paul: West Publishing Company.

Connecticut.
1945   *Connecticut Digest of Judicial Decisions, 1785-1945*. Compiled by Richard H. Phillips. 3 Vols. Hartford.

Connecticut.
1944   *Connecticut Reports*. Vol. 130: *Cases Argued and Determined in the Supreme Court of Errors of the State of Connecticut, March 1943-April 1944*. Hartford: E.E. Dissell and Company.

Connecticut.
1930   *General Statutes of Connecticut, Revision of 1930*. Compiled by Richard H. Phillips. 3 Vols. Orange and New Haven: E.E. Dissell and Company.

Connecticut.
1905   Office of the Attorney General (William A. King). *Third Biennial Report of the Attorney General, for the Two Years Ended, January 3, 1905*. Public Document, No. 40. Hartford: Hartford Press, The Case, Lockwood, and Brainard Company.

Connecticut.
1903   *Public Acts of the State of Connecticut, Passed January Session, 1903*. Hartford: The Case, Lockwood, and Brainard Company.

Connecticut.
1866   *Public Acts Passed by the General Assembly.* New Haven.

U.S. Department of Commerce. Bureau of the Census
1930   *Seventh Census of the United States, 1850* through *Fifteenth Census of the United States, 1930.*
       Washington, DC.

------------.

1900   *A Century of Population Growth from the First Census to the Twelfth, 1790-1900.* Washington,
       DC.

U.S. Department of the Interior. Census Office
1894   *Report on the Statistics of Churches in the United States at the 11th Census: 1890.* Henry K. Carroll,
       Washington, DC.

U.S. Immigration Service
1904-1905   *Annual Reports of the Superintendent of Immigration to the Secretary of Commerce* (1904,1905)
            and *Secretary of the Treasury* (1892-1902). House of Representatives Ex. Doc. 235, Part
            2, 52nd Cong.

CATHOLIC DIRECTORIES

Hoffmann's Catholic Directory, Almanac and Clergy-List Quarterly. Milwaukee: Hoffmann Brothers,
various years.

Metropolitan Catholic Almanac and Laity's Directory. Baltimore, 1837.

The Official Catholic Directory. New York: P.J. Kennedy, various years. Milwaukee: M.H. Wiltzius
Company, various years.

Sadlier's Catholic Directory, Almanac and ORDO. New York: D & J. Sadlier Company, various years.

U.S. Catholic Almanac and Laity's Directory. Baltimore, 1833-1837.

UNPUBLISHED MATERIALS

Abramson, H. J.
1970   "Ethnic Pluralism in the Central City". Paper presented at the Statewide Consultation on
       Connecticut's Ethnic and Working-Class Americans, Albertus Magnus College, New Ha-
       ven. April 17.

Antoninus, Sister M.
       "History of St. Patrick's Parish, New Haven, CT, 1853-1953". n.d.

Briggs, J.W.
1974   "Church Building in America: Divergent and Convergent Interests of Priests and Lay People in Italian-American Communities". Paper presented at Reinterpretation of American Catholic History Seminar, University of Notre Dame.

Cesaro, Rev. N.J.
1965   "Early Catholic Missionaries in Connecticut, 1638-1829". Master's thesis, St. Joseph College, West Hartford, CT.

Costa, J.
1984   "Meeting the Challenge of Education in an Ethnic Parish". Masters of Divinity Thesis, School of Theology, Immaculate Conception Seminary, Mahway, NJ.

DiGiovanni, S.M.
1983   "Michael Augustine Corrigan and the Italian Immigrants in the Archdiocese of New York, 1885:1902". Doctoral Dissertation. Gregorian University, Rome, Italy.

Hayman, Rev. R.W.
   "History of the Diocese of Providence". Typewritten. n.d.

Healy, Sister, M.M.
1966   "A Survey of Catholic Maternity Homes". Master's thesis, Catholic University, Washington, DC.

Kennedy, Msgr. J.S.
1976   "The Catholic Church in Connecticut: A Bicentennial View". Paper presented at Sacred Heart University, Bridgeport, CT. March 18.

Koenig, S.T., and D. Rodnick
1940   "Ethnic Factors in Connecticut Life: A Survey of Social, Economic, and Cultural Characteristics of the Connecticut Population". New Haven: W.P.A. Connecticut Writers Project.

Mason, Sister M.P.
1953   "Church-State Relationships in Education in Connecticut, 1633-1953". Ph.D. dissertation, Catholic University, Washington, DC.

Mierzwinski, T.T.
1971   "The Association of Polish Priests in Connecticut: An Interpretative History". Typewritten.

Murphy, J.C.
1953   "An Analysis of the Attitudes of American Catholics Towards the Immigrant and the Negro, 1825-1925". Ph.D dissertation, Catholic University, Washington, DC.

Noreen, Sister M.
1972   "The History of the Origin and Development of the Catholic Newspaper in Connecticut as Exemplified in *The Catholic Press* and Its Successor, *The Connecticut Catholic*". Master's thesis, Southern Connecticut State College, New Haven.

Parmet, R.D.
1966   "The Know-Nothings in Connecticut". Ph.D dissertation, Columbia University.

Riley, A.J.
1936   "Catholicism in New England to 1788". Ph.D dissertation, Catholic University.

Sorrell, R.S.
1975   "The Sentinelle Affair (1924-1929) and Militant *Survivance*: The Franco-American Experi-
       ence in Woonsocket, Rhode Island". Ph.D dissertation, State University of New York at
       Buffalo.

Thomas, S.J.
1977   "The Catholic Press and *Longinqua oceani*". Paper presented at the spring meeting of the
       American Catholic Historical Society, Holy Cross College, Worcester, MA.

Tybor, S., M. Martina, *et al.*, eds.
1972   "Matthew Jankola, 1872-1916: Slovak-American Priest, Leader, Educator, and Founder of
       the Sisters of SS. Cyril and Methodius". Danville, PA.: Jankola Library, July.

Vollmar, E.R.
1955   "Publication on United States Catholic Church History, 1850-1950". Ph.D dissertation, St.
       Louis University.

Wolkovich-Valkavicius, W.
1977   "Lithuanian Immigrants and Their Irish Bishops in the Catholic Church in Connecticut,
       1893-1915". Typewritten.

------------.
1976   "Lithuanian Origins in Connecticut and Reverend Joseph Zebris: The Life, Struggles and
       Tragic Death of a Pioneer Priest". Typewritten.

NEWSPAPERS

Boston Pilot

Bridgeport Post

Bridgeport Sunday Post

The Catholic Press

Catholic Standard (New Haven)

The Catholic Transcript

The Connecticut Catholic

Hartford Courant

Hartford Times

Middletown Sentinel and Witness

Morning Union (Bridgeport)

New Britain Herald

New Haven Morning Journal Courier

New Haven Palladium

New Haven Register

Newport Daily News

New York Freemen's Journal

New York Times

L'Opinion Publique (Worcester)

Pilot

Providence Journal

Sunday Republican Weekly (Waterbury)

Torrington Evening Register

Valley Catholic

Waterbury Republican

Willimantic Weekly Chronicle

Windham County Transcript

Woonsocket Patriot

Index

A

Abbelen, P., 13
Abbot, E., 165
Abbot, M., 165
Abell, A., 165, 177
Abilities, Traits, and Interests of Minor Seminarians: A Pilot Study, 177
Abramson, H.J., 2, 7, 165, 183
Acadia, 25
Agnew, W.H., 177
Agonito, J., 177
Ahlstrom, S.E., 3, 165
All Hallows Seminary, 29
All Saints Independent Lithuanian Catholic Church, 147
Ambot, J.J., 48, 57
America: A Sketch of Its Political, Social and Religious Character, 175
American Bill of Rights, 10
The American Catholic: A Social Portrait, 170
American Catholic Historical Researches, 179
American Catholic Historical Review, 178, 181
American Catholic Opinion in the Slave Controversy, 174
American Catholic Sociological Review, 179
American Catholicism: A History of the Roman Catholic Church in the United States, 171
American Catholicism and European Immigrants, 1900-1924, 172
American Catholicism and Social Action: A Search for Social Justice, 1865-1950, 165
American Catholics and Social Reform, 174
American Catholics and the Intellectual Life, 168
American Christianity: An Historical Interpretation with Representative Documents, 175
American Civil War, 32, 33, 34, 37
American College, 34, 47
American Constitution, 24
American Ecclesiastical Review, 177, 179, 181
American Immigration, 171
American Opinion of Roman Catholicism in the 18th Century, 174

The American People in the Twentieth Century, 170
American Protective Association, 86
American Quarterly, 181
American Revolution, 25, 60
"An Analysis of the Attitudes of American Catholics Towards the Immigrant and the Negro, 1825-1925", 184
Ancestors and Immigrants: A Changed New England Tradition, 175
Ancient Order of the Hibernians, 90
Andrews, G.V., 125
Andrews, T., 165
Annual Reports of the Superintendent of Immigration to the Secretary of Commerce (1904, 1905) and Secretary of the Treasury (1892-1902), 183
Anonymous Americans: Explorations in Nineteenth Century Social History, 170
Antoninus, M., 183
The A.P.A. Movement, 168
Saint Joseph College Archives, 164
Archdiocese of Boston Archives, 164
Diocese of Cleveland Archives, 164
Diocese of Providence Archives, 164
Arizona, 45
Armenia (Armenians), 61
Asia (Asians), 153
"The Association of Polish Priests in Connecticut: An Interpretative History", 184
Assumption Parish, 91
Atlantic Monthly, 180, 181
The Atlantic Reporter, 182
Australian Aid to American Catholics, 166
Australia (Australians), 60
Austria (Austrians), 57
Austro-Hungarian Empire, 49

B

Bacigalupo, L., 165
Bailyn, B., 165
Balch, E., 165

Baltimore Council of 1884, 98
Baran, F., 130
Bardeck, R., 48
Bardin, H., 165
Barry, C.J., 1, 3, 13, 165, 177
Bartlewski, G., 56, 130
Bartlewski, P., 56, 130
Barton, J.J., 165
Baumgartner, A., 165
Bay State "Blue Laws" and Bimba, 177
Beals, C., 165
Becker, 47, 95
Bedini, G., 30
Belgium (Belgians), 106
Bellerose, U.O., 48, 49
Bern, M.A., 177
Bernard Smith Papers, 32
Billington, R.A., 165
Bland, J., 166
Blejwas, S., 13, 166
Blied, B., 166
Bodnar, J., 143
Bohemia (Bohemians), 43, 133
Bojnowski, L., 48, 52, 62, 64, 89, 124, 125, 126, 127, 128, 129, 123, 166,
Bonforti F., 100
The Book of Bridgeport, Connecticut: A Handbook of Civic, Industrial and Commercial Information, 166
Borgess, C.H., 19
Boston Archdiocese, Archives of, 164
The Boston Herald, 54
Boston Pilot, 185
Boston Priests: 1848-1910: A Study of Social and Intellectual Changes, 173
Bouscaren, T., 166
Brazil (Brazilians), 30
Brennan, T.C., 177
Brewer, D.C., 166
Bridgeport Chamber of Commerce, 60
Bridgeport Post, 185
Bridgeport (Burroughs) Public Library, 164
Bridgeport Sunday Post, 185
The Bridgeport Telegram, 54, 137, 138
The Bridgeport Times Star, 139
Briggs, J.W., 97, 184
Brown, T., 166, 167, 169
Browne, H.J., 97, 166, 178
Buczek, D.S., 4, 48, 89, 124, 125, 127, 129, 166
Budapest, 50
Bukaveckas, V., 150
Burns, J.A., 166
Byrne, S., 166
Byrne, W., 166
Byzantine, 58

C

Cabrini, F., 16
Cada, J., 4, 167
Cadden, J.P., 167
Cahensly, P.P., 13
Canada (Canadians), 16, 17, 30, 37, 38, 40, 46, 55, 62, 65, 104, 106, 107, 108, 109, 111, 113, 114, 115, 116, 124
  French Canadians, 5, 22, 26, 28, 34, 35, 47, 48, 52, 58, 60, 61, 91, 105, 110, 112, 131, 132, 133, 150, 151
  Manitoba, 114
  Montreal, 46, 108
  Quebec, 48, 106, 114
  Sherbrook, 109
Canadian Dissidents of Saint James, 112
Canon Law, A Text and Commentary, 166
Capek, T., 167
Carroll, J., 8, 10
Carthy, M.P., 167
Cartier, J., 108
Catholic Charities, 54
Catholic Charities in the United States: History and Problems, 174
The Catholic Church and German Americans, 165
The Catholic Church and the Knights of Labor, 166
The Catholic Church and the Secret Societies in the United States, 172
The Catholic Church in America: An Historical Bibliography, 176
The Catholic Church in Connecticut, 4, 168
"The Catholic Church in Connecticut: A Bicentennial View", 184
The Catholic Church in the United States, 99, 174
Catholic Directory, 22
Catholic Historical Review, 177, 178, 179, 180, 181, 182
Catholic Journalism: A Study of Its Development in the United States. 1789-1930, 165
The Catholic Leader, 166
Catholic Parents and the Catholic Vocation: A Study of Parental Attitudes in a Catholic Diocese, 169
The Catholic Press, 24, 185
"The Catholic Press and *Longinqua oceani*", 185
Catholic Review, 106
Catholic Revivalism: The American Experience, 1830-1900, 168
Catholic Standard (New Haven), 185
Catholic Tract Society, 28
The Catholic Transcript, 36, 49, 50, 51, 53, 54, 55, 57, 61, 85, 86, 87, 89, 90, 118, 185
Catholic University of America, 4
  Archives of, 164
Catholic World, 182

Catholicism and the Nation's Social Development, 172

Catholicism in America, 169

Catholicism in New England to 1788, 174, 185

Catholicism in the Building of the Nation, 172

Catholics in Colonial America, 168

Catholics in Rhode Island: The Formative Era, 167

The Catholics of the Civil War, 166

Celts, 87, 92

The Century of History: The Diocese of Scranton, 1868-1968, 169

A Century of Population Growth from the First Census to the Twelvth, 1790-1900, 183

Century of Silver, 1847-1947, 173

Ceppa, J., 124, 131

Ceruti, G., 93

Cesaro, N.J., 26, 184

Chernitzky, S.F., 57, 62, 68, 142, 143, 145

Cheverus, J., 26, 27

Chiariglione, A., 100

Chicago's Catholics: The Evolution of an American Identity, 175

Chicago, Ill., 14, 15, 19, 98, 117

"Church Building in America: Divergent and Convergent Interests of Priests and Lay People in Italian-American Communities", 184

Church History, 177, 178, 180

Church of the Holy and Undivided Trinity, 28

Church-State Relationships in Education in Connecticut, 1633-1953, 173, 184

Ciesluk, J.E., 8, 167

Clancy, R., 178

Clark, G.L., 167

Clarke, R.H., 167

Cleveland Diocese, Archives of, 164

Code, J.B., 167

Code of Oriental Canon Law, the Law on Persons, 174

Commons, J.R., 167

Congregation of Notre Dame, 35

Congregation of Saint Charles, Borromeo, 41, 56, 98, 100, 101

Congregational Church, 26

Congress of French Canadians of Connecticut, 107, 110

Conley, P.T., 33, 167

Connecticut, 30, 61, 95, 96, 102, 105, 106, 109, 111, 113, 117, 118, 119, 130, 131

    Ansonia, 56, 57, 58, 61, 75, 91, 120, 150

    Baltic, 58, 106

    Bridgeport, 28, 35, 39, 42, 44, 47, 52, 56, 57, 58, 60, 64, 65, 75, 80, 93, 96, 100, 106, 133, 134, 136, 138, 139, 141, 142, 150, 151

    Bristol, 56, 75, 131

Danbury, 35, 58, 75

Danielson, 106, 109, 110, 111, 113, 114, 116, 118, 124

Dayville, 91

Derby, 28, 53, 75, 86, 91, 118, 119, 120, 121, 122, 124, 128,

East Bridgeport, 94

East Haven, 56, 101

Fairfield, 56

Foxon Park, 101

Hamden, 56

Hartford, 4, 23, 26, 27, 28, 31, 34, 35, 37, 39, 40, 42, 43, 45, 46, 47, 48, 52, 54, 58, 62, 65, 80, 85, 91, 95, 100, 106, 108, 111, 112, 113, 116, 120, 121, 123, 128, 129, 130, 132-152, 150, 155, 156,

    Archdiocesan Archives, 111, 116, 164

    Diocese of Hartford, 93, 97, 102, 103, 104, 105, 108, 109, 110, 112, 115, 117, 122, 127, 131, 164

Jewett City, 58, 75

LaSalette, 112

"Little Canada", 106

Meriden, 35, 39, 44, 55, 65, 89, 90, 96, 106, 121, 122, 123, 124, 125, 128, 144

Middletown, 28, 35, 47, 56, 57, 61, 65, 75

Naugatuck, 75

Naugatuck Valley, 61

New Britain, 34, 35, 44, 46, 48, 51, 52, 56, 57, 58, 61, 65, 80, 87, 89, 118, 121, 122, 124, 125, 127, 128, 144, 146, 147, 148, 149, 150

    All Saints, 121

New Haven, 25, 26, 27, 28, 34, 40, 41, 47, 48, 56, 57, 60, 65, 92, 96, 100, 101, 106, 120, 121, 140, 143, 150,

New London, 25, 26, 27, 28, 46, 55, 58, 65, 75, 118

Norwalk, 28, 46, 56, 65, 75, 140, 141, 142

Norwich, 28, 30, 53, 65, 75

Occum, 58

Plainfield, 58

Providence, Diocesan Archives of, 164

Putnam, 48, 58, 106

Rockville, 53, 86, 118

South Norwalk, 40, 53, 75, 142

Southington, 55, 118

Stamford, 35, 46, 56, 75, 130

Stonington, 28

Taftville, 58, 91, 110, 108

Terryville, 53, 58, 129

Thompsonville, 33, 55, 131

Torrington, 53, 56, 57, 61, 75, 94, 131, 137, 138, 140, 143

Union City, 53, 121, 127, 130, 131, 144

Voluntown, 58
Wallingford, 35, 56, 57, 94, 140, 143
Waterbury, 28, 31, 34, 35, 44, 47, 48, 51, 52, 55, 56, 61, 65, 80, 81, 91, 101, 106, 144, 145, 146, 147, 148, 151
Wauregan, 58, 91
West Hartford, 26
Wethersfield, 26
Willimantic, 47, 75, 106
Windsor, 26
Winsted, 35
Connecticut: A Study of a Commonwealth Democracy, 171
The Connecticut Catholic, 4, 36, 51, 85, 185
The Connecticut Catholic Yearbook, Being An Epitome of the History of the Church in the Diocese of Hartford From April 1876 to May 1877, 175
Connecticut Digest of Judicial Decisions, 1785-1945, 182
Connecticut Episcopal Papers, 43
Connecticut Reports, 182
Connecticut State Library, 164
Connelly, J.F., 167
The Conquest of New England by the Immigrant, 166
Conspiracy: The Fear of Subversion in American History, 167
Contemporary Catholicism, 169
Coppens, C., 57
Corish, P., 166, 172
Corporation Sole, 17
Corrigan, M.A., 15, 16
Costa, J., 184
Council of Trent, 8
Croatia (Croats), 94
Cross, R.D., 3, 167, 177
Csaba, G., 94, 141
Cullen, T.F., 178
Curry, R.O., 167
Cygan, M., 18, 178
Czech-American Catholics, 1850-1920, 167
Czech Contributions to the Growth of the United States, 168
Czechoslovakia (Czechs), 43, 133
The Czechoslovaks in America, 175
The Czechs (Bohemians) in America: A Study of Their National, Cultural, Political, Social, Economic, and Religious Life, 167

D

Dahme, H., 47, 48
Dakin, W.S., 167
DeBruycker, A., 47
DeBruycker, F., 34, 47, 106, 110
DeMarco, W.M., 18, 168

Degnan, J.A., 57, 143
Dehey, E.T., 168
Democracy of Catholicism in America, 175
Demos, J., 168
Desmond, H.J., 168
Devereux, N., 28
DiGiovanni, S.M., 16, 184
Dictionary on the American Hierarchy, 1790-1940, 167
Dignan, P.J., 168
Dilionis, V., 20
Diocesan School Report of 1890, 108
A Diverse People: Connecticut 1914 to the Present, 171
Documents of American Catholic History, 168
The Documents of the Vatican II, 165
Doherty, J.A., 57
Dolan, J.P., 3, 168
Dolin, P.J., 57
Dorn, J., 3, 178
Duggan, T.S., 4, 38, 54, 85, 86, 87, 88, 89, 90, 93, 95, 168
Dusablon, L., 110
Dvornik, F., 168
Dyrud, K.P., 4, 168

E

"Early Catholic Missionaries in Connecticut, 1638-1829", 184
Eastern Bridgeport's Catholic Churches, 94
Egan, M.F., 168
Eichstadt, Germany, 50
Ellis, A.C., 166
Ellis, J.T., 11, 168
The Emergence of Liberal Catholicism in America, 167
Encyclopedia of Biography: Representative Citizens, 169
Engels, M.H., 176
England (English), 12, 34
English Influences on Early American Catholicism, 167
Episcopal Papers, 33, 41, 51
Episcopalian (Episcopals), 28
An Episode in Anti-Catholicism: The American Protective Association, 172
Ethnic Diversity in Catholic America, 7, 165
"Ethnic Factors in Connecticut Life: A Survey of Social, Economic, and Cultural Characteristics of the Connecticut Population", 184
Ethnic Leadership in America, 171
Ethnic Parish As Compromise: The Spheres of Clerical and Lay Authority in a Polish American Parish, 1911-1930, 178
"Ethnic Pluralism in the Central City", 183

Ethnics and Enclaves: Boston's Italian North End,
  168
Europe (Europeans), 8, 22, 29, 30, 25, 37, 40,
  42, 44, 47, 49, 50, 53, 55, 62, 66, 70, 86, 92,
  101, 116, 118, 119, 129, 133, 134, 140, 144, 153
Exclusion Act, 86

F

Federkiewicz, S., 130, 131
Feehan, P.A., 15
Femminella, F., 98, 178
Fenwick, B.J., 27, 28
Fichter, J.H., 169
Fifteenth Census of the United States, 1930, 183
First Italian Congregation Church in Hart-
  ford, 97
First Vatican Council in Rome (1869-1870), 35
Fischer, D.H., 169
Fitton, J., 24, 26, 28, 169
Flannery E., 100
Flint Affair, 16
Foerster, R.F., 169
Fogarty, G.P., 169
Foley, J.S., 19
Foley, T., 15
Foner, E., 169
For God and Country: The Rise of Polish and
  Lithuanian Ethnic Consciousness in America,
  1860-1910, 170
Ford, E.E., 169
Formanek, J., 93, 132, 140
Fourth Lateran Council, 8
Fox, P., 169
France (French), 13, 16, 17, 25, 26, 31, 34, 38,
  39, 40, 50, 52, 53, 57, 58, 60, 85, 87, 92, 96,
  104, 107, 109, 11, 111, 112
    Grenoble 39, 112
    Paris, 29
    Brittany, 50
Francis Warde: American Foundress of the Sisters
  of Mercy, 170
Franciscans, 48, 68, 95
The Franciscans and the Italian Immigrants in
  American, 165
Fredericksberg, 37
Fudzinski, H., 95
Furdek, S., 20

G

Galberry, T., 36
Gallagher, J.P., 165, 169
Galush, W., 20, 178
General Statutes of Connecticut, Revision of 1930,
  182
Geography of Connecticut, 167
Germany (Germans), 4, 5, 7, 10, 11, 13, 22, 26,

27, 31, 34, 35, 38, 39, 40, 46, 48, 49, 52, 55, 57,
  65, 85, 87, 90, 91, 92, 96, 97, 99, 107, 132, 133,
  142. 151
Gibbons, J., 46
Glaab, C.N., 169
Gleason D., 2, 3, 96, 100, 169
Grant, E.S., 169
Grant, M., 169
The Great Crisis in American Catholic History,
  1895-1900, 172
The Great Hunger: Ireland 1845-49, 177
Greece (Greeks), 87
Greeley, A., 4, 170
Greene, V.R., 84, 117, 118, 178
Grikis, E., 150
Grohol, S., 64
Gross, F., 142, 143
The Growth and Development of the Catholic
  School System in the United States, 166
Guignard, M.J., 13, 16, 170
Guilday, P., 170

H

Hall, D.T., 170
Hand, J., 29
Handlin, O., 170
Handy, R.T., 175
Hansen, M.L., 170
Hareven, T., 170
Harkins, M., 54
Harrington, E.T., 172
Hart, M., 34
The Hartford Courant, 54, 115, 185
The Hartford Times, 54, 113, 185
Hatzfield, H., 182
Havey, F., 123
Hayman, R.W., 184
Hays, S.P., 170
Healy, J., 114
Healy, K., 170
Healy, M.M., 184
Heffernan, A.J., 170
Hendricken, T., 16, 34
Hennesey, J., 10, 171, 178
Herberg, W., 171
Herron, M.E., 171
Hersher, I., 179
Hibernian Crusade: The Story of the Catholic
  Total Abstinence Union, 166
Higham, J., 171, 179
Histoire des Franco-Americains, 175
Historical Aspects of the Immigration Problem,
  165
Historical Records and Studies of the United States
  Catholic Historical Society of New York, 178,
  179

The Historiography of the American Catholic Church, 1785-1943, 167
History of Bridgeport and Vicinity, 176
History of Bigotry in the United States, 173
A History of Catholic Education in Connecticut, 170
History of Connecticut, 174
A History of Connecticut: Its People and Its Institutions, 167
A History of Irish Catholicism, 166, 172
History of St. John's Seminary, Brighton, 175
"History of St. Patrick's Parish, New Haven, Ct., 1853-1953", 183
History of the Archdiocese of Boston: In the Various Stages of the Development, 1604-1943, 172
History of the Catholic Church in the New England States, 166
A History of the Catholic Church in the United States, 172, 175
A History of the Councils of Baltimore, 1791-1884, 170
History of the Diocese of Cleveland: Origins and Growth, 1847-1952, 171
History of the Diocese of Hartford, 4, 174
History of the Diocese of Providence, 184
A History of the Irish Settlers in the Irish Settlements in North America, from the Earliest Period to the Census of 1850, 172
A History of the Legal Incorporation of Catholic Church Property in the United States, 1784-1932, 168
"The History of the Origin and Development of the Catholic Newspaper in Connecticut as Exemplified in *The Catholic Press* and Its Successor, *The Connecticut Catholic*", 184
The History of Urban America, 169
Hodur, F., 19
Hoffmann's Catholic Directory, Almanac and Clergy-List Quarterly, 183
Holy Cross, New Britain, 58, 161
Holy Name, Stamford, 158
Holy Name, Stratford, 161
Holy Rosary Parish, Ansonia, 100, 160, 163
Holy Trinity Parish, Hartford, 48, 57, 150, 159, 161, 162
Horstmann, I., 123
House of the Good Shepherd, 47
How the Other Half Lived: An Ethnic History of the Old East Side and South End of Hartford, 174
Hughes, W.H., 171
Hungary (Hungarian), 5, 17, 20, 43, 44, 49, 52, 57, 60, 68, 70, 90, 94, 132, 133, 141, 143, 144, 149
The Hungarians in Bridgeport: A Social Survey, 165

Hungarian Reformed Churches, 144
Hunyady, A., 43
Hutchinson, D., 57
Hutchinson, E.P., 171
Hynes, M.J., 171

I

The Ideological Origins of the American Revolution, 165
The Ideology of the Republican Party Before the Civil War: Free Soil, Free Labor, Free Men, 169
Immaculate Conception, Hartford, 162
Immaculate Conception, Waterbury, 163
The Immigrant Church: New York's Irish and German Catholics, 1815-1865, 168
Immigrant Pastor: The Life of the Right Reverend Monsignor Lucyan Bojnowski of New Britain, Connecticut, 166
Immigrant Settlements in Connecticut: Their Growth and Character, 172
Immigrants and Religion in Urban America, 7, 173
Immigrants and the American Tradition, 174
Immigrants and Their Children, 1850-1950 171
The Immigrants in American History, 170
Immigration as a Factor in American History, 170
Immigration Restriction Act, 63
The Impact of Italian Migration and American Catholicism, 99,
International Migration Review, 178, 180, 181
International Workers of the World (I.W.W.), 62
Iorizzo, L.J., 171
Ireland (Irish), 4, 7, 10, 11, 12, 13, 14, 17, 24, 26, 29, 31, 32, 36, 43, 49, 50, 60, 64, 65, 66, 75, 82, 84, 87, 91, 94, 97, 99, 100, 103, 106, 107, 108, 112, 119, 121, 123, 127, 128, 129, 133, 140, 151, 155, 156,
    Tipperary, 46
Ireland, J., 32, 36, 46, 53
Irish Emigration to the United States, 166
The Irish in America, 173
Italian-American History, 175
Italian-American History: The Italian Contribution to the Catholic Church in America, 96
The Italian-Americans, 97, 171, 175
The Italian Emigration of Our Times, 169
The Italian Experience in the United States, 176
The Italian Problem in the Catholic Church in the United States, 1880-1900, 97
Italy (Italians), 5, 13, 16, 17, 31, 35, 36, 38, 40, 41, 42, 44, 49, 50, 52, 55, 57, 60, 61, 62, 68, 70, 80, 90, 91, 92, 96, 98, 97, 99, 100, 101, 102, 117, 156
    Bedonia, 50
    Nepi, 50
    Piacenza, 41, 50, 96, 101, 56

J

Janick, H.F., 171
Jankola, M., 133, 136, 138, 144
Jesuit Relations and Allied Documents, 176
John Carroll of Baltimore: Founder of the American Catholic Hierarchy, 173
Johnston, A., 36, 171
Jones, M.A., 103, 171
Journal of Social History, 181

K

Kaminski, S., 19
Kane, J.J., 179
Karkauskas, V., 150
Keane, J.J., 46
Keating, M., 100
Kelley A., 96, 100
Kelley, J.J., 100
Kelly C., 50, 56, 96, 101
Kenneally, F., 171
Kennedy, J.B., 168
Kennedy, J.F., 171
Kennedy, J.S., 184
Kentucky, 46
Kervick, F.W., 171
Kinzer, D.L., 172
Kish, Z., 143
Klawiter, A., 122, 123
Knights of Columbus, 90
The Knights of Columbus in Peace and War, 168
Knights of Saint Mary of Czentochowa, 90
Know-Nothing Party, 30
"The Know-Nothings in Connecticut", 184
Koenig, S.T., 172, 184
Kolko, G., 172
Komara, A., 57, 64, 136, 138, 144
Konieczny, S., 119, 121
Koslowski, A., 19
Kossalko, J., 133, 134, 135, 136
Kowalski, J., 56, 130
Krakas, P., 149
Ku Klux Klan, 86
Kucharski, C., 124
Kulik, E., 179

L

La Foi-La Langue-La Culture: the Franco-Americans of Biddeford, Maine, 170
LaSalette Fathers, 114
Lannie, V., 179
Lazarists, 48
LeProhon, E.P., A.M., 179
Leahy, W.A., 166
Leclaire, C., 109, 110, 111, 112, 113, 114

"Legion of the Freemen of Krakus", 125
Lengren, J., 143
Leopoldine Mission Society of Vienna, 29
Lincoln, A., 32
Linkh, R.M., 172
Liptak, D.Q., 179
Lithuania (Lithuanians), 5, 13, 17, 20, 39, 44, 46, 48, 49, 51, 52, 55, 57, 60, 61, 64, 68, 70, 87, 88, 90, 91, 99, 132, 144, 145, 147, 148, 149, 150, 151
"Lithuanian Immigrants and Their Irish Bishops in the Catholic Church in Connecticut, 1893-1915", 185
"Lithuanian Origins in Connecticut and Reverend Joseph Zebris: The Life, Struggles and Tragic Death of a Pioneer Priest", 185
Lithuanian Priests' League of America, 150
A Little Commonwealth: Family Life in Plymouth Colony, 168
Lives of the Deceased Bishops of the Catholic Church in the United States, 167
Loetscher, L.A., 175
Lopata, H.Z., 172
Lord, R.H., 172
Louvain, Belgium, 34, 38, 39, 47, 95
Luczycki, J., 130
Lynch, M., 101
Lynch, W.H., 64

M

MacDonald, F., C.P., 172
Maciejewski, I., 130
Madaj, M.J., 22
Madar, J., 141
The Magyars in America, 176
Maher, W., 142, 143
Maine, 45
    Biddeford, 16, 17
    Portland, 16, 17, 108, 114
Malley, J.B., 101
Mann, A., 173
Marianite Sisters of the Cross, 108
Martin, F., 55, 91
Marty, M., 180
Maryland, 2, 4, 7, 32
    Baltimore, 8, 10, 13, 20,
Marzik, T., 7, 18, 173
Mason, M.P., 173, 184
Massachusetts, 37, 38, 45, 60, 61, 107
    Amesbury, 54
    Boston, 13, 26, 27, 37, 70
    Brighton, 48
    Fall River, 16, 70
    Flint, 16
    Charlestown, 30, 37
    New Bedford, 38

Springfield, 70
 Diocese of, 114
 Diocesan Archives, 164
 Worcester, 107
Matignon, F., 26
"Matthew Jankola, 1872-1916: Slovak-American Priest, Leader, Educator, and Founder of the Sisters of SS. Cyril and Methodius", 185
May, E.C., 173
Maynard, T., 1, 12, 173
McAlenney, P., 123
McAvoy, T.T., C.S.C., 2, 3, 11, 14, 172, 179
McFarland, F.P., 30, 31, 32, 33, 34, 35, 36, 38, 46, 47, 84, 106, 155
McGee, T.D., 172
McGuire, C.E., 172
McGuire, J.F., 173
McKeown, E., 180
McLaughlin J., 100
McMahon, L.S., 35, 36, 37, 38, 46, 47, 51, 94, 96, 106, 107, 108, 110, 122, 132, 144, 155, 157
McMahon, T.J., 172
McSeveney, S.T., 173, 180
"Meeting the Challenge of Education in an Ethnic Parish", 184
Melville, A., 173
The Memorial History of Hartford, Connecticut, 176
A Memorial of Andrew Shipman, His Life and Writings, 174
Merwick, D., 173
Metropolitan Catholic Almanac and Laity's Directory, 183
"Michael Augustine Corrigan and the Italian Immigrants in the Archdiocese of New York, 1885-1902", 184
Michigan, 2, 68
 Detroit, 18, 19, 36
Middleton, T., 180
Middletown Sentinel and Witness, 186
Mierzwinski, T.T., 130, 184
Milkey, J., 64, 173
Miller, P., 175
Miller, R., 7, 18, 173
Milwaukee, Wi., 13, 36
Minority Religions in America, 177
Misicki, T., 123, 128
Missionaries of Our Lady of LaSalette, 39, 30
Missionary Zelatrices of the Sacred Heart, 57
Mnozill, T.I., 180
Mohl, R.A., 3, 173
Mondello, S., 171
Montvid, B., 149
The Morning Union (Bridgeport), 115, 186
Morse, J.M., 173
Murphy, J.C., 93, 184

Musiel, S., 47, 131
Myers, G., 173

N

A Nation of Immigrants, 171
National Council of Baltimore, 2
National Parishes in the United States, 167
The National Pastorals of the American Hierarchy, 1792-1919, 170
National Temperance Union, 54
National parishes, 8-10, 14, 15, 16, 17, 19, 18, 20, 21, 38
Nativism in Connecticut, 1829-1850, 174
Neale, L., 11
A Neglected Period of Connecticut History, 1818-1850, 173
Nevins, A.J.,173
Nevins, M.M., 173
New Britain Herald, 186
New Britain: The Hardware City of the World, 173
The New Catholic Encyclopedia, 173, 179
New England Quarterly, 180
New Hampshire, 45
New Haven Morning Journal Courier, 186
New Haven Palladium, 186
New Haven Register, 186
New Jersey, 40, 45, 51, 54, 61, 70, 144
 Newark, 15, 34, 36, 52, 70
New Jersey Catholic Historical Records Commission, 15, 164, 173
New York, 2, 27, 32, 40, 45, 51, 52, 61, 70, 98
 Brooklyn, 13, 52, 70
 Buffalo, 13, 48, 95, 117
 Fordham, 32
 Rochester, 32, 97
 Troy, 46
 Utica, 97
New York Freeman's Journal, 186
New York Times, 186
Newport Daily News, 186
Nilan, J.J., 35, 36, 54-59, 58, 62, 66, 96, 99, 100, 101, 118, 129, 130, 131, 136, 140, 141, 142, 155
Noonan, C., 1, 26, 174
Noreen, S.M., 184
Norfolk, Va, 11
North American Review, 181
Nos Enfants Canadiens de Taftville Connecticut, 108
Notes of the Life of Noah Webster, 169
Notre Dame Parish, Massachusetts, 16
Notre Dame University, Archives, 184
Novak, M., 4, 7, 168, 174

O

O'Brien, D., 100, 174
O'Connell, D., 46
O'Connor, J.J., 15
O'Connor, T.F., 180
O'Donnell, J.H., 4, 25, 27, 115, 166, 174
The Official Catholic Directory, 15, 183
Ohio, 2, 13, 54, 123
   Cincinnati, 42
   Cleveland, 20
O'Neill, M., 31
L' Opinion Publique (Worcester), 186
O'Reilly, B., 29, 30, 180
Organizational Climate and Careers, the Work Lives of Priests, 170
Ortynsky, S.S., 58
Osborn, N.G., 174
Osterweis, R., 174
The Other Bostonians: Poverty and Progress in the American Metropolis, 1880-1970, 64, 176
The Other Catholics, 168, 181
Our American Catholic Heritage, 173
Our Lady of Lourdes Church, Waterbury, 158, 163
Our Lady of Mount Carmel Church, Meriden, 101, 158, 163
Our Lady of Mount Carmel Church, Waterbury, 160
Our Lady of Pompeii Church, (Holy Rosary), Bridgeport, 56, 158
Our Lady of Pompeii Church, East Haven, 160
Our Lady of Sorrows Church, Hartford, 162
Our Yankee Heritage: The Making of Greater New Haven, 165

P

Pallen, C.B., 174
Palomba, C., 56
Panik, G., 62, 137, 144
Panik, S., 138, 139, 144
Pankus, M., 150
Parmet, R.D., 184
Parton, J., 180
Passbook to a Proud Past and a Promising Future, 1819-1969. 150th Anniversary of Society for Savings, 169
Pastor of the Poles: Polish American Essays, 166
Patrick Charles Keely, Architect: His Life and Works, 171
Pawlowski, R.E., 174
Peasants and Strangers: Italians, Romanians and Slovaks in an American City, 165
Pekari, M.A., 180
Pennsylvania, 2, 4, 20, 32, 45, 54, 61, 144
   Philadelphia, 11, 30
   Archdiocesan Archives, 164
   Pittston, 20

Scranton, 13, 117, 133
Piechocki, P., 49, 50, 55, 130
Piety and Power: The Role of the Italian Parishes in the New York Metropolitan Area, 1880-1930, 176
Pilot, 186
Podea, I.S., 180
Poland (Polish), 15, 18, 19, 20, 21, 22, 38, 39, 46, 47, 48, 49, 51, 52, 52, 55, 56, 60, 61, 62, 64, 66, 68, 70, 80, 86, 87, 88, 89, 90, 91, 92, 93, 94, 104, 105, 116, 117, 118, 119, 120, 121, 122, 123, 124, 125, 126, 127, 128, 129, 130, 131, 132, 133, 144, 150, 151
   Cracow, 50
   Kolbuszowa, 119
   Tarnow, 119
The Poles in America, 169
Polish American Studies, 177, 179, 180, 182
Polish Americans: Status and Competition in an Ethnic Community, 172
Polish Catholic Congress of Connecticut, 129
Polish Catholic School, 87
Polish Franciscans, 95
Polish National Alliance, 125, 128
Polish National Catholic Church, 19, 55, 130
The Polish National Catholic Church in America and Poland, 165
The Polish Peasants in Europe and America, 176
Polish Union, 126
Polish Vincentians, 120, 121, 129
The Politics of Depression: Political Behavior in the Northeast, 1893-1896, 173
Pontificia Americana: A Documentary History of the Catholic Church in the United States, 1704-1004, 175
Pope Leo, 98, 111
Pope Pius X, 50
Portugal (Portuguese), 11, 38, 92
Pospishil, V.J., J.C.D., 174
Preston, T.J., 109, 110, 112
Pribyl, F.J., 133
Princen, J.A., 106
Procko, B.P., 180
The Protestant Crusade: 1800-1860: A Study of the Origins of American Nativism, 165
Protestants (Protestantism), 2, 3, 5, 24, 29, 30, 31, 37, 54, 98, 144, 155
Protestant, Catholic, Jew: An Essay in American Religious Sociology, 171
Proulx, J.B., 113, 114
Providence Journal, 186
Purcell, J.R., 180
Public Acts Passed by the General Assembly, 183
Public Acts of the States of Connecticut, Passed January Session, 1903, 183
"Publication on United States Catholic Church History, 1850-1950", 185

Puritanism, 24

Q

Question of Nationality in Its Relation to the Catholic Church in the United The States, 176
Quigley, J.E., 15

R

Races and Immigrants in America, 167
Racine A., 109
Raniszewski, J., 130
Ray, M.A., 174
Records of the American Catholic Historical Society of Philadelphia, 177, 178, 179, 180, 181, 182
Redemptorists, 146
Reher, M.M., 180
Religious Census, 176
The Religious History of the American People, 3, 165
Religious Orders of Women in the United States: An Account of Their Origin, Works and Most Important Institutions, 168
Report on the Statistics of Churches in the United States at the 11th Census: 1890, 183
The Response to Industrialism: 1885-1914, 170
Review of Politics, 177, 179
The Revolution of American Conservation, 169
Rhode Island, 5, 29, 30, 32, 33, 35, 45, 60
    Providence, 16, 23, 29, 31, 46, 54, 70, 84
Rhode, P., 15
Riccio, A., 66
Richardson, J.F., 3, 173
Riggs, L., 101
Riley, A.J., 48, 174, 175, 185
Rischin, M., 4, 174, 180
The Rise of the Unmeltable Ethnics, 7, 174
Rodnick, D., 184
Roemer, T., 174
Roman Catholicism and the American Way of Life, 172
Rome (Romans), 2, 10, 13, 28, 35, 37, 40, 46, 69, 109, 113, 114, 115, 116, 118, 154
The Romanization of the American Catholic Church, 176
Rooney, J., 4. 175, 181
Rose, P.M., 97, 175
Rosko, J., 43
Roy, P.E., 48, 111, 112
Rumilly, R., 113, 175
Russell, J., 92
Russia (Russians), 49, 117, 120
Rytas, 51

S

Sacred Congregation of the Propagation of the Faith in Rome, 16, 29, 40, 41, 69, 111, 112, 113, 115, 128
Sacred Heart Church, Hartford, 39
Sacred Heart Church, New Britain, 51, 100, 125, 122, 124, 126, 127, 128, 163
Sacred Heart Church, New Haven, 162
Sacred Heart Church, Stamford, 160
Sacred Heart Church, Taftville, 108
Sacred Heart Church, Torrington, 137, 159
Sacred Heart Church, Waterbury, 163
Sacred Heart Church, Wauregan, 91
Sacred Heart of Jesus Christ, Bridgeport, 162
Sadlier's Catholic Directory, Almanac and ORDO, 183
Saint Adalbert Church, Thompsonville, 131
Saint Aedan Church, 92
Saint Albertus, Detroit, 18
Saint Andrew Church, New Britain, 51, 147, 148, 159, 163
Saint Ann Church, Bristol, 159
Saint Ann Church, Hartford, 162
Saint Ann Church, Waterbury, 56, 58, 111
Saint Anne Church, Hamden, 160, 163
Saint Anthony Church, Ansonia, 57, 161
Saint Anthony Church, Bridgeport, 163
Saint Anthony Church, Bristol, 160
Saint Anthony Church, Fairfield, 161
Saint Anthony Church, Hartford, 100, 158, 162
Saint Anthony Church, New Haven, 158, 162
Saint Augustine Church, Bridgeport, 124, 162
Saint Brendan Church, 92
Saint Casimir Church, (Sacred Heart), New Britain, 158
Saint Casimir Church, New Haven, 57
Saint Casimir Church, Stamford, 130
Saint Casimir Church, Terryville, 158
Saint Cecelia Church, Waterbury, 48, 55, 91, 151, 163
Saint Charles Church, Bridgeport, 64, 163
Saints Cyril and Methodius Church, Bridgeport, 138, 139, 159, 163
Saints Cyril and Methodius Church, Hartford, 158, 162
Saints Cyril and Methodius Church, Michigan, 68
Saints Cyril and Methodius Society, 134, 135, 136
Saint Donato's Italian Church, New Haven, 56, 101, 160
Saint Francis Church, New Haven, 162
Saint Francis Xavier Church, Waterbury, 163
Saint George Church, Bridgeport, 151, 159, 163
Saint Hedwig's Church, Union City, 130, 131, 158

Saint James Church, Danielson, 109, 110, 114
Saint John Church, Hartford, 134, 136
Saint John, Brighton, 48
Saint John, Middletown, 61, 64
Saint John Church, New Brunswick, 37
Saint John's College, 32
Saint John's Industrial School, 47
Saint John Nepomucene Church, Bridgeport, 44, 93, 162
Saint John the Evalgelist Church, New Haven, 162
Saint Joseph, Bridgeport, 162
Saint Joseph Cathedral Parish, Hartford, 123, 132
Saint Joseph Church, Ansonia, 161
Saint Joseph Church, Bridgeport, 39
Saint Joseph Church, Dayville, 91
Saint Joseph Church, Meriden, 163
Saint Joseph Church, New Britain, 163
Saint Joseph Church, New Haven, 162
Saint Joseph Church, Rockville, 158
Saint Joseph Church, Waterbury, 144, 145, 147, 159, 163
Saint Joseph College, Archives of, 164
Saint Ladislaus Church, 142, 143, 159
Saint Laurent Church, Meriden, 163
Saint Lawrence O'Toole Church, Hartford, 162
Saint Lawrence Church, West Haven, 162
Saint Louis Church, New Haven, 162
Saint Louis, Mi., 30
Saint Lucy Church, Waterbury, 160
Saint Mary Church, Bridgeport, 93
Saint Mary Church, Derby, 91, 121
Saint Mary Church, Meriden, 90, 163
Saint Mary Church, Middletown, 158
Saint Mary Church, New Britain, 163
Saint Mary Church, New Haven, 162
Saint Mary Church, Norwalk, 140, 142
Saint Mary Church, Torrington, 131
Saint Mary Church, Willimantic, 159
Saint Michael Church, Bridgeport, 47, 95, 151, 158, 163
Saint Michael Church, Derby, 89, 119, 158
Saint Michael Church, Hartford, 41, 162
Saint Michael Church, New Haven, 158, 162
Saint Michael Society, 121
Saint Michael the Archangel Church, Derby, 120
Saint Michael the Archangel Society, 124
Saint Patrick and Saint Thomas Church, Waterbury, 163
Saint Patrick's Church, Bridgeport, 162
Saint Patrick's Church, Hartford, 163
Saint Patrick's Church, New Haven, 92
Saint Paul, Mn., 97
Saint Peter Church, Bridgeport, 163
Saint Peter Church, Hartford, 162

Saint Peter Church, New Britain, 163
Saint Peter Church, Torrington, 158
Saint Raphael Church, Bridgeport, 160
Saint Rita Church, 92
Saint Rose Church, Meriden, 123, 163
Saint Sebastian Church, Middletown, 1600
Saint Stanislaus Church, Bristol, 131
Saint Stanislaus Church, Meriden, 89, 122, 124, 163
Saint Stanislaus Church, New Haven, 158, 162
Saint Stanislaus Church, Waterbury, 55
Saint Stanislaus Society, 123
Saint Stephen's Church, Bridgeport, 57, 94, 141, 142, 143, 159, 163
Saint Thomas Seminary, 47, 48, 49, 62, 63, 64, 65, 66, 68, 74, 74, 80, 81, 83, 130, 136
    Saint Thomas Seminary Library, 39, 40
Satolli, F., 46, 111, 112, 113, 115, 116
Saurusaitis, P., 146, 147
Scalabrini G.B., 16, 41, 97
Scalabrinians (See, Congregation of St. Charles, Borromeo), 41, 56, 98, 100, 101
Schaff, P., 2, 175
Scheuer, J.E., 176
Schiavo, G., 41, 175
Schneider, B., 170
Scoglio F., 100
Scrole, L., 177
Sears, C.H., 175
Sedgwick, H.D., Jr., 181
A Select Bibliography of the History of the Catholic Church in the United States, 169
Senner, J.H., 181
"The Sentinelle Affair (1924-1929) and Militant Survivance: The Franco-American Experience in Woonsocket, Rhode Island", 185
Sexton, J.E., 48, 172, 175
Shahan, T.J., 181
Shanabruch, C., 14, 15, 175
Shea, J.G., 1, 175
Shearer, D.C., 175
Sheedy, M., 181
Shields, C., 175
Shuster, G.N., 175
Silvia, Jr., P.T., 16, 181
Simeoni, G., 16
Simko, M., 43, 64
Sisters of Charity, Belgium, 108
The Sisters of Mercy in the United States, 1843-1928, 171
Sisters of Mercy, 32, 35, 92
    Archives of, 184
Sisters of Saint Joseph of Chambery, France, 109
Sketches of the Establishment of the Church in New England, 169
The Slavic Community on Strike: Immigrant Labor

in *Pennsylvania Anthracite*, 170

Our Slavic Fellow Citizens, 165

Slavics, 5, 17, 35, 36, 40, 49, 55, 58, 62, 87, 96, 97, 99, 140, 156

Slovaks (Slavics), 19, 20, 38, 39, 42, 43, 44, 52, 55, 57, 60, 64, 66, 68, 70, 75, 80, 90, 93, 94, 132, 134, 137, 138, 145

Smith, 4, 33

Smith,. C., 87

Smith, H.S., 175

Smith, M.J., 167

Smith, T., 181

The Social Systems of American Ethnic Groups, 177

Society for the Comparative Study of Society and History, 182

Sociology Looks at Religion, 176

Socquet, C., 112

Solomon, B., 175

Sorrell, R.S., 18, 185

Souders, D.A., 144, 176

South America, 153

Souvenir Volume: Three Great Events in the History of the Catholic Church in the United States, 171

Souvenir of the Consecration of St. Joseph's Cathedral, May 8, 1892, 176

Stas, J., 20

State Board of Education, 87

Stec, W., 121

Stochmal, F., 119, 120, 128

Stolarik, M.M., 19, 181

Stonington, 28

The Story of American Catholicism, 173

The Story of Religious America, 176

Strangers in the Land: Patterns of American Nativism, 1860-1925, 171

Sullivan, T., 50, 96, 100

Sunday Republican Weekly (Waterbury), 186

Supreme Court of Connecticut, 114

"A Survey of Catholic Maternity Homes", 184

Sweet, W.W., 176

Switzerland (Swiss), 49, 50, 61
    Freiburg, 50
    Lugano, 50

Symon, F., 88, 89

Synott, J., 91

Syria (Syrians), 55, 58, 62

Szobo, J., 143

T

Taft, W., 57

Tauben Blut, 133

Taylor, 28

Taylor, D., 28

Taylor, G., 176

Thayer, J., 26

Theological Studies, 180

Thernstrom, S., 64, 71, 176

Third Biennial Report of the Attorney General, for the Two Years Ended, January 3, 1905, 182

Third Order of Saint Francis, 35

Third Plenary Council of 1884, 9

Thomas, S.J., 181, 185

Thomas, W.F., 176

Three Centuries of New Haven, 1638-1938, 174

Thwaites, R.G., 176

Tierney, M., 35, 36, 45-54, 57, 58, 62, 83, 89, 90, 95, 96, 99, 100, 101, 110, 111, 112, 113, 114, 115, 118, 126, 127, 129, 130, 131, 133, 134, 135, 136, 142, 144, 146, 155

Tollino, J.W., 181

Tomasi, S.M., 16, 176

Topor, W., 56, 130

Torrington Evening Register, 138, 186

La Travailleru (Dolbec, *et al* Sept. 9, 1887), 107

Traynor, M., 93

The Triumph of Conservatism, 172

Trumbull, J.H., 176

Tully, B., 33

Twenty-Eighth Massachusetts Regiment, 37

Tybor, S. Martina, 185

Tyler, W.J., 5, 29

U

The Ukraine (Ukrainians), 58, 61

Uminski, E., 126, 127

United States, 97, 107, 108, 109, 117

The United States of America, 172

United States Catholic Almanac and Laity's Directory, 183

The United States Catholic Magazine, 181

United States Documents in the Propaganda Fide Archives: A Calender 1st Series, 171

United States Office of the Census, 34

The Urban Experience: Themes in American History, 173, 178

The Urban Wilderness, 97, 177

V

Valantiejus, J., 147

Valley Catholic, 186

Van Laar, J.G., 106

VanDusen, A.E., 60, 176

VanOppen, J.J., 39

The Vatican and the Americanist Crisis: Denis J. O'Connell, American Agent in Rome, 1885-1903, 169

Vecoli, R.J., 4, 97, 168, 181

Vermont, 45

Vienybe Lietuvninku, 146

Vincentians, 48, 68, 80

Virginia
  Antietam, 37
  New Bern, 37
  Richmond, 37
  Second Bull Run, 37
The Visit of Archbishop Gaetano Bedini to the United States: June 1853-February 1854, 167
Vollmar, E.R., 176, 185
Vygen, E., 106

W

Wade, M., 182
Wakin, E., 176
Walburg, A., 176
Waldo, G.C., Jr., 176
Walsh, J.J., 182
Walsh, L., 16, 17
Warner, S.B., 97, 177
Warner, W.L., 177
Washington, D.C., 13, 111
Waszko, P., 121
Waterbury Republican, 146, 186
Weber, N.A., 182
Webster, N., 26
West Indies (West Indians), 153
Whalen, W.J., 177
Why Can't They Be More Like Us? America's

White Ethnic Groups, 170
Wigger, W.M., 15
Willging, E.P., 182
Willimantic Weekly Chronicle, 186
Wilmington, Delaware, 149
Windham County Transcript, 186
Wolkovich-Valkavicius, W., 4, 20, 51, 177, 182, 185
Woodcock, T.L., 18, 19, 182
Woodham-Smith, C.B., 177
Woodley, R.D., 28
Woonsocket Patriot, 186
World War I, 55, 57
World War II, 92
Wueste, A.E., 177

Y

Yale University, 26, 101
Yankee Reformers in the Urban Age, 173
Yinger, J.M., 176

Z

Zebris, J., 51, 52, 57, 62, 64, 144, 145, 147, 148, 149, 150
Znaniecki, F., 176

$17.50